Entrepreneurship in the Creative Industries

An International Perspective

Edited by

Colette Henry

Head of Department of Business Studies and Director, Centre for Entrepreneurship Research, Dundalk Institute of Technology, Ireland

Edward Elgar

Cheltenham, UK • Northampton, MA, USA

Published by
Edward Elgar Publishing Limited
The Lypiatts
15 Lansdown Road
Cheltenham
Glos GL50 2JA
UK

Edward Elgar Publishing, Inc.
William Pratt House
9 Dewey Court
Northampton
Massachusetts 01060
USA

A catalogue record for this book
is available from the British Library

Library of Congress Cataloguing in Publication Data

Entrepreneurship in the creative industries : an international perspective / edited by Colette Henry.
    p. cm.
Includes bibliographical references and index.
1. Arts—Management. 2. Entrepreneurship. I. Henry, Collette.
NX163.E58 20007
658.4'21—dc22

    2007017149

ISBN 978 1 84542 610 1

Contents

List of figures   vii
List of tables   viii
Acknowledgements   ix
List of contributors   x

1   Introduction   1
    Colette Henry

PART I   THE NATURE OF CREATIVE
          ENTREPRENEURSHIP

2   The creative industries and entrepreneurship in East and
    Southeast Asia   9
    Desmond Hui

3   Art-entrepreneurship in the Scandinavian music industry   30
    Maria Aggestam

4   Creative industries in the UK: cultural diffusion or
    discontinuity?   54
    David Rae

5   Entrepreneurship features of creative industries: The Irish
    music and dance sector   72
    Barra Ó Cinnéide and Colette Henry

6   Building the film industry in New Zealand: an
    entrepreneurship continuum   87
    Anne de Bruin

PART II   SUPPORTING THE CREATIVE INDUSTRIES
          SECTOR

7   Investment and funding for creative enterprises in the UK   107
    Tom Fleming

8 Promoting entrepreneurship in arts education   126
   Ralph Brown

9 Encouraging creative enterprise in Russia   142
   Linda Moss

10 Human language technologies and entrepreneurship in
   the creative industries   159
   Brian Kenny and Julia Meaton

11 Developing relationships between higher education,
   enterprise and innovation in the creative industries   178
   Calvin Taylor

12 Conclusions   197
   Colette Henry

Index   209

Figures

2.1	The growth of employment in the creative sector, 1996–2002	25
3.1	A framework for describing corporate venturing	36
3.2	A cybernetic/life-stage model of corporate venturing in the music industry and illustrative actors and actions	38
4.1	Cultural diffusion in the creative enterprise	65
10.1	Relation between classes in ADAM	161
10.2	HLT national clusters	165
10.3	Finland's ICT strategy model	175

Tables

2.1	The economic value of creative industries: an overview of selected countries	11
2.2	Economic impact of copyright industries in Singapore	19
2.3	Composition of Singapore's total copyright industries in 2000	19
2.4	Economic impact of Singapore's creative clusters	20
2.5	The economic performance of Taiwan's cultural creative industries (CCIs)	22
2.6	Value-added of creative industries to local economy, 2001	23
2.7	Employment status and occupations of creative workforce (OCP)	26
3.1	Professional supporting bodies of the Danish music industry	40
3.2	Top ten record companies in Finland by turnover (million euro)	43
3.3	Institutional set-up of Icelandic music industry	45
3.4	The Swedish music industries' export incomes	49
4.1	Comparison of enterprises using cultural diffusion	66
10.1	HTL benchmarking: technology opportunity factors	167
10.2	Finland's world competitiveness rankings: selected characteristics	168

Acknowledgements

The authors and publisher would like to thank IP Publishing Limited for granting permission to reprint material from the *International Journal of Entrepreneurship and Innovation*, special issue on *Entrepreneurship in the Creative Industries*, 6 (3), 2005. This permission covers material from the following papers: Linda Moss, 'Encouraging small cultural enterprise in Russia: gateways and barriers in Russian society' (pp. 193–200); Ralph Brown, 'Performing arts creative enterprise: approaches to promoting entrepreneurship in arts higher education' (pp. 159–167); David Rae, 'Cultural diffusion: a formative process in creative entrepreneurship' (pp. 185–192); Barra Ó Cinnéide, 'Creative entrepreneurship in the arts: transforming "old" into "new": Irish dance and music test cases such as *Riverdance* and *Lord of the Dance*' (pp. 151–158); and Anne de Bruin, 'Multi-level entrepreneurship in the creative industries: New Zealand's screen production industry' (pp. 143–150). Copyright 2005 IP Publishing Limited, reproduced by permission.

The input of Gerard McElwee of Lincoln Business School, editor of the *International Journal of Entrepreneurship and Innovation*, which is published by IP Publishing Limited (www.ippublishing.com), is also gratefully acknowledged.

The editor is extremely grateful to all those who have contributed to this book. It has been a pleasure to work with such a dedicated team of scholars who have drawn on their particular specialist research experiences within the field of creative industries entrepreneurship. Without their expertise, dedication and patience, this international collection would not have been possible.

Thanks are also due to those who willingly gave of their time and expertise to form part of the reviewing process for this book.

Colette Henry

Contributors

Maria Aggestam, PhD, Department of Business Administration, Lund University, Sweden.

Ralph Brown, Projects Officer – PALATINE, Lancaster University, UK.

Anne de Bruin, PhD, Professor of Economics, Department of Commerce, Massey University, Auckland, New Zealand.

Tom Fleming, PhD, Director of Tom Fleming Creative Consultancy Ltd, London, UK.

Colette Henry, PhD, Head of Department of Business Studies and Director of the Centre for Entrepreneurship Research, Dundalk Institute of Technology, Dundalk, County Louth, Ireland.

Desmond Hui, PhD, Director of the Centre for Cultural Policy Research, University of Hong Kong.

Brian Kenny, PhD, Professor Emeritus, University of Huddersfield, UK.

Julia Meaton, PhD, Head of the Centre for Enterprise, Ethics and the Environment, University of Huddersfield, UK.

Linda Moss, PhD, School of Cultural Studies, Sheffield Hallam University, Sheffield, UK.

Barra Ó Cinnéide, PhD, Professor Emeritus, University of Limerick, Ireland.

David Rae, PhD, Professor of Business and Enterprise, Faculty of Business and Law, University of Lincoln, UK.

Calvin Taylor, PhD, Director for Enterprise and Knowledge Transfer in the Faculty of Performance, Visual Arts and Communications, University of Leeds, UK.

1. Introduction

Colette Henry

The creative industries represent one of the most important areas of the twenty-first century's global economy. Since the 1990s, they have been heralded as one of the fastest growing industry sectors, and are now seen as central to the success of most developing and advanced economies. The potential of the creative industries to capture both national and international markets and boost exports has been recognized in countries such as Australia (Poole, 2005), Hong Kong (CCPR, 2003), Singapore (MITA, 2002), New Zealand (NZIER, 2002) and the UK (DCMS, 2003; NESTA, 2006), among others.

Often referred to as the 'creative economy', the creative industries represent a set of interlocking, knowledge-intensive industry sectors focusing on the creation and exploitation of intellectual property (DCMS, 2001). Such industries include, but not exclusively so, the following sectors: arts and crafts; designer fashion; film, theatre and the performing arts; advertising; architecture and design; publishing; broadcast media and recorded music. Interestingly, software development, computer services, digital media, communications and a range of activities within the heritage sector also feature strongly within the creative industries, resulting in an extremely broad economic spectrum which potentially overlaps with the culture, lifestyle and non-profit sectors (British Council, 2003; Wikipedia, 2006). While in the UK, the creative industries are currently valued at £56.5 billion, accounting for 8 per cent of the British economy, in the global market their value has increased dramatically from US$831 billion in 2000 to US$1.3 trillion in 2005 (NESTA, 2006, p. 2).

Notwithstanding their economic contribution, the creative industries, with their strong cultural focus, would also seem to be particularly well positioned to respond to both social and economic agendas at the international level (Metier Report, 2002). With equality and diversity at the forefront of new millennium political correctness, music, sport, art and dance suddenly become vehicles for promoting social inclusion, encouraging cultural diversity and supporting the needs of minority groups, adding a new and interesting dimension to the creative sector. It is, perhaps, for this reason that some political leaders have been reported to focus their attention on the creative industries while 'paying no attention whatsoever to the manufacturing or service sectors' (Benson, 2005, p. 5). Thus, for a range of reasons, the creative industries present themselves as an interesting topic for research on an international scale.

This edited collection of chapters addresses a diversity of issues within the creative industries agenda from an entrepreneurial and international perspective. The objective of this book is to inform academics, policymakers, support agencies and entrepreneurs about current priority issues on the creative industries research agenda. Thus, the book contains contributions that deal with a range of pertinent and diverse topics relating to creative entrepreneurship. As editor I have endeavoured to include contributions which address a range of issues at both the national and international level; which adopt different quantitative and qualitative methodologies; and which examine the nature of creative entrepreneurship across different industry sub-sectors and in different economic and geographical contexts.

The book is strategically structured in two parts. Following this introductory chapter, Part I deals with 'The Nature of Creative Entrepreneurship' and considers various industries within the creative sector across Asia, Scandinavia, Ireland, the UK and New Zealand. In Chapter 2, Desmond Hui examines the different approaches to defining and measuring creative industries in East and Southeast Asia. The economic performance in terms of market share, number of companies and employment levels within a range of creative industries' sub-sectors is discussed, along with the different ways in which the Asian government engages with the sector. While the chapter provides a particular focus on Hong Kong, the make-up of the creative industries sector in Japan, South Korea, Singapore and Taiwan is also discussed. Desmond Hui suggests that while Singapore, Taiwan and Hong Kong may still be struggling to establish their own niche within the international creative industries sector, South Korea has become a major player in the creative global economy.

Chapter 3, by Maria Aggestam, considers the music industry in the five Scandinavian countries of Denmark, Finland, Iceland, Norway and Sweden. The concept of the music industry as an entrepreneurial-venturing endeavor is explored, and the particular facets of entrepreneurship within the sector are discussed. Maria Aggestam reminds us that, in the music industry, all entrepreneurs face uncertainties and have to take calculated risks; risks which require a certain amount of persistence. She goes on to suggest that, in the unpredictable and uncertain creative industry world, art entrepreneurs, particularly those operating within the music industry, can serve as creative magnets around which supportive ventures can consolidate.

In Chapter 4, David Rae explores the development of the creative industries in the United Kingdom (UK). Some of the key difficulties faced by creative entrepreneurs are discussed, along with issues of interest to policymakers and mainstream businesses. Rae argues that, while the creative economy works through a process of cultural diffusion, there are discontinuities between these key constituencies which stem from long-standing differences in cultural, educational, social and economic contexts. He also suggests that such discontinuities constrain the development of the creative economy in the UK.

The Irish music and dance industry is the focus of Chapter 5 by Barra Ó Cinnéide and Colette Henry. Here, Ireland is presented as a case-study of successful entrepreneurial development. The extraordinary, and somewhat unpredicted, success of the *Riverdance* phenomenon illustrates the extent of what can be achieved from an artistic piece initially designed as a short musical interlude for the Eurovision Song Contest. The chapter explains the commercial exploitation and international impact of the *Riverdance* phenomenon, which also helped to platform Ireland's existing creative culture and history, generating a renewed interest and appreciation for other Irish musicians. The key issues that can impinge on further prospective growth for the creative industries are also explored in the chapter, and recommendations are offered for further research in this area.

In Chapter 6, Anne de Bruin explores the entrepreneurial nature of New Zealand's screen production industry; more specifically, the film industry. Here, she explains the phenomenal success of the industry in terms of a continuum of entrepreneurial activity at multiple levels: national, regional, micro and individual. The support available for the film industry in New Zealand is discussed, and its importance within local development strategy-making is highlighted. The example of Peter Jackson as both an artist and a highly successful entrepreneur within the film industry is used to demonstrate the need for the key characteristics of imagination, creativity and innovation to be combined with the more 'humdrum' inputs such as finance and other organizational elements in order for the artist to be successful. De Bruin suggests that, in order to grow a project-based creative industry such as New Zealand's film industry, a comprehensive support framework alongside a continuous flow of creative projects into the country is required.

Part II of the book deals with 'Supporting the Creative Industries Sector' and considers how such industries are and, in some cases, ought to be funded, supported, encouraged and developed. Beginning with Chapter 7, the issue of investment and funding for the creative industries in the UK is discussed by Tom Fleming. The multiple barriers to creative industries investment are considered, and a range of intervention opportunities for overcoming these barriers is presented. The chapter builds on previous empirical research undertaken by Fleming on behalf of NESTA (National Endowment for Science, Technology and the Arts) which was based on interviews with policymakers, intermediaries, investors and creative enterprises. Fleming suggests that a piecemeal and 'catch-all' approach to creative industries investment exists, and argues for the co-ordination of a range of investment approaches that can flexibly respond to the distinctive business profiles of different types of creative businesses.

Chapter 8 by Ralph Brown considers the promotion of entrepreneurship amongst students of creative industries courses. In particular, the chapter focuses on performing arts entrepreneurship and platforms the increased demand for performance courses in the UK. The fact that most performing artists typically work for themselves on a freelance basis at some point in their career highlights the need for them to adopt an entrepreneurial approach from the outset. Using the PACE (Performing Arts Creative Enterprise) project as an example, Brown discusses how cultural entrepreneurship can be taught effectively. The practical and real-life nature of the PACE project demonstrates how entrepreneurial skills such as marketing and risk-taking can be taught to aspiring professional artists, providing them with the experience of both success and failure from an early stage. Brown argues that this sort of entrepreneurship teaching produces better-equipped students for careers as professional artists.

In Chapter 9, Linda Moss focuses on the creative industries in Russia. Here, she explores the nature of the creative sector, and considers the particular reasons why change within the sector has been slow and spasmodic. The importance of the creative sector to the Russian economy and the need to encourage the development of creative enterprises are discussed. The role of historical and social factors in creative enterprise development is also considered. The various problems which hinder the industry's development are outlined, and the difficulties associated with applying Western criteria to Russian creative and cultural projects are highlighted. Some examples of Russian creative enterprises that have managed to successfully balance Western models with Russian opportunities are provided. Moss suggests that the Russian government now needs to make serious choices about its role within the creative sector, and that it will have to work with both creative enterprise and consumers in order to create a more viable creative economy.

The application of human language technologies (HLT) within the creative industries sector is the subject of Chapter 10 by Brian Kenny and Julia Meaton. The nature of HLT is explained and the benefits it has brought to the software, digital and audio-visual industries are discussed. Case-studies are used to illustrate the development and entrepreneurial activities of two HLT suppliers. Finland is also used as an example of how success in HLT can be achieved in a marginalized situation. The authors of the chapter suggest that, as computer technology continues to reshape society, substantial economic and social opportunity for natural language and speech technology will be created. This, in turn, will stretch the creativity of researchers, developers and entrepreneurs alike.

Chapter 11 platforms a recurring theme throughout many of the chapters – that of relationships within the creative industries sector. In this particular chapter by Calvin Taylor, the author focuses on developing relationships between higher education, enterprise and innovation within the creative sector. The developing role of universities in relation to the creative industries, regional development and knowledge transfer is considered. The organisational characteristics of the creative industries and the types of business models within which they work are examined. A particular focus is placed on the role of institutions in regional and enterprise development. The chapter sets out some of the key issues that need to be considered by both institutions and policymakers if there is to be an effective supportive relationship between universities and the creative industries.

In the final chapter, Chapter 12 by Colette Henry, I review all of the chapters and attempt to draw together the main themes discussed in the book. I discuss the main conclusions and outline what would seem to be a logical way forward for promoting the creative industries sector in the future.

This edited collection of chapters, which essentially considers creative entrepreneurship across 14 different countries, adds some new dimensions to the current creative entrepreneurship research agenda. In so doing, it is hoped to not only highlight the valuable economic and social contribution of the creative industries sector, but also to encourage policy-makers, as well as educators and trainers, to continue to evaluate the critical role they play in the creative enterprise development process.

REFERENCES

Benson, R. (2005), Design for Life, *Guardian*, Work Section, 1 October.

British Council (2003), The Future of Creativity? How can we best encourage and develop entrepreneurship in the creative industries?, Proceedings of the British Council's European Seminar on Entrepreneurship and the Creative Industries, Scotland House Conference Centre, Brussels, 25 November.

CCPR – Centre for Cultural Policy Research (2003), Baseline Study on Hong Kong's Creative Industries, http://www.cpu.gov.uk/english/documents/new/press/baseline% 20study(eng).pdf.

DCMS – Department of Culture Media and Sport (2001), Creative Industries Mapping Document, London.

DCMS – Department of Culture Media and Sport (2003), Creative Industries Economic Estimates, London, July.

Metier Report (2002), Arts and Diversity in the Labour Market: a baseline study of research into the training and development needs of Black, disabled and female arts practitioners, managers and technicians in England, April. http://www.metier. org.uk/research/diversity_in_the_labour_market/display.php?section=8, accessed 15 December 2006.

MITA – Ministry of Information and the Arts (2002), Investing in Cultural Capital: a new agenda for a creative and connected nation, Green Paper, London, March. (http://www.mica.gov.sg/mica_business/b_creative.html).

NESTA – National Endowment for Science, Technology and the Arts (2006), Creating growth – how the UK can develop world-class creative businesses, April, available from www.nesta.org.

NZIER – New Zealand Institute of Economic Research (2002), The Creative Industries in New Zealand: economic contribution, London, May.

Poole, M. (2005), Creative leap to new industries, Vice-Chancellor – Edith Cowan University, http://www.ecu.edu.au/VC@home/Speeches/creative.html, accessed 5 January 2006.

Wikipedia (2006), Creative Industries, http://en.wikipedia.org/wiki/Creative_ Industries, accessed 17 December 2006.

PART I

The nature of creative entrepreneurship

2. The creative industries and entrepreneurship in East and Southeast Asia

Desmond Hui

INTRODUCTION

For many, the creative industries represent a variegated notion for describing a rising economic sector, the dynamics of industrial collaboration as well as the changing landscape of the employment market. The rise of the creative sector concurrently underscores the deep-seated transformation of the economic domain from a manufacturing-based economy to one that is essentially consumption-based, by which culture is rediscovered as one of the most important resources for economic development.

Creative industries are not new and could be identified in the conventional typology of economic activities. The advocacy of service-enhanced manufacturing (SEM), the notion of the 'value-added economy' and the support of small and medium-sized enterprises (SMEs) all seem to converge with the promotion of a creative economy as a result of the economic transformation and restructuring in most Asian cities in recent years. The creative industry sector, belonging mainly to the services sector which comprises around 85 per cent of the whole economy in Hong Kong, concerns transforming intangible assets into production processes as well as the distribution of goods or services of symbolic values and social meanings.

The usual means of measuring the economic value of the creative industry sector is the contribution of the sector to gross domestic product (GDP) in terms of its distribution growth, as compared to the overall economic growth, as well as the sector's potential for job creation in terms of employment share in the overall working population. The UK model of mapping has been emulated by many Commonwealth countries such as Australia and New Zealand, which also adopt the term 'creative industries' in their economic policies. Other European countries, such as Finland, Spain and Germany, prefer the term 'cultural industries' instead. However, in Asia, the notion of 'cultural industries' seems more popular than 'creative industries'.[1] Japan, South Korea and Mainland China all adopt this term, although the component industries in these countries differ substantially from one another and from those of the rest of the world.

Notwithstanding the different definitions, typologies and classifications available, it has been claimed that the creative sector is a growing economic domain with a valuable contribution to the local economy and with significant job creation potential. The percentage share of GDP and the growth rate of the creative industries in these different countries and economies vary from 2.8 per cent (Singapore's GDP) to 7.9 per cent (UK's GDP), and from 5.7 per cent (Australia's growth rate) to 16 per cent (UK's growth rate) respectively, while employment share varies from 3.4 per cent (Singapore) to 5.9 per cent (US) of the overall working population (see Table 2.1).

This chapter will examine the background and different approaches to defining and measuring creative and cultural industries in some of the major countries and regions of East and Southeast Asia including Japan, South Korea, Singapore, Taiwan and Hong Kong.[2] The case of Hong Kong will be elaborated to include analyses of the creative workforce to assess the degree and potential of entrepreneurship, with updates on policy development.

JAPAN[3]

According to the Japanese Establishment and Enterprise Census (2001), the ratio of the creative industries (CIs) in Japan to all industries, except agriculture, forestry and mining, and government, was 2.7 per cent by number of establishments and 3.1 per cent by number of persons engaged. As for Tokyo, the figures were 5.1 per cent and 7.5 per cent respectively. Accordingly, 22.3 per cent of establishments and 34.8 per cent of persons were located in Tokyo. In Japan, they generated ¥36 300 billion as income and spent ¥30 700 billion in expenses in 1999, which constituted approximately 18 per cent of all service industries. Overall, the working population in the CIs increased to 1.6 million in 2000, which was 2.4 per cent of the total working population, 20 per cent of which were in Tokyo.

As regards government policy, CIs are divided into two areas: media contents industry, under the Ministry of Economy, Trade and Industry (METI), and arts and culture, under the Agency for Cultural Affairs (ACA). However, advertising, architecture and design are not covered by these policies. On the whole, enterprises in these three categories manage themselves commercially. The Japanese government does not directly support these businesses, although sometimes it encourages them to establish business associations in their community.

The METI did not pay attention to the media and content industry area until the early 21st century. Since then, the Media and Content Industry

Table 2.1 The economic value of creative industries: an overview of selected countries

Country/city	Concept	Year	Value added	Share of GDP	Average annual growth % of CIs / % of overall economy (period for comparison)	Numbers employed (share of national employment)
Britain	CIs	1997–98	£112.5 billion	<5%	16% / >6% (1997–98)	1.3 million (4.6%)
Britain^	CIs	2000–01	£76.6 billion	7.9%	9% / 2.8% (1997–2001)	1.95 million#
London	CIs	2000	£21 billion	–	11.4% (1995–2000)	546 000
New Zealand	CIs	2000–01	NZ$3526 million	3.1%	–	49 091 (3.6%)
United States	CRs	2001	US$791.2 billion	7.75%	7% / 3.2%* (1977–2001)	8 million (5.9%)
Australia	CRs	1999–2000	AU$19.2	3.3%	5.7% / 4.85% (1995–2000)	345 000 (3.8%)
Singapore	CRs	2000	S$4.8 billion	2.8%	13.4% / 10.6% (1986–2000)	72 200 (3.4%)
Taiwan	CCIs	2000	TW$702 billion	5.90%	10.1% (1998–2000)	337 456 (3.56%)

Notes:
* This figure only stands for 'core copyright industries'; CIs: Creative Industries; CRs: Copyright Industries; CCIs: Cultural Creative Industries
^ The UK figures in 2000 were based on the Office for National Statistics Annual Business Inquiry, which are different from those in the mapping documents. Hence figures of 1997–98 and 2000 are not comparable.
\# This figure is for 2001.

Sources: Britain: DCMS (2001), *Creative Industries Mapping Document*; DCMS (2002), *Creative Industries Fact File*, April; Greater London Authority (2002), *Creativity: London's Core Business*, October, http://www.london.gov.uk/approot/mayor/economic_unit/docs/create_inds_rep02.pdf.
New Zealand: New Zealand Institute of Economic Research (INC.) (2002), *Creative Industries in New Zealand: Economic Contribution, Report to Industry New Zealand*, March.
United States: Stephen E. Siwek (2002), *Copyright Industries in the U.S. Economy: The 2002 Report*, International Intellectual Property Alliance.
Australia: Allen Consulting Group (2001), *The Economic Contribution of Australia's Copyright Industries*.
Singapore: ERC Services Subcommittee Workgroup on Creative Industries (2002), *Creative Industries Development Strategy: Propelling Singapore's Creative Economy*, September.
Taiwan: Taiwan Institute of Economic Research (2002), *Cultural Creative Industries Mapping Study*, Interim Report, November.

Division of the METI has been promoting broadcasting, newspapers, publishing, film, music and digital entertainment. The total value of production of these industries was ¥10 600 billion in 2000. Three major issues in these industries are: the oligopolistic structure in the distribution system, the subcontract status of content producers, and the immaturity of broadband systems, which collectively prevent talented creators from producing attractive productions and interrupt smooth circulation of content.

In view of this, the METI established two principles for media and content industry policy: the equal relationship between creators and distributors, and a healthy circulation of media content. The METI plans to develop circulation infrastructure and to encourage competition among distribution routes by the following measures: improvement of the broadband system with secured safety, creation of the alternative distribution routes, and elimination of piracy for overseas promotion. In addition, the METI aims to improve the environment for vital markets by ensuring fair competition, developing a fundraising strategy, and developing human resources.

In contrast to the media contents industry, there is a history of policy for arts and culture in Japan. For example, the Japanese government established the Agency for Cultural Affairs (ACA) in 1968 by integrating the Cultural Bureau of the Ministry of Education and the Cultural Properties Protection Commission. For many years, the ACA's primary purpose was to preserve and maintain cultural properties and promote traditional arts. In 1990, the ACA founded the Japan Arts Fund (JAF) to support arts and cultural activities, including art companies, theatres, performing groups, artists and so on. The total amount of support to art activities was doubled as a result of the establishment of the JAF. Since then, the ACA has strengthened the promotion of creative and artistic activities by enhancing support measures. For example, the ACA launched the Arts Plan 21 in 1996 to reinforce these measures (ACA, 1997). In 2002, the ACA further developed the Plan, resulting in the New Century Arts Plan, and again doubled its budget frame to ¥20 billion in 2003. The total budget of the ACA also increased rapidly in these three years, while other areas suffered from severe budget cuts. Through the Plan, the ACA promotes the creation and presentation of drama, dance, opera, music, film, visual arts, and so on. The Plan also nurtures artists by granting international and domestic fellowships. However, the Japanese government does not seem to recognize these arts and cultural areas as industrial entities.

SOUTH KOREA

The South Korean government has developed a series of cultural policy plans since the mid-1970s in an effort to become a nation with vibrant arts and culture. The Culture and Arts Promotion Act was introduced in 1972, and this defines culture and arts as literature, fine arts, music, dance, theatre, film, entertainment, traditional music, photography, language and publishing. The Ministry of Culture and Tourism (MCT) is the national body responsible for setting out cultural policy for Korea. The MCT was established in 1998 and oversees areas of culture, the arts, religion, tourism, sports and youth. In 2002, the MCT was operating on 1.06 per cent of the government's total annual budget.

The setting up of policies on cultural industry by the South Korean government was largely due to confrontation with the domination of foreign cultural products in domestic markets, especially in animation, video and film. A major cultural support initiative was the Cultural Industry Bureau, which was established within the Ministry of Culture and Sports in 1994 (renamed in 1998 as the Ministry of Culture and Tourism). The bureau comprises six divisions: Cultural Industry, Publication and Newspaper, Broadcasting and Advertising, Film and Video, Interactive Media, and Cultural Contents Promotion. Traditional arts and culture, on the other hand, are looked after by the Arts Bureau, under the MCT, for programmes in performing, visual and folk arts. The Arts Bureau is composed of the Cultural Promotion Division, Performing Arts Division, Traditional Regional Culture Division and Cultural Exchange Division.

In 1999, the Cultural Industry Promotion Law (amended in 2002) was enacted, together with a five-year plan for the Development of the Cultural Content Industry, followed by the publication of *Content Korea Vision 21* in 2000, and *Culture Contents Industry Vision 21* in 2002. Policies on cultural industries were also driven by the enhanced promotion of high-tech industries and communication technologies. According to the Ministry of Finance and Economy, 'culture and entertainment content technology (CT)' is 'one of the six state-of-the-art industries of the 21st century with excellent potential for long-term growth'.[4]

In 1995, the local autonomy system was introduced, and the provincial governments were designated to share direct responsibility for enhancing provincial culture. Accordingly, provincial governments began to engage in fund raising and establishing cultural infrastructures, such as performing arts centres, libraries and cultural industry complexes. In 1994, provincial cultural expenditure totalled 102.5 billion (KRW). The South Korean government has also developed distinctive policy and organization frameworks to promote the culture and content industries. For example, specialized intermediary public agents have been established to offer industry practitioners support ranging from financial subsidies for start-ups, to marketing and exports services, tax reductions, equipment and technology advancements. Among these are the Korea Culture and Content Agency (www.kocca.or.kr),

Korean Game Development and Promotion Institute (www.crocess.com) and the Korean Film Commission (www.kofic.or.kr).

According to the Cultural Industry Promotion Act (1999), the scope of cultural industries includes visuals, games, music, broadcasting, advertising, publishing, design, crafts, characters, fine arts, video, film, animations and digital content. The Cultural Industry Policy Department of the Korea Culture and Tourism Policy Institute also defines 'cultural industries' as a 'service industry related to development, production, manufacturing, distribution and consumption of cultural contents'. Such industries are knowledge-intensive and based on the utilization of cultural technology $(CT)^5$ for practical use. Falling within the above criteria are mainly the media and entertainment industries, including movie, animation, music, character, cartoon, game, broadcasting, and other digital content. This strategic emphasis on digital content is also reflected in the government's organizational framework through the bolstering of the culture and content sector. This strategy ties in with the government's pursuit of digital society and technologies.

According to the report from the South Korea Culture and Tourism Policy Institute (South Korea Culture and Tourism and Policy Institute, Cultural Industry Policy Department, 2002), the annual growth rate of cultural industries was expected to be 10 per cent by 2005. Furthermore, the four major cultural industry sectors (movie, music, broadcasting, games) were forecast to grow at an average rate of 22.8 per cent, significantly outperforming the annual economic growth rate of a mere 6 per cent as a whole. The South Korea Ministry of Culture and Tourism estimated the export size of cultural content industries in 2001 to be US$328 million, contributing 0.2 per cent of total exports. Based on the same data, the domestic market share of Korea's culture content industry could be broken down as: character industry 35 per cent, comic industry 37.4 per cent, music industry 76 per cent, film industry 46.1 per cent and animation industry 15 per cent. The animation industry, for instance, had a total value of US$270 million and a 0.4 per cent share of the world market. In 2005, there were 200 companies in the animation industry employing 15 000 workers. By comparison, the character, game and music industries had an estimated market size of US$3.8 billion, US$3.2 billion and US$340 million respectively.

SINGAPORE

With the challenge of an economic recession in 1985, the Singapore government formed the Economic Committee (the forerunner of the present Economic Review Committee) to revise strategies on economic developments. 'Cultural and entertainment services' – defined as 'performing arts (popular music, symphony, drama), film production (for theatres and television), museums and art galleries, and entertainment centres and theme parks' – were identified as a potential contributor to economic growth. Initial recommendations were made to foster the development of the respective cultural businesses in order to forge Singapore as an international cultural hub for tourists and business talents.

The publication of the *Report on Advisory Council on Culture and the Arts* (ACCA, 1989) was regarded as a watershed for the arts and cultural policy of Singapore. The report paved the way for the formation of statutory boards such as the National Arts Council (NAC), National Heritage Board (NHB) and National Library Board (NLB). It also initiated the development of infrastructure such as the Singapore Arts Museum (SAM), Asian Civilizations Museum (ACM) and The Esplanade.

In the early 1990s arts and cultural business in Singapore was overseen by the Economic Development Board (EDB). A Creative Services Strategic Business Unit was set up within the EDB in 1990.

> Its main task was to formulate a blueprint on how creative services can enhance the quality of life and the economy. Nineteen taskforces brainstormed on separate sectors from design to performing and visual arts. In addition, EDB also recommended the formation of institutes to nurture creative skills, and this recommendation resulted in the formation of Ngee Ann Polytechnic's School of Film and Media Studies, and funding support from SIA to La Salle College of the Arts. (MITA, 2002)

This responsibility for promoting creative services as business was transferred in 1995 to the Singapore Tourism Board (STB), which launched its strategic plans to circumscribe benefits of cultural tourism and economic spin-offs leveraged by the arts business cluster.

In December 1996, the Committee on National Arts Education released a report entitled *The Next Wave of Creative Energy*. This report emphasized the need for a coherent national arts education policy to develop the creative competencies for Singapore. It was followed by a report by the Committee to upgrade La Salle-SIA and NAFA in July 1998, *Creative Singapore – A Renaissance Nation in the Knowledge Age*, which outlined recommendations on the improvement of arts education at the tertiary level as a preliminary aspiration to raise artistic excellence and creative talents. In March 2000, the *Renaissance City Report* was issued by the Ministry of Information and the Arts (MITA), which explicitly endorsed the government's determination to build world-class arts and cultural activities.[6]

The MITA's Green Paper on 'Investing in cultural capital: a new agenda for a creative and connected nation' was published in March 2002 (MITA,

2002). The notion of 'cultural capital' was officially brought forth as a pivotal contributor to cultural policy and economic agendas. The use of 'cultural capital' in the paper accounts for three major resources: the 'creative cluster', 'creative people, creative workforce' and the 'connected nation'. Following this was a report on implementation strategies completed by the Creative Industries Working Group, Subcommittee on Service Industries of the Economic Review Committee (ERC) in September 2002.[7] The report entitled 'Creative industries development strategy: propelling Singapore's creative economy and creating new job possibilities for Singaporeans' further envisaged steps to achieve the 'creative economy'. The ERC report designates three broad categories of creative clusters: arts and culture, design and media. In relation to the three categories outlined, three major initiatives were formulated (ERC, 2002):

1. Renaissance City 2.0:
    a. build creative capabilities;
    b. stimulate sophisticated demand;
    c. develop creative industries.
2. Design Singapore:
    a. integrate design in enterprise;
    b. develop a vibrant and professional design community;
    c. position Singapore as a global design hub;
    d. foster a design culture and awareness.
3. Media 21:
    a. develop a media city in Singapore;
    b. position Singapore as a media exchange;
    c. export made-by-Singapore content;
    d. augment the media talent pool;
    e. foster a conducive regulatory environment and culture.

The 'creative cluster' recognized in the ERC report and upheld by the Singapore government includes:

● Arts and culture: performing arts, visual arts, literary arts, photography, crafts, libraries, museums, galleries, archives, auctions, impresarios, heritage sites, performing arts sites, festivals and arts-supporting enterprises.
● Design: advertising, architecture, web and software, graphics, industrial products, fashion, communications, interior and environmental.
● Media: broadcast (including radio, television and cable), digital media (including software and computer services), film and video, recorded music and publishing.

It is important to note that an addendum to the MITA Green Paper highlights strategies to develop 'the software', that is, education and human resources, in parallel with 'the hardware' for the creative economy.[8] It envisages four levels of creative capabilities: Expert, Enrichment, Embedded and Everywhere, and outlines specific recommendations for them. Thus, for the Expert level where the objectives are for employability in the arts and opening up of new career possibilities, the recommendations are to offer visual arts, design and media education at university level and to set up specialized arts and design secondary schools. For the Enrichment level, where the objectives are to promote arts for individual fulfilment and inspiration and to cultivate audiences, the recommendations are to expand the base of schools offering music and art electives at 'O' and 'A' Level, to renew emphasis on literature and to restructure tertiary education to allow broad-based education before specialization. For the Embedded level where the objective is to inculcate a 'creative mindset', the recommendations are to encourage the use of arts, design and media as tools for teaching other subjects and to include enhanced design curricula in business and engineering courses. Finally, for the Everywhere level, where the objective is to enhance Singaporeans' (or the general public's) artistic and cultural quotient, the recommendations are to set up an 'Arts Everywhere' Initiative and to promote lifelong learning for arts and culture. Although brief (nine bullet points all contained within one page of the addendum), these strategies constitute a complete and comprehensive conceptual framework for creative education, which is not seen in the creative industries strategies of other countries examined in this context.

Interestingly, Singapore carried out its mapping of creative industries following the methodology adopted by Australia and the USA, which differs from the UK model. The Singapore Department of Statistics conducted the study by identifying copyright industries to constitute three activities: core, partial and distribution. Thirteen industries were mapped out: advertising, architecture, the art and antiques market, crafts, design, designer fashion, film and video, interactive leisure software, music, the performing arts, publishing, software and computer services, television and radio.[9] The results of these statistics reveal that the creative cluster contributed S$4.8 billion to the economy, or 2.8 per cent of GDP in 2000. The 'core copyright industries', largely composed of publishing, broadcasting media and computer services, accounted for S$2.6 billion, or 55.4 per cent of the total value added, while the 'partial' (mainly advertising and architectural services) and 'distribution industries' (mainly wholesale trade of photographic equipment, toys and sporting goods) shared S$1.2 billion, or 24.4 per cent of the total value-added, and S$1 billion, or 20.2 per cent of the total value-added respectively. Although the sector is regarded as being at a nascent stage, its growth is impressive. The value-added of the total copyright industries expanded from S$0.8 billion in 1986 to S$4.8 billion in 2000, representing an annual growth of 13.4 per cent, figures which outperform the economy's average annual increase of 10.6 per cent over the same period. The promising result of the creative cluster is shown in the growth of employment. The sector employed 72 200 workers in 2000, representing an average annual increase of 6.3 per cent. As a result of these statistics and the government's determination to boost the sector, the key priorities became establishing Singapore as a New Asia Creative Hub, and doubling the percentage GDP contribution of the creative cluster from an estimated 3 per cent in 2000 to 6 per cent in 2012 (ERC report 'Vision 2012'). Tables 2.2, 2.3 and 2.4 illustrate the economic performance of Singapore's copyright industries.[10]

TAIWAN

In the early 1990s, the economy of Taiwan thrived with financial and economic activities clustered in cities. Conversely, in rural regions traditional industries such as craft, agriculture and fishing were threatened with obsolescence. The Taiwanese government imported the experience of Japan in deploying traditional crafts as a means to revitalize the local craft business as well as the local culture and communities. In 1994, the programme for Promoting Integrated Community Development was first launched with the purpose of enhancing the traditional cultural assets of regional areas. The first conference, entitled 'Culture Industries' was held in 1995. The term 'cultural industry' first appeared in government policy as a strategy to regenerate the diminishing rural industries.

Later the scope was no longer limited to crafts but also encompassed the production and distribution of cultural products and services. In August 2002, the Executive Yuan released the *Challenge 2008 Report – The Six-year National Development Plan 2002–07* as 'the latest effort to foster the creativity and talent Taiwan needs to transform itself into a "green silicon island".' The development of a 'cultural creative industry' is among ten strategic policies to empower the cultural and economic strengths of Taiwan.

As outlined in the report, the Ministry of Economic Affairs, Council of Cultural Affairs, Government Information Office and Ministry of Education share responsibility for the various schemes and projects listed. The estimated investment by the central government in cultural creative industries totalled NT$224.91 billion from 2002 to 2007. As proposed in the policy plan, a specialized Cultural Creative Industry Promotion Unit was to be established to formulate and govern parameters and strategies of development and implementation with respect to the relevant industries.

Table 2.2 Economic impact of copyright industries in Singapore[a]

Year	Value-added (S$)	Average annual growth	% of total GDP	No. of establishments	No. of employment	% of national employment	Export (S$)
1986	0.8 billion	–	2.0%	5000 (1990)	30 700	–	–
2000	4.8 billion	13.4% (CAGR)	2.8%	8100	72 200	3.4%	4 billion

Note: [a] Ibid.

Table 2.3 Composition of Singapore's total copyright industries in 2000[a]

	Core copyright industries[b]	Partial copyright industries[c]	Distribution of copyright industries[d]	Total
Value-added (S$)	2.6 billion	1.2 billion	1.0 billion	4.8 billion
%	55.4%	24.4%	20.2%	100

Notes:
[a] Ibid.
[b] Ibid. The core copyright industries: mainly data processing services, printing of newspapers and publishing of periodicals, books and magazines.
[c] Ibid. The partial copyright industries: mainly advertising and architectural services.
[d] Ibid. The distribution copyright industries: wholesale trade of photographic equipment, toys and sporting goods.

Table 2.4   Economic impact of Singapore's creative clusters[a]

	Arts and cultural activities	Design industry[b] (1999/2000)	Media industry
1986 Value-added (S$) / (% of GDP)	$43 million/ (0.11%)	–	$1.2 billion (1990)
2000 Value-added (S$) / (% of GDP)	$470 million/ (0.29%)	$2.7 billion/ (1.9%)	$2.6 billion/ (1.6%)
Output multiplier	1.66	1.76	–
Establishments	–	3 657	More than 3 500
Employment	–	Some 25 000	Some 37 000

Notes:
[a] Ibid.
[b] The original statistics were published in a 2001 study commissioned by IE Singapore and conducted by the NUS CBRD (Centre for Business Research and Development). The design cluster surveyed included software and multi-media, advertising, art and graphic design services, and industrial design activities.

Five focuses were listed for the coming six years:

1. The establishment of the Cultural Creative Industry Promotion Unit.
2. The cultivation and education of talent in arts, design and creative industries.
3. The improvement of the regulatory environment for creative industries.
4. The enhancement of creative design industries development.
5. The enhancement of cultural industries development.

The Taiwanese government aims to double the employment levels and triple the production value of the cultural creative industries for the six-year period.

In 2002 the Council of Cultural Affairs of the Executive Yuan commissioned the Taiwan Institute of Economic Research (TIER) to conduct a comprehensive mapping exercise and to recommend strategies for Taiwan's cultural creative industries. The December Interim Report (TIER, 2002) shows some deviations from the definition and spectrum of industries adopted in the 'Challenge 2008' report (Taiwan Executive Yuan, 2002). The TIER Report identifies three major categories:

1. Cultural arts industry: fine arts, such as performing arts (music, drama, and dance), visual arts (painting, sculpture, public art), and traditional folk arts.

2. Design industry: Application of cultural arts, such as popular music, costume designing, layout design, imaging and broadcasting production, and software game design.
3. Peripheral industries: The relevant sectors that support the above industries, such as management of exhibition facilities, professional exhibitions, agency, programme planning, publishing, advertising, planning, and pop culture packaging.

The TIER Report employs UNESCO's definition of cultural goods and services[11] in identifying the scope of industries. Accordingly, it maps out 13 industries: publishing, film and video, crafts, antiques, broadcasting, television, performing arts, social education, advertising, design, architecture, software and digital entertainment and creative living. Interestingly, in comparison with the policy report released by the Executive Yuan, the TIER Report also adds categories of social education (for example libraries, museums and cultural facilities) and creative living industries (for example tea houses, wedding photography and so on).

As illustrated in Table 2.5, the cultural creative industries in Taiwan reached a total value of NT$570 billion, or 5.9 per cent of GDP in 2000.[12] The sector experienced a consistent growth in both its value and share of GDP. Over the period 1998–2000, it reported an average increase of 10.2 per cent; employed 337 456 workers, and contributed to 6.46 per cent and 2.6 per cent of total employment in service industries and national employment respectively. The statistics also illustrate a rapid expansion in the number of people working in the sector: that is, in 1998, there were only 245 412; however, by 2000, another 92 044 employees had moved into the sector.[13]

HONG KONG

In Hong Kong, the idea of creative industries was first suggested by some cultural NGOs around 1999–2000. It became a buzzword when, in 2002, the Hong Kong government decided to undertake a similar mapping study to the British. After two rounds of proposal competitions, the Centre for Cultural Policy Research at the University of Hong Kong was chosen to carry out the Baseline Study on Hong Kong's Creative Industries, and the report was released in September 2003 (CCPR, 2003).

The CCPR Report defines the creative industries as 'a group of economic activities that exploit and deploy creativity, skill and intellectual property to produce and distribute products and services of social and cultural meaning – a production system through which the potentials of

Table 2.5 The economic performance of Taiwan's cultural creative industries (CCIs)

Year	Value of CCIs (NT$ million)	Annual growth rate (year-on year-based)	Annual GDP (NT$ million)	% of GDP	Employment of CCIs	% of national employment
1998	469 368.298,381	–	8 938 967	5.25%	245 412	2.64%
1999	499 953.610,353	6.52%	9 289 929	5.38%	243 647	2.60%
2000	570 210.576,015	13.96%	9 663 388	5.90%	337 456	3.56%

Source: TIER (2002).

Table 2.6   Value-added of creative industries to local economy, 2001

Industry category (relevant codes of HSIC)	2001 (HK$ million)	% share of aggregate value
Jewellery and related articles, manufacturing (HSIC 3902)	1 199	2.6
Advertising and related services (HSIC 8336)	3 179	6.9
Architectural, survey and project engineering services related to construction and real estate services (HSIC 8334, 5311 and 5318)	9 568	20.8
Design services (HSIC 8339)	768	1.7
Motion picture and other entertainment services (HSIC 9401, 9402, 9403, 9406 and 9407)	1 111	2.4
IT and related services (including software development, data processing, and related services) (HSIC 8333)	4 433	9.6
Internet and telecommunications services (HSIC 7329)	7 854	17.0
Photographic studios (HSIC 9592 and 9593)	596	1.3
Printing, publishing and allied industries (HSIC 3421, 3422 and 3429)	12 309	26.7
Television, radio stations and studios, theatrical production and performance, and other recreational services (HSIC 941)	4 870	10.6
Electronic games centres (HSIC 9497)	214	0.5
Aggregate value of creative industries	46 101	100
Share of GDP		3.8

wealth generation and job creation are realized.' The study identifies a number of creative industries as foci of analysis, to include advertising, architecture, arts, antiques and crafts, design, digital entertainment, film and video, music, performing arts, publishing and printing, software and computing and television and radio. Discounting some limitations imposed by the Hong Kong Standard Industrial Classification (HSIC), the creative industries in Hong Kong were estimated to contribute a total of HK$46 101 million to the local economy in 2001, accounting for 3.8 per cent of the whole GDP. As illustrated in Table 2.6, of this, 32.1 per cent belongs to content production industries, 26.8 per cent to production input industries and 41 per cent to reproduction and distribution industries. Between 1996 and 2001, the total value of the sector decreased from HK$47 665 million in 1996, to HK$46 101 million in 2001, and the sector also witnessed a declining share of GDP from 4.1 per cent to 3.8 per cent during the same period.[14] The overall contraction of the creative industries could be attributed to the economic downturn since 1997. The creative sector as a whole recorded an average annual growth of −0.7 per cent, while the average annual growth of GDP during the same period was maintained at 1 per cent.[15] The average annual growth pattern of the sector was invariably due to the volatile nature of the creative industries, which tend to rebound rapidly when the general economic climate improves.

Only a handful of industries demonstrated average annual growth during the period of 1996–2001. For example, the software sector, media and entertainment industries, as well as newspaper printing and publishing, enjoyed positive growth of 7.5 per cent, 10.7 per cent, 4.2 per cent and 2.4 per cent respectively. Other industry segments' performance was less sanguine, for example, architecture design recorded an annual average growth rate of −1.3 per cent, advertising −5.6 per cent, film −5.3 per cent (although showing a significant rebound of 71.1 per cent in 2000), design −1.8 per cent. For Internet and telecommunication services, and jewellery manufacturing – industries closely related to manufacturing, production or production input – growth rates of −1.6 per cent and −8.2 per cent were recorded, respectively.

In terms of employment, there were 25 342 establishments engaging 153 190 persons in the sector in 1996. However, adverse economic conditions since 1997 had entailed some job loss, but despite the intermittent decline, the sector as a whole demonstrated a gradual employment growth during the seven years between 1996 and 2002. The number of establishments increased to 30 838, with total employment reaching 170 011 in 2002. Generally speaking, the creative sector demonstrated consecutive growth on a year-on-year basis, and rebounded from the lowest ebb of −5.8 per cent in 1998. Throughout the period of the CCPR study, the creative sector demonstrated an average annual growth of 1.8 per cent against an average of 0.8 per cent total employment growth in the same period. The creative sector's share of total employment is also growing: 5.3 per cent in 2002, against 5 per cent in 1996, as illustrated in Figure 2.1.

Characteristics of the Creative Workforce

The core creative workforce in Hong Kong is not homogenous in terms of attributes, nor in terms of the structure of employment. Indeed, those within the workforce share some common characteristics, but with diversity and discrepancy. The workforce is predominantly male – at 68.8 per cent; generally young – half of those working in the sector fall within the

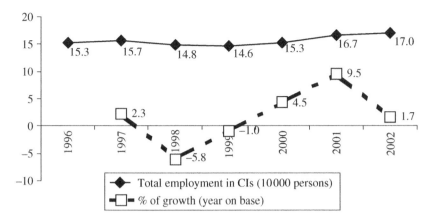

Figure 2.1   The growth of employment in the creative sector, 1996–2002

age range of 25–34; highly educated – 64.7 per cent possess tertiary degrees; mostly working as employees – 94 per cent (with only 2.4 per cent as employers and 3.7 per cent self-employed) and comparatively well paid – only 11.7 per cent earning less than the median monthly income of HK$10000.

Employment Status and Entrepreneurship

Analysis of the creative sector in Hong Kong reveals that creative workers, unlike those portrayed in Western countries as self-employed and, hence, entrepreneurial, are indeed mostly employees. Among all occupations within the sector, writers and creative artists, and performers and entertainment personnel, have more self-employed workers. However, as shown in Table 2.7, self-employment levels in these two categories, despite being higher than other occupational groups, are only 12.6 per cent and 10.1 per cent respectively. In addition, secondary employment among creative labour is 5.3 per cent, which is high when compared to that of the whole working population at 2.3 per cent. Among all the OCP, 11.5 per cent of performers and entertainment personnel report avocation, as do 9.3 per cent of writers and creative artists, while the proportion of sideline employment for the remaining occupations ranges between 2.3 per cent and 8.1 per cent. While the low percentage of entrepreneurs in the creative sector indicates slow growth in the creative industries, it also offers a huge untapped market of creative individuals who could become entrepreneurs should the conditions for enterprise become favourable. Hence, the potential for growth in new venture creation is huge.

Table 2.7   Employment status and occupations of creative workforce (OCP)

Occupations	% of employers	% of employees	% of self-employed
Architects, town/traffic planners and surveyors	2.5	95.2	2.3
Translators and interpreters	3.5	92.4	4.1
News editors and journalists	0.9	98.2	0.9
Writers and creative artists	5.4	82.0	12.6
Librarians and related professionals	–	100.0	–
Application system dev. professionals	1.7	97.3	1.0
Internet/multimedia content dev. professionals	4.5	92.5	3.0
IT research and product dev. professionals	2.7	94.5	2.8
Performers, entertainment and sports	2.5	87.4	10.1
Internet/multimedia content dev. associate professionals	2.7	93.7	3.7
Sub-total of OCP by economic activity status	2.4	93.9	3.7

Policy and Future Prospects

As a policy directive, the Hong Kong government first employed the term 'creative industries' in its Policy Address of 2003. Subsequent annual Policy Addresses reinforced this initial interest with some concrete measures until January 2005, when it was elaborated as the priority work of the then Chief Executive, Mr Tung Chee Wah, for his remaining term of office.[16] The Home Affairs Bureau of the HKSAR Government also produced a Creativity Index in the same year (HAB & CCPR, 2005). The term was then amended to 'cultural and creative industries' to take account of the differences between the primarily British 'creative industries' concept and the already prevalent term 'cultural industries' adopted in Mainland China. Ironically, Mr Tung stepped down in March 2005 and was succeeded by Mr Donald Tsang, who announced his Policy Address in October 2005. Although Mr Tsang reiterated the importance of promoting the cultural and creative industries at the end of his address, he was not as adamant as Mr Tung in pushing this agenda.[17]

CONCLUSION

Of the five countries studied in this chapter, with the exception of Japan, the four 'economic tigers' – South Korea, Singapore, Taiwan and Hong Kong – have, since the late 1990s, all developed policies and strategies of some kind to promote cultural and/or creative industries. In this regard, as South Korea probably suffered the most during the Asian Financial Crisis of 1997–98, it was possibly the most determined and focused in its endeavours. With hindsight, South Korea's efforts and determination seem to have paid off, as their film, TV, music and animation industries have taken off since the late 1990s, creating not only a regional but also a world market for their creative products. Korean culture – in Chinese *han liu* (Korean trend) – has, in the last few years, conquered the whole of East and Southeast Asia. Korean music and movie stars have become the new idols of the Asian audience, and their animation industry has the second-biggest share of the market after Japan. In contrast, Singapore, Taiwan and Hong Kong are still struggling to find their own niche in the cultural creative milieu. Until they can really consolidate their efforts to forge this new frontier of creative economy and achieve results similar to South Korea, Mainland China will undoubtedly remain the land of attention and opportunity, as it becomes the fourth-largest global economic entity.[18] How China will promote and develop its cultural and creative industries will have an everlasting impact not only on East and Southeast Asia, but also on the rest of the world.

NOTES

1. Recent development in Hong Kong and Mainland China seems to converge with Taiwan in using the term 'cultural and creative industries'.
2. Mainland China is not included in this study because of lack of comprehensive data in their cultural industries. It is important to note that they came up with a new National Classification System for Cultural Industries in 2004.
3. I commissioned the NLI Research Institute in Tokyo to carry out a similar baseline study to mine on the creative industries in Japan in 2003. This section is summarized from their report. I am grateful to Mitsuhiro Yoshimoto of NLI for double-checking this part for any missing information and updates.
4. Ministry of Finance and Economy, Republic of Korea: http://www.mofe.go.kr/.
5. A term coined by KOCCA, according to Haksoon Yim who was the Director of Policy Development of the Korea Culture and Contents Agency (KOCCA) in 2003.
6. The MITA was subsequently reformed as the MICA (Ministry of Information, Communications and the Arts) in 2004. For their latest strategies on developing creative industries, please see http://www.mica.gov.sg/mica_business/b_creative.html.
7. http://app.mti.gov.sg/data/pages/507/doc/ERC_SVS_CRE_PressStatement.pdf.
8. http://app.mti.gov.sg/data/pages/507/doc/ERC_SVS_CRE_Annex1.1(e).pdf.
9. http://app.mti.gov.sg/data/pages/507/doc/ERC_SVS_CRE_Exec.pdf.

10. The latest update with 2002/03 data was done by the IP Academy in collaboration with WIPO (see IP Academy, 2006).
11. According to UNESCO, 'cultural goods generally refer to those consumer goods which convey ideas, symbols, and ways of life. They inform or entertain, contribute to build collective identity and influence cultural practices. The result of individual or collective creativity – thus copyright-based cultural goods are reproduced and boosted by industrial processes and worldwide distribution. Books, magazines, multimedia products, software, records, films, videos, audio-visual programmes, crafts and fashion design constitute plural and diversified cultural offerings for citizens at large.' While 'cultural services are those activities aimed at satisfying cultural interests or needs, such activities do not represent material goods in themselves: they typically consist of the overall set of measures and supporting facilities for cultural practices that government, private and semi-public institutions or companies make available to the community. Examples of such services include the promotion of performances and cultural events as well as cultural information and preservation (libraries, documentation centres and museums). Cultural services may be offered for free or on a commercial basis.' http://www.unesco. org/culture/industries/trade/html_eng/question2.shtml.
12. This figure was drastically amended when the Cultural Creative Industries Steering Committee was set up under the Executive Yuan in 2004 and announced that the total value added of CCI in 2001 was only 2.9 per cent of GDP. Unfortunately we never saw the final report of the study by TIER and this is not available at their website or that of their commissioning body, the Council of Cultural Affairs.
13. For latest news on CCI in Taiwan, please visit http://w2kdmz1.moea.gov.tw/index. asp?P1=searchandP2=actionandidx=news,ecobook,chief,eventandquery=文化創意產業 &Item=10&qc=0&At=1&dfmt=d&chkDate=&meandex=0&transfer=0.
14. The year-on-year change in CIs value does not include the year 1996 because of inconsistency of data (in particular the IT sector in 1995).
15. This result contradicts the international trend of a generally higher growth rate of the creative industries over the average annual growth of GDP. My survey base years unfortunately were among the worse economically in the recent past of Hong Kong. If the base years were to include the positive growth periods, for example the early 1990s, the picture might have been very different. It can be observed that the positive growth figures of creative industries as quoted by other countries are either taken during their economically better times or over a very long and extended period of say, 14 to 24 years (see Table 2.1).
16. According to the January 2005 Policy Address: 'In the Asia-Pacific region, with over 2 billion people, Hong Kong is well positioned to develop cultural and creative industries: we have a highly open and free society, where information, capital, talent and goods can move freely. We have the rule of law, providing effective protection for intellectual property. We are a pluralistic and inclusive society, a confluence of Eastern and Western cultures, and a cultural cradle for overseas Chinese. We have a rich variety of cultural activities and life styles conducive to inspiring creativity. We stand to benefit from the many opportunities now arising in the Mainland following its own promotion of cultural industries in recent years. We have people who have always been good at learning, skilful at adaptation and strong on creating things. Yet, there are apparent limiting factors in some key areas, such as cultivating creative talent, fostering creativity, commercializing creative ideas and financing the establishment of creative industries, which have held back the full development of cultural and creative industries in Hong Kong. At present, cultural and creative industries account for only about 4 per cent of our GDP, compared with 8 per cent in the United Kingdom. Obviously, there is still scope for growth.' Point 84, http://www.rthk.org.hk/special/ce_policy2005/.
17. Mr Tsang set up in 2005 a Subcommittee on Economic Development of the Commission on Strategic Development (CSD) to be responsible for the development of cultural and creative industries. The latest reshuffling of policy portfolio in 2007 resulted in a new reform bureau – to be responsible for the development of creative industries.

18. China's GDP output was just behind that of the US, Japan and Germany, and had over-taken UK and France in 2006. See http://www.chinadaily.com.cn/english/doc/2006-01/26/content_515819.htm.

REFERENCES

ACA (1997), http://www.bunka.go.jp/english/2002-index-e. html.

ACCA (1989), *Report on Advisory Council on Culture and the Arts*, Singapore.

CCPR (2003), *Baseline Study on Hong Kong's Creative Industries*, http://www.cpu.gov.hk/english/documents/new/press/baseline%20study(eng).pdf.

ERC (2002), Report of the ERC Services Subcommittee Workgroup on Creative Industries, *Creative industries development strategy: propelling Singapore's creative economy*, September, http://app.mti.gov.sg/data/pages/507/doc/ERC_SVS_CRE_Exec.pdf.

HAB & CCPR (2005), *A study on creativity index*, http://www.hab.gov.hk/file_manager/en/documents/policy_responsibilities/arts_culture_recreation_and_sport/HKCI-InteriReport-printed.pdf.

IP Academy (2006), *Economic contribution of copyright-based industries in Singapore: an update*, http://www.ipacademy.edu.sg/site/ipa_cws/resource/executive%20summaries/Exec_Sum_Economic_Upd.pdf.

Japan Establishment and Enterprise Census (2001) Korea Cultural Policy Institute (1995–98, 1999–2001), *The Abstracts of the Reports on Cultural Policy Study*.

MITA (2002), Ministry of Information and the Arts Green Paper on *Investing in Singapore's cultural capital: a new agenda for a creative and connected nation*, March, http://app.mti.gov.sg/data/pages/507/doc/ERC_SVS_CRE_Annex1.1(a).pdf.

South Korean Culture and Tourism Policy Institute, Cultural Industry Policy Department (2002), *The Cultural Industry Policies in Korea*.

Taiwan Executive Yuan (2002a), Challenge 2008 National Development Plan highlight – survey and estimation on cultural creative industries (2002.09.01–2003.02.10).

Taiwan Executive Yuan (2002b), Challenge 2008 National Development Plan highlight – planning on the systematic services of promoting cultural creative industries (2002.09.01–2003.02.10).

TIER (2002), Survey and estimation on the value added of cultural creative industries: interim report.

Yue Kuo-hua (2003), Culture–creativity–industry: the development of 'industries' in Taiwan's cultural policy in the last 10 years, http://www.artouch.com/story.asp?id=2003051018848016.

3. Art-entrepreneurship in the Scandinavian music industry

Maria Aggestam

INTRODUCTION

Music industries, part of the creative industries, represent an evident example of the contemporary socio-economic changes moving from production industries to knowledge and creativity-oriented businesses. Creative industries are defined as activities which have their origin in individual creativity, skill and talent and which have a potential for wealth and job creation through the generation and exploitation of intellectual property (DCMS, 2001). Developments in the creative industries provide an example of business survival in post-industrial economies. The Scandinavian countries have fairly small domestic markets but remarkably large international business activities. The international markets are critical for Scandinavian industries. Their successes are highly dependent on art-entrepreneurs and their creative entrepreneurship. Creative entrepreneurship, especially in the music industry, is a significant international billion-euro business. The music business is highly specialised and consists of a wide variety of support activities, knowledge and technology. In Scandinavia, the music industry is continuing to grow in terms of sales, employment and global reach.

The aim of this chapter is to shed light on the dynamics and dimensions of the music industry as a part of the creative industry sector, in particular, popular music as a setting for art-entrepreneurs in Scandinavian countries. As individual entrepreneurs move into so-called creativity-oriented societies and the post-industrial age, creative entrepreneurship, with its immense capabilities to produce new commodities, has not yet begun to elicit interests within entrepreneurship scholarship. This study attempts to fill some of these gaps by looking at the conglomerate of art-entrepreneurs each of whom contributes in some measure to corporate venturing in the music industry.

The chapter examines the context and the background conditions of the music industry in Scandinavia. More specifically, the chapter focuses on the music industry as a venue for art-entrepreneurs in the five Scandinavian countries: Denmark, Finland, Iceland, Norway and Sweden. The Scandinavian music industry is conceptualized as an entrepreneurial-venturing endeavour, corporately constituted, involving creators (for example musicians, artists, performers), brokers (various agents, studios and publishers), and media outlets in the worldwide commodification of its products.

THEORETICAL BACKGROUND

The music industry is an entrepreneurial-venturing process, individually or corporately representing the activities of actors who have an interest in particular music production and in the commodification of its products and who leverage resources to create novel music. Thus, the industry comprises musicians, artists, performers, various agents, studios, publishers and media outlets. There are many facets of entrepreneurship in the music industry. These facets involve a variety of art entrepreneurs each of whom contributes in some measure to venturing within the industry. In various degrees all entrepreneurs in the music industry face uncertainties and take calculated risks. Those risks require a certain amount of persistence. Background conditions of the music industry in Scandinavian countries influence the creative work of art-entrepreneurs in the corporate venturing process. The main contributions of art-entrepreneurs in the music industry emerge out of their imaginations and in their actions and interactions with others. Here it is suggested that, in the unpredictable and uncertain creative industry world, art-entrepreneurs serve as creative magnets around which supportive ventures consolidate.

ART-ENTREPRENEURSHIP

Defining and identifying an entrepreneur continues to be problematic in the research literature on entrepreneurship. Defining the term 'art-entrepreneur' is even more difficult. The concept of the art-entrepreneur may differ in its dimensions but the art-entrepreneur can generally be conceived as a holder of tacit knowledge that is realized as a part of human capital and includes individual skill, competence, commitment and creativity-based mindsets. Livesay, for example, suggests that 'successful entrepreneurship is an art form as much as, or perhaps more than, it is an economic activity, and as such is as difficult as any other artistic activity to explain in terms of origins, method or environmental influence' (1982, p. 13). In this light, the entrepreneur is a creative individual who thinks in trans-disciplinary, multifaceted ways and is attentive to the commodification of that thinking. Art-creating entrepreneurs are likely to be creative in unique and sometimes unexpected ways rather than only in conformist ones. It is the aesthetic and artistic knowledge of the individual entrepreneur that provides a harmonious set of skills that, used in multifaceted ways, enable creative and expressible performance. Entrepreneuring (Aggestam, 2004; Bjerke, 1989; Fletcher, 2003), which is what entrepreneurs do, is an act of creation and a pursuit of opportunity (for example, De Koning, 2003; Venkataraman, 1997). All entrepreneuring begins with creative ideas (Aggestam, 2004; Bjerke, 1989). Art-entrepreneurs, it is argued, as representative of the music industry, operate close to the root processes of entrepreneuring that involve ideas conceived, shaped and transformed into unique creations and eventually into commodities. An art-entrepreneur is defined here as an individual who has an entrepreneurial mindset[1] in response to two triggers for the entrepreneurial act: extrinsic, that is, contextual and business-driven; and intrinsic, that is, involving internal desire to create something aesthetic and focused on a sense of personal achievement. Enhancing their own creativity and success in this process, art-entrepreneurs help provide social models, meanings and products that influence the lives of their followers. The sense of cognitive and artistic experiences that characterize art-entrepreneurs can be regarded as commercial exploitations of artistic knowledge. Given these strong pressures towards commodification, art-entrepreneurs produce 'cultural products' that are defined as 'nonmaterial goods directed at a public of consumers, for whom they generally serve an aesthetic or expressive, rather than a clearly utilitarian function' (Hirsch, 1972, p. 641). This overarching influence of aesthetics on individualized cognition and creativity is perhaps best recognized in the music industry.

ART-ENTREPRENEURS AND THE MUSIC INDUSTRY

The long association of music, especially popular music, with individual artists and personal appearances has been expanded to include other areas of art-related entrepreneurship. The music industry now comprises art-industry commodities that are deliberately produced by art trendsetters to be consumed by music followers. The logic of the contemporary music industry is to generate products and/or ideas for the purpose of incessant consumption. Music trendsetters (for example radio, TV) drive consumption by persuading prospective buyers to discard existing fashions in favour of new ones. The logic of the music industry sector and popular music, in particular, is to respond to, as well as stimulate, pressures for rapid change, novelty and freshness, providing for uncertainties since, as Caves (2000) points out, 'nobody knows what will happen'. Music is a social phenomenon in which not only the experience of musical sound, performers and events but also the possession and use of a great variety of music-related products can confer social status and prestige. In many ways, the music industry has far-reaching influence. Enhancing its own creativity and success in the process, it helps provide social models, meanings and products that shape life.

The music business has become a significant resource generator within countries and as an export commodity. It works through many intricate linkages among multitudes of interactions that unfold among a variety of actors in the value-added succession. Along the way, the value-added succession within the music business involves corporate venture creation (Baron, 2006; Block and MacMillan, 1993). Characterized by uncertainty, the venture creation includes entrepreneurial acts oriented toward novelty and commodification, and initiated internally or externally with significantly high risk of failure.

The long value-added process within the music industry starts with art-entrepreneurs beginning their journey through musical avenues with their creative designs (melody and lyrics), and continues until it reaches a customer in the form of recorded music, live performance or other media. The commodification process involves a system of interconnected efforts toward export earnings. For example, in the process of music production as a commodity for export purposes, corporate venturing includes: artists (for example composers, songwriters, technicians); producers (for example representing the process from selection of music to industrial production of records); salespeople (for example sale chains, distributors, stores) and supporters (for example management and marketing, legal services, technical equipment, public agencies).

The creative industries, and in particular the music industry, can be considered as the commercial exploitation of artistic knowledge. Insights concerning the exploitation of artistic knowledge can be drawn from the experiences in Scandinavian countries. One critically important international in-character event that can greatly impact upon future developments in those industries is the Eurovision Song Contest. The first prize, for example, which has been garnered in the past by Swedish contestants (ABBA, Carola or Charlotte Nilsson), Danish contestants (The Olson Brothers), Norwegian contestants (Secret Garden) or Icelandic contestants (Selma Björnsdottir) is both the cause and consequence of the new convergence, at the local, national and global levels, of creative industry and artistic knowledge-based modes of production. Individual acts of creativity are often idealized as key drivers for success and inspiration for corporate creativity or 'creative willingness' (Boden, 1990; Groth and Peters, 1999). With these facts in mind, it is instructive to reflect on the consequences for the whole country and, where radical changes occur after such events, it is also instructive to consider the influence of music's historical heritage on the artistic knowledge of art entrepreneurs.

THE DISTINCTIVE NATURE OF THE MUSIC INDUSTRY

The concept of the music industry has not received much scholarly attention over past decades (Bjorkegren, 1993; Power and Hallencreutz, 2002). The music industry is steadily growing and is a significant contributor to national economies. The explosion of small, independent record companies in Scandinavian countries since the disco music boom of the 1970s and 1980s has been seen as a challenge to the domination of the music industry by multinational corporations. There is increasing consensus that music is an important part of everyday life. Music is a powerful product because of its important influence on people and society.

As an industry, music is multifaceted, complex and under constant technological change. Radical technological changes not only affect its products, instruments and musical styles, but also the infrastructures of the industry (Jones, 2002). Advances in new audio file formats, Internet progress and other new technologies of cheap and easily mass-produced records have opened a new era for music industries (Alexander, 1996) promoting the corporate venturing of art-entrepreneurs. These new technologies are forcing a constant restructuring of the industry and, where radical changes occur after such events, it is also instructive to consider the channels of mass distribution of music, and to its illegality through copy-allowing programmes such as Napster and Gnutella.

The production of music is a process that often involves the intrinsic, hyper-vivid fantasy and creativity of venturing individuals who are both cooperating and competing, and who are driven by extrinsic commercial forces in the hope of multi-million-dollar deals. The potency and prominence of music is largely the result of intrinsic and external demand-related forces. From a commercial point of view, the outcome of the music production process faces the high unpredictability of the market response. It can vary from overnight celebrity, one-hit wonder to big-budget spectacles and long high-concept performances that bring 'money' into the company. According to Bjorkegren (1993), it is still unclear and difficult to predict which product becomes a successful money maker. Art-entrepreneurs do not have much control over the outcomes or over the receivers – the audience. The audience define the way the music is regarded. The products of art-entrepreneurs are judged mainly on the audience's terms (Gans, 1974). DiMaggio (1987) shows how art-entrepreneurs may struggle for professional status and material success (money). He notes that the need to become professional is most prevalent where the artistic field is relatively autonomous: where artistic work is patronized outside the market by individuals and companies that delegate monitoring and control to the artists and others in the art field (p. 451).

THE SCOPE OF ART-ENTREPRENEURS IN THE CORPORATE VENTURING PROCESS

A central contribution of the corporate venturing approach lies in its argument that corporate entrepreneurial efforts frequently lead to the creation of new business ventures (Biggadike, 1979; Burgelman, 1983; Chell, 2000; Shane, 2003). The conditions that define corporate venturing reflect the creative mindsets of entrepreneurs, in particular, entrepreneurial mindsets that lead them to the creation of newness either within or outside the company. McGrath and MacMillan (2000) defined an entrepreneurial mindset as a 'way of thinking about your business that captures the benefits of uncertainty'. Entrepreneurial mindsets are aimed at either creating new ventures or creating new values in existing ventures (Aggestam and Keenan, 2003). In the context of the music industry, corporate venturing refers to collectivities of individuals or companies who act together to bring about paced and innovative outcomes for profit in the face of uncertain market conditions (Baron, 2006; Kirzner, 1985). In short, the art-entrepreneur could be presented as passionate and playful (Steyaert and Hjorth, 2003) initiators who can bring about the creation of newness, novel products (music), and processes or technologies, and who are also able to extend these skills or ways of working to corporate venturing for profit. A framework for illuminating the corporate venturing of art-entrepreneurs is presented in Figure 3.1. The framework includes four dimensions: art-entrepreneurs involved in the creation of music (for example education, need for achievement, risk-taking, job satisfaction, playfulness); supportive organizations (for example technological base, geography, services, customer contacts, distributions); the context that influences the new music creation (for example venture capital availability, availability of supporting services, attitudes of the area population, industrial base) and the processes which include all actions taken by the art-entrepreneurs to create this venture (for example location of opportunity, accumulation of resources, building the process of production, using individual knowledge, marketing the end product).

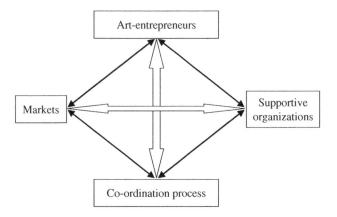

Figure 3.1   A framework for describing corporate venturing

The underlying assumption of corporate venturing is that supra-individual and collective mindsets (Weick and Roberts, 1993) improve chances of entrepreneurial success (Aggestam and Keenan, 2003). Art-entrepreneurs, accordingly, integrate their own resourcefulness and artistic knowledge into the corporate creativity that results from cooperation of the supporting companies involved in the successful launching of the new product.

STUDIES OF THE MUSIC INDUSTRY

In discussing the phenomenon of creative arts (Bjorkegren, 1993) and the music industry, researchers (Henry et al., 2004; Hallencreutz et al., 2004) draw attention to the absence of accurate data on the economic status of the music industry. While entrepreneurship and corporate venturing have not been easy to study (Low and MacMillan, 1988), the music industry may be even more difficult to examine because of its frequently covert and hidden characteristics. In recent years, studies of the music industry in Scandinavia have been on the rise and have provided some glimpses into the area. The studies have provided a macro-level perspective in describing the music industry. Macro-level studies have largely been influenced by ideas and theories from economic geography and economics that award primacy to the localization and agglomeration of the industry. Literature on the creative arts industries has included studies of the film industry (Bjorkegren, 1993), the media industry (Baines and Robson, 2001) and the music industry (Power and Jansson, 2004).

Macro-level studies of the music industry tend to look broadly at the large population of companies rather than at the individual entrepreneur. This has resulted in emphasizing environmental conditions such as political, cultural, economic and specialized infrastructure that influence music creation from the birth to maturity of the end product. Hallencreutz et al., (2004) in their study of the music industry in southern Sweden, for example, observed that the music industry includes a dimension of location with particular technological advancements. Location introduces supportive industries into the process of music creation. Such industries can offer professional insights about product development. In this situation the 'creative-technical' influence of the supporting industry is introduced into the 'aesthetic and artistic product' of the art entrepreneur and the emerging music product is further refined. That might be what Stinchcombe (1959) calls 'craft administration of production'. The location provides a creative milieu and supportive professionals in technical areas. This kind of situation allows production in the music industry to follow the lead and ideas of the art-entrepreneur rather than bureaucratic motifs (Hirsch, 1972; Stinchcombe, 1959).

The movement towards protection and enforcement of intellectual property rights has become crucial for the industry's profitability. Studies of actual industrial situations tend to confirm the tendency of declining incomes from global sales of recorded music (Power and Jansson, 2004). These tendencies showed falling world sales of recorded music by 7 per cent in 2002, 10 per cent in the number of units sold in the USA, and 9 per cent in Japan (IFPI, 2003). Other studies concerning the music industry have focused on music creation, highlighting the creative artists, their products, record companies and the consumers (Hesmondhalgh, 1996, 1998, 2002; Power and Hallencreutz, 2002).

THE MUSIC INDUSTRY AND CORPORATE VENTURING

The music industry is both a domestic and an export-oriented industry that requires specialized skills and competencies. According to Power (2002), musical skills and competencies are often not matched by business skills. The music business includes many intricate local and international linkages and interactions unfolding among a variety of actors contributing to the value of the product. The involvement of related industries contributes to the creation of values. Such music-related industries include music videos, talent agencies, art managers, broadcasting firms, journals, songwriters, recording studios, digital distribution and software houses. These industries

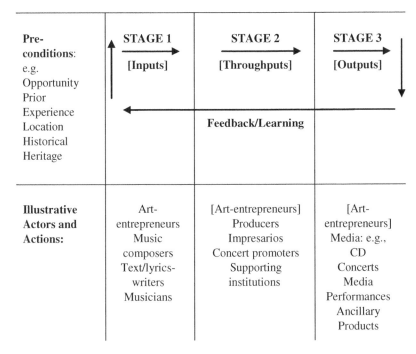

*Figure 3.2   A cybernetic/life-stage model of corporate venturing in the
music industry and illustrative actors and actions*

function variously in the creation, production, distribution and sales of the
product (see Figure 3.2). Those processes work together in the value-adding
sequences and corporate venturing (Block and MacMillan, 1993; Hirsch,
1992, 2000) of music-making business. Corporate venturing in the music
industry involves partnerships and cooperations both within the industry
itself and between the internal and external actors from related industries
including the public sector. Boundaries between those partnership types are
blurred. For example, relationships between record companies, promotion
and publishing companies are often part of the same business structure, for
example under the same ownership or tied together in alliances.

Characterized by uncertainty and risk-sharing, corporate venture creation includes entrepreneurial acts oriented toward 'money-making' products initiated with a significantly high risk of failure. Corporate venturing
can be viewed as a set of activities shared by a group of people or companies, which help the individual (art-entrepreneur) to decide how musical
products should be made and who should be making them. Figure 3.2 provides some examples of elements involved in corporate venturing.

The review of research literature on the process of corporate venturing illustrated in Figure 3.2 reveals some converging ideas. Firstly, it is broadly agreed that the music industry is a corporate venturing process and the output product significantly depends on the aesthetic skills and talents of art-entrepreneurs. In terms of Figure 3.2, the art-entrepreneur has significant roles in all stages of the music product's life. Secondly, as the music product matures, so also does the art-entrepreneur. Studies underscore corporate venturing as a dynamic process. Depending on the art-entrepreneur's reasons for launching the product, the music product may be transformed and new related products spawned. Thirdly, there is a close fit between the art-entrepreneur's input and the tightness of couplings such as resource sharing, effectiveness of technical infrastructure or availability of internal corporate capital in the throughput stages. Effective corporate venturing has been described as a balancing act with needs for creativity and change on one side and demands for cohesiveness and complementarity on the other (for example Lengnick-Hall, 1992; Thornhill and Amit, 2000). This understanding suggests that art-entrepreneurs tend to construe situations corporately and that their entrepreneurial orientation is creativity-driven. Hence, the focus of this chapter is the music industry conceptualized as an entrepreneurial-venturing endeavour.

ART-ENTREPRENEURS IN SCANDINAVIAN COUNTRIES

The intention of the following sections is to provide a short overview of music industries in five Scandinavian countries. They are presented as case-studies of each country that illustrate common territorial and, to some extent, similar socio-economic backgrounds. The case material is based on aggregated data such as: *Behind the Music – Profiting from Sound: A Systems Approach to the Dynamics of the Nordic Music Industry* (Power, 2003, www.step.no/music), academic journals, Internet and media information. Each of these sources provided only a fragmented picture of the industry that limited the author in learning details about the work of art-entrepreneurs.

Denmark

In recent years, the role of art-entrepreneurs in the Danish music industry has become particularly noticeable in terms of start-ups, turnover, growth and increased export revenues. The role of art-entrepreneurs in stimulating growth in the small business economy grew by 19 per cent (in the number of companies) between 1992 to 1999, while in the same period of time, the total

Table 3.1   Professional supporting bodies of the Danish music industry

Art-entrepreneurs/core sector	Supporting industries and organizations
Artistic creators, composers, artists	KODA
	GRAMEX
	Danish Musicians Union (DMF)
	Danish Artist Association (DAA)
	Danish Songwriters Guild (DPA)
	Danish Composers Society
	Danish Council of Performing Artists' Organization
	Council of Danish Artists
	The Danish Society for Jazz, Rock and Folk Composers (DJBFA)
	Fajabefa (The Association for Amateur Rhythmic Musicians)
Industrialists: record companies, publishers	International Federation of Phonographic Industries (IFPI)
	Spillestad DK
	Society of Danish Impresarios
	Association of Danish Music Festivals
	Danish Music Publishers' Association
	Association of Phonogram Suppliers
Distribution	GDC

number of Danish firms decreased by 4.5 per cent. Most of the companies are small and medium-sized, with less than nine employees. For the most part (80 per cent), the companies are single art-entrepreneur companies. The music industry experienced a 63.4 per cent growth between 1992 and 1999, while national GDP grew only 31.7 per cent over the same period.

In 2005, Denmark has about 7500 organized professional musicians, singers and composers connected to various associations (as illustrated in Table 3.1) in order to obtain support and collaboration (www.komponister. dk). Art-entrepreneurs connected, for example, to Fajabefa support 5800 members across 110 local branches with numerous venturing opportunities.

The patterns of music product consumption in the Danish market have changed dramatically. For example, in 2000, 30 per cent of the sales origi-nated from domestic pop music while 65 per cent originated from the inter-national market. In 2000, 19.3 million units were sold. Total export values grew from US$44.2 million in 1992, to US$96.7 million in 1999. From 1995 to 2005, the export of Danish music grew considerably. The value of Danish record sales in 2000 increased to US$233 million. According to IFPI (2002), the Danish music industry (retail value) was the twentieth-largest in the world. In terms of employment, the music industry, particularly pop music, employs 3057 full-time employees in 1918 companies producing music in the venturing process. Furthermore, employment has seen an increase of 20 per cent since 1995.

Big music scenes and music festivals in Roskilde and in Odense have influenced the creative mindsets of younger generations. Big cities such as Copenhagen attract almost 46 per cent of the companies in the creative industries. The Copenhagen region has the highest rate of start-up companies. This explosion of small, both dependent and independent music companies, has been a challenge to domination by multinational corporations (EMI, BMG/Bertelsmann, Sony/CBS, Universal/Vivendi, AOL Time Warner). The five majors dominate the recording business in Denmark. These five, along with other independent firms, account for 95–98 per cent of the sales of recorded music in Denmark (Lorenzen and Fredriksen, 2003). According to Lorenzen and Fredriksen (2003), there is very little horizontal venturing within the industry. IFPI/Denmark plays a role as corporate coordinator between its members and associates. The distribution system is essentially run by the five major companies and the few independents that formed GDC, and covers 90 per cent of all Danish music products. There are three main types of Danish music retailers: specialized independent record shops (for example GUF, TP Music), the large national and international music retail chains (for example Fona, HMV), and supermarkets such as FDB, Fötex, Bilka and OBS.

Danish music is homogenous, and mostly dominated by domestic music production. For example, among the ten best-selling CDs in 2000, five were produced by Danish art-entrepreneurs. Further, on the Singles Top 50, the five best-selling singles are all of Danish origin (IFPI, 2002). The volume of records sold in 1998 in Denmark amounted to 3.3 units per capita, while the USA had four, Sweden 2.9, and UK 3.9 units (Eurostat, 2002).

The Danish music industry is influenced by three governmental agencies: the Ministry of Cultural Affairs, the Ministry of Education and the Ministry of Trade and Industry. In 2000, the Ministry of Cultural Affairs drafted a White Paper on the development of the creative industries which was aimed at increasing corporate venturing and closer cooperation between art-entrepreneurs and business.

Finland

The Finnish music industry is difficult to grasp due to scarce information and accurate data. The description here relies on Virtanen's (2003) study as well as journal articles.

The only authentic form of Finnish music, which has influenced pop, rock and popular music, is the tango. Despite its roots and popularity in Argentina, the Finns think that the tango is as Finnish as their sauna or midnight sun. The main difference between the Argentine and Finnish tango is that the Argentine tango captures the fun part of life, while the Finnish version touches on the tragedy in life within two to three minutes (Ilpo Hakasalo, 1994). Tango music is a major part of the Finnish language record market and continues to attract massive public attention to various media-related performances. According to Isokangas (1994), 50 per cent of the Finnish population choose tango as the favourite music form. The tango is an integral part of Finnish culture. The power of the music is contained in its heavily codified content, which makes the music a strong bond between men and women. Dancing and dance halls have become an important element in this music art form. In particular, the Tangomarkkinat Festival, which attracts more than 70 000 tango dancers every year, encourages interest in music at all ages. Young as well as older people are fond of these events.

The tango was first brought to Finland in 1913 by an art-entrepreneur, and has since become the most characteristic Finnish form of music. It has been developed by many performers, including Toivo Karki, Unto Mononen, Olavi Virta, Taipale, Sorsakoski, Koriseva and Eino Gron. In 1964, Kari Kuuva recorded a parody of Finnish tango melodramatic contents by producing the song 'Tango Pelargonia' which became the most humorous Finnish tango ever made. Lyrics are essential to understanding Finnish tango. Indeed, the main barrier to making the Finnish music industry more international is the language. Other export barriers in the Finnish music industry include the lack of professional marketing skills, lack of commercial resources and the fact that Finnish artists retain the domestic language.

Based on Standard Industrial Classification codes, the Finnish music industry employed over 5000 joint-venturing entrepreneurs in 1999. That number included the chain of entrepreneurs from creators to performers. In 1999, 2100 firms were related to the music industry. Most of the companies were very small, employing 1 to 4 individuals, with an annual turnover of less than US$200 000. The total revenues of the Finnish music industry amounted to some US$300 million. Here, as in other Scandinavian countries, more than 50 per cent of firms are concentrated in the attractive metropolitan areas of Helsinki and Southern Finland.

The sales of records represent only a small portion of the total revenues of the Finnish music industry. Broadly speaking, 60 per cent of the record sales in Finland are channelled through subsidiaries to five major international companies (Muusikko Online, 2001). As illustrated in Table 3.2, the Finnish recording market is dominated by multinational companies such

Table 3.2   Top ten record companies in Finland by turnover (million euro)

Record company	Corporate company (mother)	Net sales in millions euro
Warner Music Finland Oy	AOL Time Warner (US)	15.0
Oy EMI Finland AB	EMI Group (UK)	12.6
Universal Music Oy	Vivendi Universal (France-US)	11.7
BMG Finland Oy	Bertlesmann AC (Germany)	10.7
Sony Music Ent. Finland Oy	Sony Corporation (Japan)	9.9
Edel Records Finland Oy	Edel Company Music AC (Germany)	6.0
Spin-farm Oy	Vivendi Universal (France-US)	4.5
Poko Records Oy	EMI Group (UK)	3.5
Oy Fg-Naxos Ab	HNH International Ltd (Hong Kong)	2.1
Johanna Kustannus Oy	Love Music Publishing Ltd (Finland)	1.7
Total		77.7

Source: Adapted information from Trade Register of the National Board of Patents and Registration of Finland (2000).

as Warner, Sony, Universal, EMI and BMG, with smaller record companies such as Poko Records Oy playing a less significant role. The market leaders in the music publishing sector are Warner Chappel Music Finland Oy and the wholesaler Pec Corporation which is jointly owned by EMI, Universal, Sony and BMG. In 2001, the value of record sales was US$113.3 million, of which 50 per cent came from domestic music (ÂKT ry, The Finnish National Group of IFPI). In 2001, the expenditure on records in Finland was US$21.8 per capita. According to the International Federation of the Phonographic Industry, domestic music piracy currently amounts to 20 per cent of the total market, giving Finland the highest piracy level in Scandinavian countries. Bootleg music is imported mainly from neighbouring Russia and Estonia. Lost sales are also caused by the low demand for CD players and broad demand for live and dance-related music. The record retailing industry is concentrated in department stores which hold 36 per cent of the market (ÂKT ry).

The recent international achievements by art-entrepreneurs such as HIM, Bomfunk MC's and Darude have increased the interest of the international community in the Finnish music industry. These breakthroughs have not only resulted in increased interest of international financiers, but also substantive increases in the quality of the music products. In 2002, a music export agency was created by the Finnish Ministry of Foreign Trade and Industry as a first initiative for supporting the venturing process.

Iceland

As a proportion of the total population, the Icelandic music industry is tiny, with just 300 000 people. The detailed data concerning the Icelandic music industry are not available. Thus, this chapter relies on Adalsteinsson and Ragnarsdottir's (2003) study.

Iceland has always had its own art-entrepreneurs who have provided creative models to new generations of art-entrepreneurs. The history began in 1993, when the former lead singer of the Sugarcubes, a popular rock band from Iceland, released an album called *Debut*. So began the most extraordinary musical trajectory of the decade in Iceland. Ten years later that singer, Björk, became the art-entrepreneur of the contemporary Icelandic music industry. She has released many solo albums, each one expanding the bounds of what seems possible in the music industry, and inspiring other musicians. As an art-entrepreneur, her desire is 'to invent a new Icelandic modern musical language' with unconventional song-writing. The critics view her as a true sonic innovator, one who has extended the frontiers of music in general and electronic music in particular.

Recently, there has been increased awareness of the Icelandic music industry. This has resulted in increasing support both at the new business venture level and also at the institutional level. At the institutional level, major steps to improve the art-entrepreneurs' situation have been proposed. For example, the Trade Council, Samtonn, the record companies, performers and all involved in creative music industries, including the Federation of Icelandic Industries, have agreed to promote activities within the art-entrepreneurial sector. New legislation is focusing on improving the environment for musical activities by increasing the support available for art-entrepreneurs. The New Business Venture Fund and Trade Council of Iceland have involved themselves considerably in the music industry by providing institutional and financial support. The various institutions, industry organizations and festivals which support the Icelandic music industry are listed in Table 3.3.

The capital region of Reykjavik is the only centre of music venturing in the country. All the venturing companies such as record companies, all major concerts, stores, pop music performers, economic resources and international connections are situated in the capital area.

The value of domestic record sales increased by 50 per cent between 1991 and 2001. In 2001, 740 000 copies of records were sold. The market is divided between one large company and 3–4 smaller ones. Skifan, the largest firm, holds the distribution rights for international companies such as Sony, BMG, Warner Music and EMI-Virgin, who together dominate the market with 80 per cent of the share (in 2001). Skifan have record sales of US$5.9 million (ISK 501 million).

Table 3.3   Institutional set-up of Icelandic music industry

Supporting institutions	The Ministry of Industry and Commerce
	The Ministry of Education, Science and Culture
	Trade Council of Iceland
	Technological Institute of Iceland (IceTec)
	The New Business Venture Fund
Industry organizations	The Federation of Icelandic Industries
	Performing Rights Society of Iceland (STEF)
	Collecting Society for Performing Artists and
	Phonogram Producers (SFH)
	Icelandic Musicians' Union (FIH)
	Collecting Society (IHM)
	The Icelandic National Group of IFPI (SHF)
Music festivals	Iceland Airwaves
	Musiktilraunir

The music industry in Iceland is a slowly growing industry. Until recently, much of the public attention has been devoted to cultural policy rather than the industrial policy that supports its needs. The national bodies discovered that the music industry was growing, and identified it as being a sector of strategic importance. The Adalsteinsson and Ragnarsdottir (2003) study found that there are a variety of areas in which both national government and investors can help the industry better achieve its intellectual potential.

Norway

The Norwegian music industry has been receiving increasing attention both nationally and internationally. This description relies heavily on Bugge's (2003) study.

The Norwegian music industry's finest years were between 1997 and 2000, when, according to the Norwegian daily *Dagens Næringsliv*, the annual turnover passed NOK1 billion. Compared to 2002, the volume of music products is down 9 per cent, and its value is down 8 per cent. In total, 13.6 million albums, singles and DVDs were sold in 2003, according to data from the Association of Norwegian Record Distributors. The total turnover in 2003 was NOK905 million (US$134 million/€106 million).

Music Export Norway A/S is a new organization established in 2000 by the Norwegian music industry. It provides access to information on Norwegian artists and companies, and assists the Norwegian music industry by organizing international trade show participation and presentations designed to increase the worldwide awareness of Norwegian music. The six organizations behind this new initiative are IFPI Norway, FONO – the Norwegian Independent Record Companies Association, NOPA – the Norwegian Society of Composers and Lyricists, GramArt (the Recording Artists Association), MFO – the Musicians Union and the Music Information Centre Norway. The aim of Music Export Norway A/S is to be a service and resource centre for exporters of Norwegian music products. Primarily, the company will concentrate on strengthening the commercial value of Norwegian music products.

The front-runner in the Norwegian music market is domestic repertoire. Norwegian acts have strengthened their grip on the home market with a 32 per cent increase in volume in 2004, and 27 per cent in value compared to the previous year. Total music product sales closed at 14.3 million units, generating revenues of NOK923 million (US$147.8 million/€112.5 million). Norway has the fourth-highest expenditure on music products per capita globally. In 2004, 13.2 million albums (including CD, MC/LP, SACD and DVD-A) were sold on the Norwegian market. This represents a 6 per cent increase in sales volume over the previous year. Singles sales closed at 800 000 in 2004 – a decline of 21 per cent in volume compared to 2003. DVD sales in 2004 numbered 300 000 music units – a decrease of 21 per cent in volume compared to the previous year.

The Norwegian music industry consists of about 20 major record companies (IFPI members) representing the Norwegian branches of all the major, as well as a number of smaller, international firms, and also 100 independent record labels (FONO members). About 50 per cent of all companies are located in Oslo and surrounding areas (Akershus, Østfold, Buskerud and Vestfold). The Norwegian independent sector is dominated by three firms: Grappa, Kirkelig Kultur Verkstad and Norske Plateproduktiojon. The total turnover in 2004 was NOK123.9 million (US$19.8 million/€15.1 million).

The following companies shared the market in 2004:

- Universal: 23.4 per cent
- EMI Recorded Music: 20.3 per cent
- Sony: 13.5 per cent
- Warner: 11 per cent
- BMG: 8.7 per cent
- Bonnier Amigo: 6.1 per cent
- Tuba: 3.3 per cent
- Bare Bra/Tylden: 2.9 per cent
- Master Music/Naxos: 2.6 per cent
- MO: 2.5 per cent

- Playground: 2.4 per cent
- VME: 2.4 per cent
- KKV: 0.9 per cent

The Norwegian music industry includes about 12 000 companies employing a total of about 9000 people (in 1999). The majority (90 per cent) of the firms within the music industry employ less than ten people. The Norwegian music industry has never been as internationally visible as its Danish or Swedish counterparts. However, there are performers such as Trina Rein, Morten Harket, Sissel Korseby and Wild Seed which have developed and promoted domestic models for others to follow within the industry.

Sweden

In 1995, within the Swedish music industry, approximately 75 per cent of the global market was controlled by major international companies such as TNC, EMI Group plc, Bertelsmann AC, Vivendi-Universal, Sony Corporation and AOL Time-Warner Inc. Entrepreneurial developments within the music industry in Sweden have two predominant characteristics: they are agglomerated in the main city areas and they are largely dependent on foreign ownership.

The Swedish music industry has drawn impressive international media attention over the past few decades, beginning in April 1974 when ABBA won the Eurovision Song Contest with 'Waterloo' and the Blue Swede made first place on the American *Billboard* list with 'Hooked on a Feeling'. Between 1975 and 2005, the Swedish music industry has had a significant impact on international creative industries. According to the Swedish Institute (2003, http://www.sweden.se/templetes/artickle) Sweden is the third-largest music-exporting nation after the USA and the UK. Names such as ABBA and Blue Swede have been number one in the American and other big markets for a long time. Other well-known groups have included Secret Service (1980), Roxette (1988), Herreys, Carola Haggqvist, Army of Lovers, Ace of Base, The Cardigans (1990) and others like Robyn, Dr Alban, Emilia. Meja, Eagle-Eye Cherry De-De, The Hives, Soundtrack of our Lives and E-Type.

The effect that ABBA has had on Swedish music is considerable. Between 1995 and 2005, children who watched ABBA were growing up and forming their own bands. European MTV was launched, providing European artists with the same opportunity as the Anglo-Saxon countries had previously. The children of ABBA were ready to invade the world (Roxette, Europe, Ace of Base, Rednex). The peak came in the mid-1990s, when, on the

Continental Top 20 hits – a list of the top European songs – nine were Swedish, including Emilia, Roxette, Meja, The Cardigans, Jennifer Brown, Jessica Folcker and Eagle-Eye Cherry (http://www.sweden.se/templetes/art/5393.asp).

Live music scenes are strongly supported in Sweden. Big music scenes in Stockholm and music festivals in Huldsfred have influenced the creative mindsets of younger generations. Stockholm's scenes have hosted more shows than many major cities in the US and Europe, and have attracted well-informed and open-minded audiences who are eager to learn about new fashions and trends. Media exposure has been an important factor for artist development, and the media landscape has changed drastically over recent decades. Music exposure has also changed with the addition of commercial radio to the media mix (this was previously monopolized or state-owned and controlled) to popularise recent music trends. The print press has also played an important role. As *Billboard* concluded: 'Generally speaking, the press here has been interested, knowledgeable and keen, and that's why bands have broken here faster than in other parts of the world' (*Billboard*, 2001, Vol. 113.51, p. 3). Creative acts by music entrepreneurs gaining European and international attention have included Lisa Miskovsky, Escobar, The Ark, Millencolin and Titiyo. Also the breakthrough of Ace of Base put songwriting, production teams and production houses in Sweden on the international map where they all benefited from the success.

There are various aspects of corporate venturing in the music business: selling goods (for example CDs, tapes), selling services (for example mixing in studios, video production) and through royalties. One particular sector of music product exporting is songwriting. International artists such as Britney Spears, Celine Dion, Jennifer Lopez and the Backstreet Boys have all had number one hits with songs written by Swedish songwriters, produced by Swedes, and using Swedish backing techniques. All the Backsteet Boys' global hits are Swedish; Christina Aguilera's song 'Come on Over Baby', Britney Spears's 'Baby One More Time', and Jennifer Lopez's 'Play' are all Swedish. These are strong indications that Swedish music exports are growing. Japan has been a strong market and has provided significant export earnings for the Swedish music industry. Groups such as The Cardigans, Meja, Pandora or Cloudberry Jam found their niche in this market. In addition, some groups that are almost unknown in the Swedish domestic market sell more than 50 000 units in Japan (*Billboard*, 1997, Vol. 109.52, p. 3).

The music industry over the years has become more international which makes it hard to study. Many of the figures are estimates. Figures relating to exports and royalty incomes are more reliable. The total export earnings from this sector in 2002 were SEK 6759 million. Levels of exports such as

Table 3.4   The Swedish music industries' export incomes

Year	Export volume in million SEK	Changes from year to year
1997	2200	
1998	2375	+8%
1999	3150	+33%
2000	2918	–7%
2001	2757	–5%
2002	4767	+73%

Source: Adapted and selected data from National Bureau of Statistics (NBS), Sweden (2003).

all CDs as well as hardware, for example, in the form of equipment for production houses, that are exported from Sweden are provided in Table 3.4.

Musical products also generate income from services connected to the production at home or abroad both by Swedish and international groups producing in Sweden. It is estimated that total revenues from the sales volumes were SEK 325 million in 2002 (Foss, 2003). Royalties are the third source of revenues in creative industries. There are several types of royalty income. They vary depending on whether they are based on mechanical rights (collected by NCB, a Nordic organization) or royalties paid to the artist.

CONCLUSION

In discussing the music industry in Scandinavian countries, an attempt has been made to highlight how art-entrepreneurs and their entrepreneurial venturing are constituted. It was argued that art-entrepreneuring involves a mix of interrelated resources marshalled towards the commodification of new ideas. Previous research has not focused much on art-entrepreneurship. The idea that individuals may act in unpredictable and wide-ranging environments in ways they find beneficial has significant intuitive appeal. A point of interest for entrepreneurship research, therefore, would be to investigate the variety of models that current creative entrepreneurs provide to society that might influence future generations of art-entrepreneurs. For both theorists and practitioners, this information would force a consideration of art-entrepreneurs as diversely creative, commercial exploiters of artistic knowledge. In addition, highlighting the interplay between different local environments and art-entrepreneuring provides new insights into the entrepreneurial mindset and its use in the music industry.

This chapter highlights entrepreneurship in the music industry as being constituted within a system of resources. But generalizing from this point of view is difficult because of the obvious and important varieties of cultures and artistic heritage. In addition to the roles of culturally different art-entrepreneurs, there is an important difference in how government in the Scandinavian countries is involved both politically and economically in the music industry. Clearly, new research data are needed to understand how cultural and inter-cultural factors affect the dynamics of art-entrepreneurship and the potency of entrepreneurs to develop music commodities. The fact is that the music industry in Scandinavia is internationally and inter-culturally entwined. This makes it difficult to accurately describe the interplay of the many influences within the system of people, processes and products.

The production of music as a part of the creative industries has become an international multi-billion-dollar industry during the last 30 years. While previous research has focused largely on the aesthetic characteristics of the music products, it is timely that attention be given to the industry's entrepreneurial exploitation of artistic knowledge. Highlighting this process of artistic knowledge carried out by art-entrepreneurs is an important contribution to entrepreneurship research and practice, mainly because it shows how individual art-entrepreneurs take actions that result in the commodification of their products. Few studies to date have focused on such commodification by art-entrepreneurs. Conceptualizing art entrepreneurs as triggers for corporate venturing within the creative industry would appear to have large potential for guiding future research in the field of entrepreneurship. For researchers and practitioners alike, such an avenue of research might be to provide prescriptive paths for envisioning the new possibilities and future scenarios for creating ideas, new directions and artistic products.

In this chapter a tentative step has been taken towards recognizing and understanding the commodification of artistic knowledge-production in Scandinavian societies. Such production is characterized by the mass creation and distribution of art-music products in knowledge-intensive industries and settings. The chapter provides an indication of the complex relationship between economic and artistic capital within art-entrepreneurship in the Scandinavian music industry.

In summary, this chapter concludes that the Scandinavian creative industries, and the music industry in particular, have accumulated a significant amount of artistic knowledge. Operating within a high level of uncertainty about the commercial response to the commodification of art products, the industries have succeeded and generated high economic yields. By investing in art-entrepreneurs, individuals and companies have built many important bodies of work involving the promotion and connection of various avenues of music. The Scandinavian music industry has gained an international leadership position and is an important model for the work and financial successes of future generations of art-entrepreneurs in Scandinavia and, indeed, elsewhere.

NOTE

1. Entrepreneurial mindset is defined and structured through corporate venturing interaction.

REFERENCES

Adalsteinsson, G. and Ragnarsdottir, H. (2003), Iceland. In Power, D. (ed.), *Behind the Music*, Nordic Industrial Fund, Oslo, pp. 49–68.

Aggestam, M. (2004), Entrepreneuring as sensemaking, sensemaking as entrepreneuring. Conference paper presented at SCOS, Halifax, Canada.

Aggestam, M. and Keenan, J. (2003), Entrepreneurial mindsets during environmental jolts: vessels and vaults. In Steyaert, Ch. and Hjort, D. (eds), *New Movements in Entrepreneurship*, Cheltenham, UK and Northampton, MA, USA: Edward Elgar, pp. 258–86.

Alexander, P. (1996), Entry barriers, releases behaviour, and multiproduct firms in the popular music recording industry, *Review of Industrial Organization*, **9**, 85–98.

Bains, S. and Robson, L. (2001), Being self-employed or being enterprising? The case of creative work for the media industries, *Journal of Small Business and Enterprise Development*, **8**, 349–62.

Baron, R. (2006), Opportunity recognition as pattern recognition: how entrepreneurs 'connect the dots' to identify new business opportunities, *Academy of Management Perspective*, **1**, 104–19.

Biggadike, R. (1979), The risky business of diversification, *Harvard Business Review*, **79**, 103–11.

Bjerke, B. (1989), *Att Skapa Nya Affärer*, Studentlitteratur, 'Behind the Music. Profiting from Sound: A System Approach to the Dynamics of the Nordic Music Industry' 2003, Copenhagen: Nordic Industrial Fund.

Bjorkegren, D. (1993), Managing art-related businesses, *Scandinavian Journal of Management*, **9**, 175–87.

Block, Z. and MacMillan, I. (1993), *Corporate Venturing*. Cambridge, MA: Harvard Business School Press.

Boden, M. (1990), *The Creative Mind: Myths and Mechanisms*, London: Weidenfeld and Nicolson.

Bugge, M. (2003), 'The Independent Dependency and the Resonance of Buzz: Creation and Co-ordination of Competencies in the Norweigen Pop Music Industry', in D. Power (ed.), Behind the Music – Profiting from sound: a systems approach to the dynamics of the Nordic music industry. Final Report. Oslo: Nordic Industrial Fund, Centre for Innovation and Commercial Development.

Burgelman, R. (1983), Corporate entrepreneurship and strategic management: Insights from a process study, *Management Science*, **29**, 1349–64.
Chell, E. (2000), Towards researching the 'opportunistic entrepreneur': a social constructionist approach and research agenda, *European Journal of Work and Organizational Psychology*, **9**, 63–80.
Caves, R. (2000), *Creative Industries: Contracts between Art and Commerce*, Cambridge, MA: Harvard University Press.
DiMaggio, P. (1987), Classification in art, *American Sociological Review*, **52**, 440–455.
Eurostat (2002), *Statistics on Sound Recordings – EU sound recordings market stagnating in 2000*, Brussels: The European Commission.
Fletcher, D. (2003), Framing organizational emergence: discourse, identity and relationship, in Steyaert, Ch. and Hjort, D. (eds), *New Movements in Entrepreneurship*, Cheltenham, UK and Northampton, MA, USA: Edward Elgar, pp. 103–125.
Gans, H. (1974), *Popular Culture and High Culture*, New York: Basic Books.
Groth, J.C. and Peters, J. (1999), What blocks creativity? A managerial perspective, *Creativity and Innovation Management*, **8**, 179–187.
Hakasalo, I. (1994), *The Melancholy Finnish Tango*, FIMIC (Finnish Music Information Centre), www.fimic.fi/.
Hallencreutz, D., Lundequist, P. and Malmberg, A. (2004), *Populärmusic från Svedala*, Stockholm: SNS Förlag.
Henry, C., O'Cinneide, B., Aggestam, M. and Johnston, K. (2004), Where art meets the science of entrepreneurship: a study of the creative industries sector and the case of the music industry, *Irish Academy of Management*, Dublin, Ireland, 2–3 September.
Hesmondhalgh, D. (1996), Flexibility, post-Fordism and the music industries, *Media, Culture and Society*, **18**, 469–488.
Hesmondhalgh, D. (1998), The British dance music industry: a case study of interdependent cultural production, *British Journal of Sociology*, **49**, 234–251.
Hesmondhalgh, D. (2002), *The Cultural Industries*, London: Sage.
Huygens, M., Baden-Fuller, Ch., Van den Bosch, F. and Volberda, H. (2001), Co-evolution of firm capabilities and industry competition: investigating the music industry, 1877–1997, *Organization Studies*, **22**, 971–1011.
Hirsh, P. (1972), Processing fads and fashions: an organization-set analysis of cultural industry systems, *American Journal of Sociology*, **77**, 639–659.
Hirsch, P. (1992), Globalization of mass media ownership, *Communication Research*, **19**(6), 677–681.
Hirsch P. (2000), Cultural industries revisited, *Organizational Science*, **11**, 356–361.
International Federation of Phonographic Industry (2002), *Global Music Sales down 5% in 2001*, www.ifpi.org.
International Federation of Phonographic Industry (2003), *Global Sales of Recorded Music down 7% in 2002*, www.ifpi.org.
Isokangas, A. (1994), 'Finish Tango: Once a Fad, the Dance is Now a Tradition', *Billboard*, **106**(49), www.billboard.org.
Jones, S. (2002), Music that moves: popular music, distribution and network technologies, *Cultural Studies*, **16**, 213–232.
Kirzner, I. (1985), *Discovery and the Capitalist Process*, Chicago: Chicago University Press.

De Koning, A. (2003), Opportunity development: a socio-cognitive perspective, in Katz, J. and Shepherd, D. (eds), *Cognitive Approaches to Entrepreneurship Research*, Oxford: Elsevier, 265–315.

Lengnick-Hall, C. (1992), Strategic configurations and designs for corporate entrepreneurship: exploring the relationship between cohesiveness and performance, *Journal of Engineering and Technology Management*, **9**, 127–154.

Livesay, H. (1982), *Entrepreneurship History. Encyclopaedia of Entrepreneurship*, Englewood Cliffs, NJ: Prentice-Hall.

Lorenzen, M. and L. Fredriksen (2003), *Experimental Music: Product Innovation, Project Networks and Dynamic Capabilities in the Pop Music Industry*, Proceedings of the Druid PhD Winter Conference, January, Aalborg, Denmark.

Low, M. and MacMillan, I. (1988), Entrepreneurship: past research and future challenges, *Management Science*, **29**, 770–791.

McGrath, R. and MacMillan, I. (2000), *The Entrepreneurial Mindsets: Strategies for Continuously Creating Opportunity in an Age of Uncertainty*, Boston, MA: Harvard Business School Press.

Power, D. (2002), The cultural industries in Sweden: an assessment of the place of the cultural industries in the Swedish economy, *Economic Geography*, **78**, 103–127.

Power, D. (2003), *Behind the music – profiting from sound: a systems approach to the dynamics of the Nordic music industry*. Final Report. Oslo: Nordic Industrial Fund, Centre for Innovation and Commercial Development.

Power, D. and Hallencreutz, D. (2002), Profiting from creativity? The music industry in Stockholm, Sweden and Kingston, Jamaica, *Environment and Planning*, **34**, 1833–1854.

Power, D. and Jansson, J. (2004), The emergence of a post-industrial music economy? Music and ICT synergies in Stockholm, Sweden, *Geoforum*, **35**, 425–439.

Shane, S. (2003), *A General Theory of Entrepreneurship*, Cheltenham, UK and Northampton, MA, USA: Edward Elgar.

Steyeert, C. and Hjorth, D. (2003), *New Movements in Entrepreneurship*, Cheltenham, UK and Northampton, MA, USA: Edward Elgar.

Stinchcombe, A. (1959), Bureaucratic and craft administration of production: a comparative study, *Administrative Science Quarterly*, **4**, 168–187.

Thornhill, S. and Amit, A. (2000), A dynamic perspective of internal fit in corporate venturing, *Journal of Business Venturing*, **16**, 25–50.

Weick, K. and Roberts, K. (1993), Collective mind in organization: heedful interrelating on flight decks, *Administrative Science Quarterly*, **38**(3), 357–381.

Venkataraman, S. (1997), The distinctive domain of entrepreneurship research: an editor perspective, in Katz, J. and Brockhouse, R. (eds), *Advances in Entrepreneurship, Firm Emergence and Growth*, Greenwitch, CT: JAI Press, pp. 119–138.

Virtanen, H. (2003), 'Digital Diversity of Popular Music: The Case of Finland', Research Institute of the Finish Economy, Articles, **4**, 58–64, available from: http://www.etla.fi/files/954_FES_03_4_popular_music.pdf.

4. Creative industries in the UK: cultural diffusion or discontinuity?

David Rae

INTRODUCTION

This chapter explores the development of the 'creative industries' in the United Kingdom. It plots the ascendance of the creative economy and comments on its attractiveness for policymakers in the context of the UK's relative economic decline in other areas. Key issues in the creative economy that are faced by creative entrepreneurs, together with other stakeholders including policymakers, mainstream businesses, higher education establishments and the wider community who interact with the creative industries, are discussed. It is then argued that there are deep-seated discontinuities in British life between 'the creative' and 'the mainstream' which stem from long-standing differences in cultural, educational, social and economic contexts and which affect interactions between the creative industries and the other constituencies. There is evidence that these discontinuities constrain the development of the creative economy in the United Kingdom. These need to be addressed for the mainstream economy to become more creative, an outcome desired by policymakers. The need to diffuse a culture of creative thinking and practices to overcome these discontinuities is proposed.

Entrepreneurs in the creative and cultural industries have always faced the challenge of how to transform their ideas into viable enterprises, and there are a rapidly increasing number of examples of how this can be achieved. The concept of 'cultural production and consumption' has an established position in the literature on creative enterprise (Du Gay, 1997), but it is argued that the phenomenon of creative entrepreneurship is more complex than is suggested by this industrial metaphor. It is proposed that the creative economy works through a process of cultural diffusion, for which a conceptual understanding of cultural diffusion is outlined. The chapter suggests that the concept of cultural diffusion can be extended to enable participants in the creative and mainstream economies to interact more effectively.

THE ASCENDANCE OF THE CREATIVE INDUSTRIES IN THE UK

The creative industries are now of considerable social and economic significance within the United Kingdom. UK government statistics indicate that the creative industries generated revenues of £112.5 billion in 2000, employed almost 1.9 million people in 2003, constituted 8 per cent of gross value-added to the economy, and had grown at a rate of 6 per cent per annum between 1997 and 2003 (DCMS, 2001, 2004; DTI, 2005). The Cox Review (Cox, 2005) signals strong interest from the Treasury in the potential of the creative economy, which has moved from marginal to central importance in policymaking over an eight-year period. It is, therefore, necessary to precis the role of enterprise in the significant development which has taken place in the creative economy.

The development of a publicly funded arts and media sector in the UK can be traced to the period after 1945 when the Arts Council and regional bodies were created to support national and regional cultural activities. Previously, artistic and cultural activity was privately sponsored or self-funded, hence state funding transformed a hand-to-mouth *petit entrepreneur* culture of creative businesses into one of increasing government dependence. However, state sponsorship of the arts and media was often contentious, privileging 'high culture' and fine arts, whilst support for 'popular' art forms was generally partial or non-existent (Hall, 1997). This reinforced the stereotype of 'the arts' as being intended for a bourgeois audience of the elite. Yet the long tradition of cultural enterprises performing popular entertainment for commercial risk continued, with music, theatre and dance traditions emerging from popular folk culture and collective social creativity (Bruner, 1990).

Independent creative activity flourished alongside and beyond publicly sponsored arts in post-1945 Britain. The growth of the creative industries beyond the state results largely from creative entrepreneurship – creating or identifying an opportunity to provide a cultural product, service or experience, and bringing together the resources to exploit this (Leadbeater and Oakley, 1999). These creative entrepreneurs sprang from diverse backgrounds, ranging from self-employed artists to owners of global businesses (Björkegren, 1996). Commercial films, book publishing and popular music grew mainly through private sector enterprise. In the public sector, the BBC expanded over a 60-year period from solely a radio broadcaster into a global multi-media organization which competes on every spectrum with commercial creative enterprises.

The creative industries, a term which gained prominence from the work of the Department of Culture, Media and Sport (DCMS, 1998), are defined much more broadly than the limited connotations of highbrow culture formerly embodied in 'the arts'. The creative industries are classified by the DCMS to include 13 subsectors, from fine and applied art, design, dance and entertainment, to advertising, publishing, media, architecture, leisure software and fashion design. The creative economy embraces the entire process from creating the artefact to its marketing, retailing and consumption, as the DCMS 'production chain' concept recognized (DCMS, 2004). This creative economy is synergistic, requiring the involvement of many agents, some large and capital-intensive, some small and skill-expert, in its productive processes. Individual creative workers have generally been self-employed independents, for whom staying in work is a major concern (Baines and Robson, 2001). Any cultural production, be it a music or video recording, computer game or theatrical play, requires the involvement of a group of independent enterprises acting interdependently in complex and specialized ways. The self-employed person selling their ideas, talent and skills has to join forces with production and distribution companies in a shared enterprise. The existence of these complex and tightly wrought networks of workers and enterprises in the cultural economy is essential, giving rise to the pervasive concept of the cultural cluster (Scott, 1999).

Technology has played a vital role, as the explosion in electronic media following the mass adoption of colour TV in the late 1960s was exploited largely by private sector entertainment businesses. Increasing leisure time and disposable incomes fuelled the growth of independent television and local radio, firstly audio and video tape, and then digital media, from the compact disc in the 1980s to include, within 20 years, digital video, cable and satellite media. The development of digital media and creative applications has an increasingly significant effect on the growth of the creative industries which are being transformed by the Internet and by high-speed broadband and other technologies, including mobile phones and the Sony iPod, enabling instant mass access to cultural media of all kinds. The UK is a leading centre in computer game design and together with computer software and other digital applications these now constitute 37 per cent of the creative economy, by far the biggest segment (DTI, 2005). This fusion of technology, creative and commercial activity with constant innovation is a powerful attraction for consumers, students, creative producers and other businesses such as publishers and distributors.

THE POLITICAL ATTRACTION OF THE CREATIVE ECONOMY

The term 'creative industries' denotes the economic significance of creative activity, yet creative production in itself is insufficient, for it must attract a market and support viable enterprises to be sustainable. 'Industry' traditionally referred to manufacturing and mechanized processes, yet originally meant 'diligence' and 'the intelligent application of skill', terms appropriate to cultural production. However, the term 'creative industries' has a postmodern ring, suggesting the decline of traditional forms of wealth creation and their replacement by industrialized culture (Lash and Urry, 1994). This has been manifested physically in many post-industrial cityscapes, where cultural attractions such as multiplex cinemas have replaced steelworks and mills, or where 'creative quarters' have emerged, bringing new economic life and cultural vibrance to run-down urban districts. The Lace Market area of Nottingham, for example, has been rejuvenated by artists, designers, independent retailers and cinema, developing a distinct 'creative ecology' based on informal collaborative networks (Shorthose, 2000).

Entrepreneurial activity is creating new value from discarded assets of the old economy, yet risks being displaced by a 'bar culture' of pure consumption as such districts become fashionable destinations and property values increase. Between 1997 and 2005 the creative industries, and their wider impact on trade, commerce and consumption in the creative economy, grew rapidly. This has both been assisted by and has led to increasing attention from economic policymakers at local and national levels. There was a view that the policy attention from the DTI in the early years of the New Labour government, signalled in the 1998 Competitiveness White Paper, masked the absence of serious policies for mainstream industrial development, and that the 'great expectations' invested by government in the creative industries were exaggerated (DTI, 1998; Heartfield, 2000). Since then, the growth of the creative economy has outstripped the performance of the mainstream economy, and the competitive position of the UK in relation to developing economies – not only India and China, but potentially Russia and Brazil (the BRIC economies) – is an increasing concern (DTI, 2005). UK investment in research and development, start-up rates of new firms, the exploitation of innovation and the knowledge base, especially by small firms, are all indicators in which UK performance is lagging behind its competitors. This led to the initiation of the Cox Review (Cox, 2005) by the Chancellor of the Exchequer, Gordon Brown, aiming to explore the potential of creativity as 'the key to competitive success' by exhorting 'all industries to be creative', and by exploiting higher value-adding activities of creativity, innovation and design more effectively, especially within the small firm and manufacturing sectors.

The period between 1998 and 2005 was one in which the creative industries became highly fashionable as an agent of policy, and possibly a deceptively easy answer to policy development difficulties. All Regional Development Agencies (RDAs) developed creative industry strategies, and several adopted the creative industries as one of their key 'clusters' for growth. The development of initiatives for creative quarters, clusters, networks, incubators, workspace and entrepreneurial training became widespread, and no doubt some of the growth in the sector can be attributed to such initiatives. Where cities have engaged seriously in creative development as part of a wider strategy, such as in Newcastle and Gateshead in the UK, the results have been impressive in starting to change the cultural identity of the region and to attract visitors. Others have so far been less successful. However, as at national level, this privileging of the creative industries masks the relative decline of the private sector mainstream economy in a number of regions outside London and the South East. It is also the case that investment in the creative industries is much less costly than in industries which are more intensive in their use of science and technology, whilst jobs can be created relatively quickly by attracting graduates into subsidised training and workspace to start new businesses. A major challenge, as the Cox Review identifies, is how the growth in the creative industries to date can be translated to assist in renewing the mainstream economy through increasing the value-adding factors of innovation and design.

KEY ISSUES FOR STAKEHOLDERS IN THE CREATIVE ECONOMY

It is clear that the development of the creative economy is of general cultural, societal and economic concern, not only to creative entrepreneurs; it is also of increasing importance to a number of other stakeholders who interact with it. These include policymakers in central, regional and local government; those in education and especially higher education; the 'mainstream' business community which is not recognized as part of the creative economy; and people in the community who are consumers, taxpayers or simply affected by the creative industries in some way. Each of these stakeholder groups has an engagement with the creative economy, yet their needs and priorities often differ. This section addresses the development of the creative economy from the perspective of each of these groups, and identifies some of the issues which need to be considered.

Creative Entrepreneurs

The issues faced by entrepreneurs in the sector include the distinctive challenge of building and sustaining a business from creative activities, as well as those challenges normally faced by small businesses, especially: finding and attracting their market to grow the demand for their businesses; attracting able people, financial and technical resources; making strategic choices on how to compete, collaborate and specialize in order to adapt to the changing environment; and, at a personal level, considering whether a long-term career within the creative industries is sustainable, since certain segments of these industries are dominated by fashion, taste and a young demographic. Creative businesses often exist in an environment characterised by rapid technological and social change, extreme competition, and transient relationships with customers, and may require assistance from other stakeholders to gain the skills required to manage, and especially to grow, in this dynamic context, since one of the challenges identified by Cox (2005) is the very low incidence of UK creative companies which grow to dominate their market sector.

Policymakers

Significant political capital is invested in the growth of the creative economy, nationally, regionally and locally. Will this investment be repaid by the creation and sustainability of businesses, jobs and economic activity, or will it prove to be an ephemeral period of economic and social transition? Policymakers increasingly rely on the creative industries to help 'deliver' their policy agendas of enterprise, innovation, competitiveness and skills, but they work within public sector organizations which cannot usually be described as creative. A key issue is the transfer of skills and culture from within the creative industries to the broader economy and especially to organizations perceived as 'not creative'. This is a long-term shift which, as discussed below, is affected by deep cultural divides.

Education

Higher education (HE), especially creative, art and design courses, is vital for the continuing flow of skilled people into the creative industries. There has been a critique of the relevance of higher education provision for the needs of creative enterprise which institutions are seeking to address. As HE becomes an open market, the future of creative course provision will depend increasingly on the ability to attract students who have developed creative skills within the school system and who perceive the sector as a source of good career opportunities. The educational system in general itself experiences tensions between introducing creative teaching methods, such as Creative Partnerships[1], within a regime of controls, standards and accountability.

Mainstream Businesses

The challenge of the 2005 Cox and DTI reports is for the mainstream business sector to invest in innovation and especially design in order to provide higher value-added and more attractive products and services, but the evidence (for example, that 50 per cent of businesses say that design has no role in their business) is not encouraging. This low appetite for innovation is similarly found in the Lambert Report (Lambert, 2004) which highlighted the disappointing levels of small business engagement with universities. There are issues which affect many business managers which include distrust of external expertise, not appreciating the value of creative input, failing to recognize opportunities for improvement, and a perceived lack of business relevance of creative activity.

Community

The broader community of taxpayers and people, almost all of whom also purchase or consume the products of the creative industries, are inextricably involved, although their relationships with the industries themselves are inevitably distant and one-way in most cases. There are continuing and widespread (mis)perceptions of creative organizations in general to be elitist, frothy, state-subsidized and remote from 'ordinary' people's lives, depicted for example in a film such as *Billy Elliott*, yet there is also a great popular appetite for participation in cultural experiences.

CULTURAL DISCONTINUITY

There are considerable tensions between the stakeholder groups and their respective interests within the creative industries. These act as discontinuities between the groups, and stem from historic cultural differences, attitudes and perceptions about the role of creativity in society in the UK. Creative activity has tended to be seen as distinct and marginal from, rather than an integral part of, the mainstream culture of British society. These tensions, if they are not addressed, are likely to continue to frustrate efforts to bring the creative economy into the mainstream. The Cox Review reflected this and concluded that the main obstacles faced by businesses in becoming more creative were: a lack of awareness and experience; lack of belief in the value of, or confidence in, the outcome; not knowing where to turn for specialized help; limited ambition or appetite for risk; and too many other pressures on the business (Cox, 2005). Four broad themes of culture, education, economy and society can be used to explore these discontinuities.

Culture

The values, behaviours and attitudes to society often tend to differ markedly between people in creative organizations and those in the mainstream. For example, officials in government departments and regional development agencies are rewarded by a value system which emphasises conformance, formal control structures and systems, planning and procedure. Creative people are more likely to value tolerance of difference, informality and spontaneity, and challenging the orthodox. They prefer independence and to be in control rather than to be regulated. The Treasury and regional government agencies may espouse creativity but are not noted for practising it. Leadbeater and Oakley (1999) referred to the 'missing middle' in public policy, in which the characteristics of 'this new generation of entrepreneurs' were little understood by policymakers. There have certainly been advances since then, and the notion of 'the creative classes' (Florida, 2002) has significantly influenced policymakers. However a cultural disconnection still exists between the 'base culture' of government and large organizations which emphasises control and direction, whereas the underlying culture of the creative enterprise is freedom of action and expression.

Education

The educational system emphasises rational knowing, whilst national curricula from primary school to university are predicated on the formal identification of goals, targets, standards and skills. Creative education encourages experimentation and discovery, praxis, and more rounded personal development. The two approaches should not be incompatible, and educational practice through Creative Partnerships and enterprise in the curriculum, for example, has become more open to creative approaches, although it is sometimes remarked that business schools are especially resistant to this (Gibb, 2005). However, while most creative practitioners will have studied in a school of art, design or computing (and there has been criticism of the relevance of this experience as a preparation for creative enterprise), the Creative Industries Task Force recommended that both creative and business skills are necessary for people to succeed (DCMS, 2001).

Economy

The driving force in the UK economy since the 1980s has been the search for efficiency and the lowest-cost provider. This drive for cost leadership has been evidenced in every aspect of life from public sector procurement, from the Gershon Review (Gershon, 2004), and school meal provision, to the inexorable rise of Tesco and Wal-Mart. This remorseless drive for economy results in every consumable item being commoditised and 'Tesco-ised', or sourced in mass quantity at least cost. The tension between efficiency and creativity acts to drive out the cultural and symbolic value of creativity because creativity costs, yet is hard to value in purely monetary terms. It is increasingly hard for creative innovators to establish a sustainable niche market faced with international competition from low-cost economies. UK clothes designers, for example, find their work is rapidly imitated by low-cost producers, although premium-priced 'designer' brands retain a higher value. The challenge is how to create and retain the high added-value of creativity whilst using technology and low-cost production to deliver scale and cost efficiency, as Dyson have done by moving production outside the UK.

Society

The creative economy relies on social networks and clusters, and a feature of creative industry development in the UK has often been the formation of local creative networks. However, a distinctive feature of these tends to be that they are almost exclusively where creative people meet other creative people, with a smattering of development agency, local government and academic involvement. Seldom do they reach out to engage with the business networks in which potential mainstream business clients participate. There is a need for creative networks to become more permeable and to use their marketing activities to engage with business people who, through participating, can learn to recognize the potential for external creative input to their organizations. One example of this was a well attended meeting of the Creative Industries Network, in a Midlands city not previously noted as a cultural centre, which had become a vibrant organization within a three-year period. The meeting was addressed by the designer Wayne Hemingway, who delivered a highly effective critique of the lack of design in modern housing developments, yet the gathering was almost exclusively attended by members of the creative producers together with academics and business support organizations; the mainstream property developers and local authority planners, who could have benefited from his ideas, were not present.

As a result of the four factors discussed above, people in the creative economy are often perceived as living in a different, separate culture which does not engage closely with the mainstream. Consequently, creative activity does not cross over to flourish in or enrich the mainstream as quickly as it might, and opportunities for innovation are lost. Clearly there are geographical exceptions to this, as Florida (2002) argues in the case of Manchester. But more generally, the creative economy has developed its own culture, networks and ways of working, as outlined in the next section. The question is whether and how these can engage with the mainstream.

FROM PRODUCTION AND CONSUMPTION TO CULTURAL DIFFUSION

In writing about the creative industries, the distinction is frequently made between 'production' and 'consumption', a producer-centric perspective which has been reified in policy (Lash and Urry, 1994; Hall, 1997; Du Gay, 1997; DCMS, 2004). This distinction oversimplifies the intermediary roles which enterprises in areas such as media, entertainment and advertising play, where their activity is neither simply producing nor facilitating cultural consumption. Dewey (1934), in *Art as Experience*, long ago rejected the notion of the artist as active creator and audience as passive recipient of art, proposing that the appreciator actively engages with the work (Dewey, 1934). As Leadbeater and Oakley (1999) argue, cultural entrepreneurs 'blur the demarcation lines' between consumption and production, work and non-work, individualism and collaboration. Membership of creative communities is central to their working, and many cultural businesses engage their audience with the cultural product or experience in creative ways. The 'art-house' cinema, such as The Broadway in Nottingham, does not simply screen films to allow a public to consume them. It designs a themed programme of films which are selected to appeal to a particular niche market, both meeting and leading their expectations, then provides an ambience of café culture in which they are experienced and given life by the audience. Culture is a live social experience, actively constructed with the audience as an interactive symbolic exchange, even when this occurs through technology rather than in person, and is not just consumed by them. It has a quality beyond the Tesco-ised consumption of a mass-produced, lowest-cost commodity.

Cultural diffusion occurs where the primary activity is not simply the production of creativity, but rather the sharing of cultural discourse with a distributed audience. Rogers (1983) advanced the theory of the diffusion of innovation through social networks, and a similar process takes place in creative enterprise. Cultural diffusion advances from the static and limited notions of 'cultural production and consumption' by exploring the social and creative processes through which symbolic and commercial value is created through interaction between the audience and the creative enterprise. Cultural diffusion is a creative process applied to a business activity, communicated discursively with its audience. The business performs a narrative and often visual act, 'telling a good story' or 'putting on a good show'. Forming and managing such a business is, therefore, not only an economic but also a creative act, involving shaping a complex cultural web of identity, relationships, communication, language and technology. Technology and communications media, such as design and print, audio and video broadcasting, and the Internet engage the audience creatively with the cultural message. The reflexivity of cultural diffusion with the audience, gaining their attention through the deployment of cultural symbols and discourse, and enabling their expectations to shape the story, is essential in managing the creative enterprise. The development of interactive media and broadband Internet technology enables this reflexive diffusion of culture to take place rapidly, remotely and in new ways.

THE FIVE PROCESSES OF CREATIVE DIFFUSION

Cultural diffusion distributes and shares a discourse of symbols, ideas, language and artefacts with an audience by means of diverse communications technologies, enabling a viable commercial enterprise to be developed and managed. (Björkegren, 1996; Spinosa et al., 1997; Rae, 2005). The five generic processes of cultural diffusion are described below and illustrated in Figure 4.1:

1. Creating a unique identity invested with a personality or branding, which appeals to individuals and networks of intended customers, and with which they can identify.
2. A creative product, service or experience which meets a recognized market need or stimulates an opportunity, attracting a specific audience who interact with it in acts of symbolic exchange.
3. A business process which generates and captures commercial value in the symbolic and economic interaction between the business and customer.
4. Innovative use of technology in engaging, communicating and interacting in creative discourse with the customer.
5. Managing the creative enterprise as a social organization in which distinctive culture, language, behaviour and work style interact in support of the identity, product and process.

By way of comparing creative and mainstream enterprises using cultural diffusion, four cases of creative enterprises and one 'mainstream' manufacturing business are presented from recent research to illustrate the processes of cultural diffusion (Rae, 2005). All five enterprises started as independent small businesses based on applied creativity, although one is

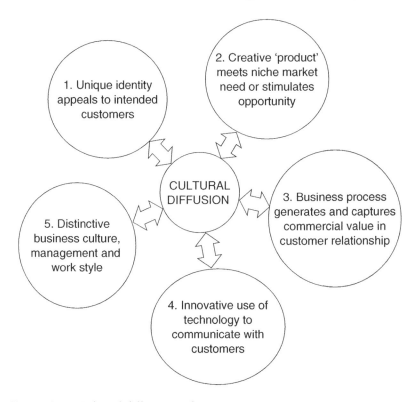

Figure 4.1   Cultural diffusion in the creative enterprise

now an international corporation. The analysis in this section includes each
of the five processes of cultural diffusion illustrated in Figure 4.1.

- Home Stagers®, a property restyling and design service.
- Shires FM, an independent regional group of music radio stations.
- Blue Fish Design, a corporate, product and marketing design business.
- Games Workshop plc, an international producer of fantasy war
  games and published media.
- Phoenix Fabrications, a designer and manufacturer of architectural
  aluminium fabrications.

(The identity of Shires FM and Blue Fish Design has been disguised.)

All businesses depend on their ability to attract and engage their
customers or audience as active participants through cultural diffusion.
Each enterprise in Table 4.1 has attracted a 'fan base' of customers, rec-
ommenders, employees and associates around the business, through which

Table 4.1 Comparison of enterprises using cultural diffusion

Process case	1. Unique identity appeals to intended customers	2. Creative product meets market need or opportunity	3. Business process generates and captures commercial value	4. Innovative use of technology to communicate with customers	5. Distinctive business culture, management and work style
Home Stagers®	Appeals to home owners restyling homes to sell; and to self-employed home stylists	Demand stimulated by TV-led 'home makeovers' and property market	Clients contact stylists via Home Stagers Network and pay for home restyling	Constantly updated website and monthly e-mail magazine create online community	Founder's personal touch, female-focused, branding and networking
Shires FM	Group of FM radio stations with local identities aimed at wide listener spectrum	Local news and pop music radio with advertising	Advertisers pay to reach audited audience numbers	Use of digital studio technology and DAB, basic websites	Culture of fun to keep staff motivated and retain audience
Blue Fish Design	Identity based on being innovative and different, aimed at long-term corporate clients	Design and identity for organizations and products	Clients buy design ideas, studio time and media services	Regular client mailshots and projects on website, training in website updating	'Buzz' factor to retain staff and clients; values of fun, ethics and integrity
Games Workshop plc	Hobby business aimed at male youth market, war gaming clubs	Fantasy wargames, books and magazines	Product sales by retail and resellers, mail order via call centre and website	Website, online wargaming community	Staff selected to join the club, promote belonging and membership for customers
Phoenix Fabrications	Design-led brand identity, confident image targets top construction industry clients	Design of architectural aluminium fabrications for construction projects	Design and manufacture using innovative automated production technology	Website enables customers to create drawings, calculate and place orders online	Strategies to attract, empower and develop employees

further 'fans' are attracted. All five businesses market themselves increasingly by diffusing their identity and creative product via these informal, word-of-mouth, social networks, and through virtual communication, especially e-mail newsletters. The inclusion of a comparative enterprise from outside the creative industries, Phoenix Fabrications, a design and manufacturing business, illustrates that the concept and principles of cultural diffusion can be applied to mainstream businesses. The only principle which needed to be interpreted more flexibly in the case of Phoenix was the product, a design and manufacturing service for innovative products rather than a purely creative process or artefact. The business has innovated constantly, expanded to create new ventures, and grown consistently over five years. The success of a business such as Phoenix demonstrates that managing a business in the way suggested by the cultural diffusion model is transferable beyond the creative industries. The founder has applied a creative approach to the business identity, has developed and marketed it in a way quite different from the traditional norm in the 'metal-bashing' industry, and encouraged a work culture which empowers employees. It is this type of business which demonstrates that the aspirations of the Cox Review (2005), of stimulating creativity in small businesses, can really be achieved. However, the question that now must be asked is: how can more of this interaction be developed?

The other businesses illustrate the intuitive nature of cultural diffusion in a creative enterprise, in which 'what works' is a combination of the enacted values of innovation, emotional engagement and responsibility to people, and the 'feel' and 'approach' which has been learned through experience. For example, in Shires FM, the success of cultural diffusion depends on the outcome of the continuous processes of negotiation between Ofcom, the advertisers who provide revenue in return for listeners, and the community of listeners who provide the audience. Only by producing a cultural product which meets the perceived needs of each of these groups can the radio station be established and continue to operate.

This harmonization between individual creative effort, the management of creative activity within the business, and channelling this into a commercial application is necessary for success in creative enterprises; it is, as Björkegren (1996) observed, a fusion of creative and commercial strategies. For creative production alone has no intrinsic value, and finding opportunities to exploit it is essential. There may be tensions between creative activity and commercial exploitation. None of the examples given pretends to be creating 'pure' or 'high' culture. Rather, they apply a repertoire of creative ideas and discourse to commercial needs and opportunities. The ability to do this successfully, whilst retaining the attention of the chosen audience, is a vital aspect of entrepreneurial activity. These negotiated meanings, practices and culture, enacted within the businesses, are socially learned ways of entrepreneurial working which enable creative and commercial activity to occur (Wenger, 1998).

There is often a quality of shared emotional engagement and energy in creative businesses which goes beyond rationality, expressed in such words as 'buzz', 'excitement', 'fun' and 'passion'. This is produced in the language, practices and repertoire of creative enterprises, as people express their identities, channelling their emotional energy and their creative abilities through their work. This distinctive quality of creative businesses is culturally diffused and shared with the audience. The radio disc jockey, the copywriter, the games designer, each share their creative production and emotional engagement with the audience. Their performance needs to be consistent and consonant with the ongoing expectations and values of the audience, aiming to gain attention, to entertain and, in a marketing sense, to result in a decision to buy.

Cultural diffusion requires the customer to engage as an active participant, not simply as a passive consumer. Cultural diffusion offers the audience a narrative conversation of ideas and language through creative media, requiring new ideas to attract and maintain their interest. Innovating – working in new, distinctive ways – is a negotiated process which meets cultural needs in a different way, drawing customers with it, and distinguishing the particular enterprise from others. Cultural value is generated in the symbolic exchange between producer and consumer, and just as the producer is giving something of themselves, so the customer identifies with the enterprise. The cultural identity of the enterprise is formed and enacted through the interactions between it and the groups with which it engages. Participating in selected networks, influencing opinion-formers, and being 'talked about' in the 'right' way are significant and learned aspects of entrepreneurial working in the creative economy (Leadbeater and Oakley, 1999).

Every creative enterprise is unique in some aspects, but all face similar challenges in forging a business from cultural tastes and discretionary spending. This transformation of creative discourse into economic and social activity is more complex than simple 'production and consumption'. Cultural diffusion provides a practical and conceptual means of understanding the negotiated, interactive, informal and relational aspects through which the creative enterprise is enacted, and from which other businesses can learn. Enterprises which are able to enact the processes of cultural diffusion effectively are more likely to succeed, by working in dynamic and socially connected ways in a rapidly evolving environment, than those which persist with static notions of production and consumption.

CONCLUSION

The Cox Review (2005) offered five principles in its recommendations to increase the impact of creativity in UK business:

1. Tackle the issue of awareness and understanding, including by taking the Design for Business programme, which has been developed and piloted by the Design Council since 2001, and making it widely available to small and medium-sized enterprises (SMEs) throughout the UK and those that work with them.
2. Improve the effectiveness of government support and incentive schemes, prominent among which is the research and development (R&D) tax credits system.
3. Tackle the issue in higher education of broadening the understanding and skills of tomorrow's business leaders, creative specialists, engineers and technologists.
4. Take steps to use the massive power of public procurement, both centrally and locally, to encourage more imaginative solutions from suppliers.
5. Raise the profile of the UK's creative capabilities by way of a network of centres of creativity and innovation across the UK, with a national hub in London (Cox, 2005).

These five themes connect with the earlier discussion in this chapter of the challenges of culture, education, economy and society related to the discontinuities between the creative and mainstream economies. The creative economy has developed to a point where it is a significant generator of both economic and cultural activity in the UK, and there is an expectation that it can contribute to a regeneration of the mainstream economy to stimulate creativity, innovation and growth. This can only happen through a convergence between the creative and mainstream economies, in which the discontinuities between them are overcome.

The concept of cultural diffusion can, perhaps, assist in this. It is vital to develop an enhanced social awareness of the relevance and value of creativity in society, and an openness to change. Education at all stages has an essential role to play in this process of social formation, and as remarked, creativity can increasingly be found within the educational system. Popular aspirations need to be raised, so that creativity enhances the quality of everyday life beyond the Tesco-ised experience. At a societal level, creative problem-solving, innovation and design have myriad applications in changing the established thinking and developing new solutions in such areas as affordable housing, regeneration of urban space, transportation, and environmentally sustainable production. The generation now being educated will be more aware and more skilled overall in the application of creative skills than those currently in the workforce, who will remain the majority for some time to come.

One of the major changes which is likely to come about only through time, education and generational change, as Cox (2005) implicitly acknowledges, is the general move in society from simply consuming creative products, to actively using enhanced creative skills in order to work more effectively in everyday life. When we stop using clichés such as 'thinking outside the box' to represent creative working, but rather apply creative skills and techniques which have been diffused to everyone as part of their cultural formation, we will have moved beyond the discontinuity.

NOTE

1. Creative Partnerships in the UK Government's flagship creativity programme for schools and young people, www.creative-partnerships.com.

REFERENCES

Baines, S. and Robson, L. (2001), Being self-employed or being enterprising? The case of creative work for the media industries, *Journal of Small Business and Enterprise Development*, **8**(4), 349–362.

Björkegren, D. (1996), *The Culture Business: Management Strategies for the Arts Related Business*, Routledge, London.

Bruner, J. (1990), *Acts of Meaning*, Cambridge, MA: Harvard University Press.

Cox, G. (2005), Cox Review of creativity in business: building on the UK's strengths, www.hm-treasury.gov.uk/coxI

DCMS – Department of Culture, Media and Sport (2001), The Creative Industries Task Force, *The Cultural Industries Mapping Document*, London.

DCMS – Department of Culture, Media and Sport (2004), Creative Industries Toolkit, www.dcms.gov.uk

Dewey, J. (1934), *Art as Experience*, New York: Perigee Books.

DTI (1998), *Competitiveness White Paper*, London.

DTI (2005), Economics paper no.15, Creativity, design and business Performance, London.

Du Gay, P. (1997), *Production of Culture: Cultures of Production*, London: Sage.

Florida, R. (2002), *The Rise of the Creative Class*, New York: Basic Books.

Gergen, K. (1999), *An Invitation to Social Construction*, London: Sage.

Gershon, P. (2004), Releasing resources to the front line: Independent review of public sector efficiency, HM Treasury, London.

Gibb, A. (2005), Towards the Entrepreneurial University: Entrepreneurship Education as a lever for change, National Council for Graduate Entrepreneurship, Birmingham.

Hall, S. (1997), Representation: Cultural Representations and Signifying Practices, London: Sage.

Heartfield, J. (2000), Great expectations: the creative industries in the new economy, Design Agenda, London.

Lambert, R. (2004), Review of University and Business Collaboration, HM Treasury, London.

Lash, S. and Urry, J. (1994), *Economies of Signs and Space*, London: Sage.

Leadbeater, C. and Oakley, K. (1999), *The Independents: Britain's New Cultural Entrepreneurs*, London: Demos.

Rae, D. (2002), Entrepreneurial emergence: a narrative study of entrepreneurial learning in independently owned media businesses, *International Journal of Entrepreneurship and Innovation*, 3(1), 27–34.

Rae, D. (2003), Entrepreneurial capability and identity: the role of learning. Unpublished PhD thesis, Nottingham Trent University, Nottingham.

Rae, D. (2004). Entrepreneurial learning: a practical model from the creative industries, *Education and Training*, 46(8–9), 492–500.

Rae, D. (2005), Cultural diffusion: a formative process in creative entrepreneurship?, *International Journal of Entrepreneurship and Innovation*, 6(3), 185–192.

Raffo, C. O'Connor, J. Lovatt, A. Banks, M. (2000), Attitudes to formal business training amongst entrepreneurs in the cultural industries: situated business learning through 'doing with others', *Journal of Education and Work*, 13(2), 215–230.

Rogers, E.M. (1983), *Diffusion of Innovations*, New York: Free Press.

Scott, A.J. (1999), The cultural economy: geography and the creative field, *Media, Culture and Society*, 21(6), 807–817.

Shorthose, J. (2000), 'The ecology of the creative community in Nottingham's Lace Market', in R. Aubrey and H. David (eds), *Greater Nottingham in the 21st Century*, The Work Institute, Nottingham Trent University, pp. 223–228.

Spinosa, C., Flores, F. and Dreyfus, H. (1997), *Entrepreneurship, Democratic Action and the Cultivation of Solidarity*, Cambridge, MA: MIT Press.

Weick, K. (1995), *Sensemaking in Organizations*, California, CA: Sage.

Wenger, E. (1998), *Communities of Practice: Learning, Meaning and Identity*, Cambridge: Cambridge University Press.

5. Entrepreneurship features of creative industries: The Irish music and dance sector

Barra Ó Cinnéide and Colette Henry

INTRODUCTION

There is increasing recognition of the growing significance of creative industries within the economy. The sector has significant potential for wealth and job creation through the generation and exploitation of intellectual property, covering a wide range of industries, from crafts to advertising, designer fashion to antiques, entertainment to leisure software, and an extensive range of support services. The creative industries continue to benefit from high growth rates, outpacing growth in the economy as a whole, while the communications revolution and the arrival of digital networks are creating new opportunities, as well as challenges for creative entrepreneurs.

Despite recent efforts on the part of policymakers to improve awareness and understanding of the creative industries, this sector has not been the subject of concerted academic research. Studies to date have made valuable contributions in particular sectors, such as film (Blair et al., 2001), media industries (Baines and Robson, 2001), creative arts (Welsch and Kickul, 2001), designer fashion (Moore and Fairhurst, 2003) and creative industries enterprise curricula (Carey and Naudin, 2006). However, several questions remain unanswered. For example, at the fundamental level, how can enterprise development principles be applied to the commercialization of creative, artistic talent? Additionally, at the economic level, how should the sector be supported to ensure future growth and sustainability?

This chapter begins with a consideration of the importance of the sector for economic growth and employment generation. This is followed by a discussion on the main barriers facing the sector, the particular characteristics of creative entrepreneurs, and the degree to which entrepreneurs in the creative sector have special development and support needs. The chapter then considers the music and dance industry, presenting Ireland as an example of successful entrepreneurial development. Finally, the chapter considers the key issues that can impinge on further prospective growth for the creative industries, offering recommendations for further research.

BACKGROUND AND CONTEXT

Overall Importance and Growth Factors

The creative industries have become a priority economic sector for governments worldwide. As noted by Wolf (1999): 'entertainment – not autos, not steel, not financial services – is fast becoming the driving wheel of the new economy' (p. 4). The reasons for this are as follows. Firstly, the sector is central to everyday life, and is, 'all around us: the shoes and clothes we wear, the buildings we live and work in, the computer software we use for business and pleasure, the music we listen to, the books and TV programmes we enjoy at leisure' (M2 Presswire, 2001).

Secondly, the globalization of communications networks and the rapid advance of digital technologies have propelled growth in the creative industries. In the UK, for example, this sector is growing significantly faster than the economy as a whole. Between 1997 and 2001, the creative sector grew by 8 per cent, compared to under 3 per cent for the whole UK economy, and contributed £11.4 billion to the balance of trade. Moreover, it is estimated that 2 million people are employed, directly and indirectly, in the sector. Their contribution to UK exports is around £10.3 billion and the industry accounts for 5 per cent of GDP, greater than the contribution of any of the UK's manufacturing industries. Similar growth rates have been documented in Australia, Canada and Hong Kong, among others.

Thirdly, the variety of industries that make up the creative sector are connected, either directly or indirectly, to the information, communication and entertainment sectors of the economy, and are typically very receptive to foreign collaborations. Hence, there is huge potential for exports, international partnerships and foreign direct investment. Finally, by their very nature, the creative industries are constantly absorbing new technologies, processes and management expertise in order to add value to the content of their outputs. As a result, there is a large business opportunity, in terms of sales, knowledge and technology transfer, to be exploited.

Recognizing the above factors, over the last number of years, there has been a concerted effort on the part of policymakers to improve awareness and understanding of the creative industries. Governments have been keen to promote the sector through the establishment of specialist task forces, unique initiatives and official commissioned reports. However, the findings from a number of recent publications on the component industries high-light significant weaknesses in current government approaches. In the UK, for example, the National Endowment for Science, Technology and the Arts – NESTA (2004) report entitled *New Solutions to Old Problems: Investing in the creative industries*, found that traditional British investors have no confidence in the creative industries. Moreover, this lack of investment confidence translates into a serious economic loss for the UK, as innovative and exciting developments are either lost to other countries, or never fully realized through underfunding.

In the case of Ireland, much has been achieved within the creative industries as a result of the Arts Plan 1995–1997 (Arts Council, 1994) and other studies published subsequently (Coopers and Lybrand, 1994; Durkan, 1994; Goodbody, 2003). However, in the ensuing debate on the way forward, several critical issues were overshadowed, such as the role of entrepreneurship, the need to foster a creative 'enterprise' culture within the sector, and a new-business development system, through education and training appropriate to the arts. The Arts Plan featured positive national aspects, such as a strong indigenous imaginative tradition and the natural spontaneity of the Irish people, both of which provide encouragement for entrepreneurial development in the sector. In particular, devolution of the arts within the regions has enabled a new dynamic to be released, based on indigenous skills, such as traditional music and dance (Ní hAodha, 1997). The value that local initiatives can add to the development process has been attested by several observers (Smilor, 1986).

Creative Entrepreneurship and Economic Development

Developments in the creative industries provide a clear example of business survival in post-industrial economies (Hill, 1996). The sector has clearly followed and has been a dynamic part of societal change, especially in terms of facilitating the move from a production-based to a knowledge-based socio-economy. The business of the creative industries is 'multi-rational'; that is, it is governed by both aesthetic as well as individualized creativity, aimed at commodification of the end product. However, defining and identifying an entrepreneur continues to be problematic in the context of the research literature. Livesay (1982), for example, suggests that 'successful entrepreneurship is an art form as much as, or perhaps more than, it is an economic activity, and as such, is as difficult as any other artistic activity to explain in terms or origins, method or environmental influence' (p. 13).

In researching the topic of entrepreneurship in creative industries, the authors of this chapter recognize that not only are such industries and enterprise interrelated, but they can also be highly effective partners. For example, the cultural sector can provide an attractive platform for entrepreneurship, while the arts is a dynamic factor in supporting a creative 'can-do' environment, as well as influencing enterprise development mechanisms and regional enhancement (Griffin, 1996). Since the early 1990s, there has been an unprecedented upsurge in the number of entrepreneurs who start their own arts organizations. This growth coincides with the market demand and opportunities seen in the culture and entertainment industry. In the United States, nearly 3 million people earn their living within entertainment enterprises, while in California, job creation in this sectoral economy has helped to compensate for devastating losses in the aerospace industry (Welsch and Kickul, 2001).

Interestingly, in analysing economic performance in general over the past decade, commentators have been inclined to concentrate on the performance of the manufacturing sector, often in relation to FDI (foreign direct investment) policies, particularly in relation to Ireland. In more recent times, however, there has been heightened awareness of the contribution to the economy of the indigenous sectors. Consequently, 'natural resource' sectors, in particular, creative elements, such as music, dance, literature and film, are now recognized as significant economic contributors. This is especially the case in Ireland, where the creative sector's growth in popularity was foreseen a decade ago (Forte Report, 1996).

The economic case for supporting the creative industries is strong. In India, for example, the creative industries were estimated to be worth £2 billion in 2003, and in Hong Kong, the creative industries were responsible for exports totalling HK$10 billion in services, equivalent to 3 per cent of the total services sector. As outlined above, in the UK, the sector is estimated to account for 8 per cent of UK GDP, far more than any of the preferred industries, employing 2 million workers. Moreover, Asian countries such as Taiwan, Singapore and Korea all recognize and have begun to focus on the creative sector as a means of diversification for the economy as well as providing an important export base. However, the actual benefits are not confined simply to economic outputs but can also be seen to enrich a broad span of society. Mitchell and Wall (1989), for example, argue that creative forms can have a much wider brief in today's society (Johannisson, 1990; Arts Council, 1994). In addition, the indirect benefits of developing creative enterprises, such as music, including the traditional music sector, have also been strongly expressed:

> In addition to the direct employment, the enormous benefit that the indigenous music industry generates in other sectors of the economy should not be overlooked. (Forte Report, 1996)

Furthermore, it has been recognized that culture, for example, can become a most potent force, especially in terms of economic and regional development, when it is developed in tandem with tourism. The mushrooming of cultural music centres and summer schools throughout Ireland is testimony to this (Ó Cinnéide, 1997).

THE CREATIVE ENTREPRENEUR

Barriers Facing the Creative Industries Sector

Economic, social, political and aesthetic pressures are forcing creative entrepreneurs and their support services to face tough options at the start-up stage. The decisions they make must balance conflicting interests in the context of ever-tightening resources, more intense competition and greater demands for accountability. All these factors must be confronted without losing the creative dynamic.

One of the most problematic aspects of engaging in creative entrepreneurship is the necessity to balance artistic, financial and self-development considerations. Using the example of artists, Welsch and Kickul (2001) have succinctly outlined how creative entrepreneurs also encounter problems and opportunities critical to the success of a creative enterprise. As in the case of traditional entrepreneurs, they are confronted with the need to make major decisions and take options to advance their careers.

In the first instance, artists, for example, usually encounter difficulties in promoting their expertise to their audiences. This is where coaching and mentoring in self-assessment skills, networking and marketing techniques can be of significant help in career guidance. In no other industry sector is the dilemma of balancing the art and the science of entrepreneurship (Jack and Anderson, 1998) more evident.

Secondly, finding financial support is critical in business venturing, particularly at the early stages, or the so-called 'valley of death' phase. In this regard, intending creative entrepreneurs need to obtain sound advice with regard to preparing financial applications and operational budgets in addition to being guided towards appropriate funding sources, such as foundations, corporations, business angels, state agencies, enterprise boards, and so on. The funding issue within the creative sector, particularly at the start-up stage, is paramount, as highlighted by the UK NESTA report (2004). According to the report, while over two-thirds of investors believe that the UK has the potential to be a world leader in the creative field, less than a quarter actually consider investing in the sector. Lack of understanding between funders and creative businesses is considered central if the two are to 'move towards a common ground'.

In addition, it is widely recognized that entrepreneurs in general can encounter a wide range of legal and technical issues associated with their businesses, and significantly so at the start-up stage. Such issues apply equally to the creative industries and include choice of the most appropriate legal structure, contractual agreements, copyright and other forms of intellectual property protection such as trademarks and patents (Grant, 1994; NESTA, 2004).

Finally, promoting and encouraging 'creative entrepreneurs' is a difficult concept. While creating clusters is fundamental to the sector, it has been shown that creative industries in the UK, for example, still face a number of important issues which are inhibiting critical mass. Specifically:

- meeting the demand for key skills;
- the need for improved access to finance;
- coordinated and focused export promotional activities;
- the protection of intellectual property rights.

Moreover, these issues are further complicated by the fact that creative enterprises are characterized by uncertainty. For example, venture creation includes entrepreneurial acts, oriented toward novelty and commodification, with a significantly high risk of failure. While it could be argued that all entrepreneurs, in both creative and non-creative sectors, experience these problems, there are further complications to promoting creative entrepreneurs, namely in the unique characteristics of creative people, as outlined below.

Characteristics of Creative Entrepreneurs

There is some evidence in the literature to suggest that creative entrepreneurs are different to those in more traditional industry sectors and are, to some degree, part of a new and emerging social group (Fussell, 1983). They represent the valuable new knowledge workers (Drucker, 1993); the basic tools and materials of creativity which are beginning to form a new type of creative class (Florida, 2002). Their uniqueness notwithstanding, creative entrepreneurs display certain common core entrepreneurial characteristics within their particular creative sector. In music, for example, risk-taking propensity is a core attribute, as artists take risks with freshly composed tunes and songs, new interpretations, and the creative integration of different types of music formats. Musician entrepreneurs can range from administrators of musical cultural centres, to music school directors, and on to producers and impresarios of theatrical musicals. As such, 'entrepreneurial' musicians could be deemed to be particularly well endowed with the necessary skills and expertise to deal with risk factors. Furthermore, it has been posited that artists, including those in the music sector, share many of the entrepreneurial personality traits cited in the academic business literature, particularly locus of control, risk-taking propensity, innovation, creativity and achievement motivation.

There is a widely held belief in the business literature that creativity and innovation are key qualities in entrepreneurship (Drucker, 1988; Hisrich and Peters, 1989). In business, as well as in the arts, individuals need to be in touch with the wellsprings of creativity and imagination. According to Schumpeter (1934), entrepreneurs are the innovators who shatter the status quo through new combinations of resources and new methods of business. They could be deemed to act as a force of 'creative destruction', challenging current practices and replacing them with enhanced activities. It could be argued in relation to this chapter that such traits are particularly evident in creative entrepreneurs. For example, a high tolerance for ambiguity, perseverance, self-reliance, adaptability, autonomy and creativity are characteristics that have been attributed to artists (Pufal-Struzik, 1992; Dubek et al., 1991). These traits have also been identified in traditional entrepreneurs.

THE MUSIC INDUSTRY

As one of the largest segments within the creative industries, the music sector, makes for particularly interesting study in terms of entrepreneurship. Part of the reason for this is that music involves a wider range of activities than can be found in many of the other components of the creative industries. The music industry includes composition, publishing, performance, production and retailing of recorded items, together with the manufacture and sale of musical instruments. It has experienced considerable growth since the mid 1980s, with the UK, for example, presenting itself as the third-largest music record sales market in the world and the market leader in Europe. Between 1997 and 2000, music sales more than doubled and the sector continues to attract significant investment and growth. Moreover, the music recording industry is extremely dynamic, undergoing significant changes since its establishment at the turn of the nineteenth century.

The major music companies battle constantly against copyright infringement in an attempt both to defend their artists' intellectual property and to protect their own market share. The advent of video and DVD; the concept of manufactured bands (that is, the Spice Girls, Boyzone, Blue and WestLife); the introduction of virtual artists (that is, DB Boulevard and The Gorrillazs), and the increasingly popular and painstakingly coached

Pop Idol and *X-Factor* creations, might suggest that today's music industry is more to do with packaging, image and marketing strategy, than actual musical talent.

Music offerings have evolved from conservative, traditional markets to liberal, modern ones, with jazz, rock, pop, soul and rap making their debut along the way. Twenty-first-century music continues to reinvent itself and demonstrates a trend for new and unusual combinations, evidenced in the 1990s by such unlikely partnerships as Lulu and the Pet Shop Boys, and Tom Jones and the Art of Noise. More recent musical double acts have included Kylie Minogue and Robbie Williams, Brittany Spears and Madonna, Leanne Rimes and Ronan Keating, and the paradoxical combination of the controversial lesbian Kay de Lange and the traditional romantic crooner Tony Bennett (Murray, 2003).

Further evidence of the creative dynamism of the music industry can be found in established artists' approaches to marketing their records and their own self-image. For example, The Artist Formerly Known As Prince has long dispensed with the services of the big record companies, choosing instead to market his music directly over the Internet. In a similar, but slightly more magnanimous vein, George Michael recently stated that he has earned so much money from the music industry he felt it was now time to give something back. Michael indicated that he would make his next album available for free through the Internet but with purchasers encouraged to contribute small amounts as donations to charity (Parkinson, 2004). Puff Daddy, 'a unique blend of businessman, producer and performer', has practically become a professional marketer, extending his brand to restaurants, frozen foods, clothing and the film industry (Welsch and Kickul, 2001, p. 168).

The long value-added process within the music industry (Block and MacMillan, 1993), starts with art-entrepreneurs beginning their journey along musical avenues by their creative designs (melody and lyrics), and continues until it reaches a customer in the form of recorded music, live performance or other media. For example, in the process of music production as a commodity for export purposes, corporate venturing would include the artists (composers, songwriters, technicians), the producers (representing the process from the selection of music to the industrial production of records), the salespeople (sales chains, distributors, stores) and the support teams (management, marketing, legal services, technical equipment and public agencies).

Case-Study: the Irish Music and Dance Industry

Insights into the commercial exploitation of artistic knowledge in the creative industries, particularly within the music sector, can be gained from the experience of Ireland. An important catalytic effect occurred through Ireland's successes achieved when competing in Eurovision, the international song contest staged annually by the European Broadcasting Union. In particular, the accolades garnered by the Irish *Riverdance* dance troupe led to global recognition of new national talents within the Creative Industries.

Acts of creativity that may have been sparked by what might be termed providential inspiration or 'stroke of genius' are often seen as key drivers for corporate success or 'creative willingness' (Groth and Peters, 1999; Boden et al., 2000). It is instructive, therefore, to reflect on the consequences for Ireland as a result of competing in the Eurovision Song Contest and to identify the quantum effects that transpired.

Music and dance are two of the most popular symbols of Irish culture, representing an integral part of Ireland's national identity abroad. In recent years, the commercial dimension of Irish music and dance has been more fully appreciated, with an increased national focus on the arts and entertainment industry and its potential economic benefits. However, it has been argued that Irish music has always had an economic dimension, ever since the eminent harpist Turlough O'Carolan was paid his first patronage fee. While musicians have always played for money to supplement their incomes, it was often on an unstructured, ad hoc basis.

The relatively newly found status of the sector has brought with it structures, guidelines and support organizations. For example, in 1993, the Department of the Arts, Culture and the Gaeltacht was established in Ireland, and this enhanced the music sector's ministerial status, allowing Irish music and dance, as it were, to progress from its pub backroom scenario towards the boardroom. Since 2001, it has been enabled to act as a forum in providing advice on how the government and support agencies might better promote the sector.

Economic Significance of the Irish Music Industry

The size of the Irish music industry in terms of economic value is significant. According to the Goodbody Economic Consultants report (2003), the industry generated €478 million in 2001. The output of Irish recording performers is also impressive. Sound recording output by Irish artists is almost 30 times the worldwide average, per capita of the population, with Ireland's music output, overall, being eight times the average of music's contribution to gross domestic product per capita in the US.

Irish music and performers have achieved universal recognition, with artists like The Corrs, Enya, U2, Christy Moore and The Chieftains demonstrating that a small nation can make its voice (and music) heard on the world's stages. Their achievements have been exceptional, taking into consideration that Ireland has only 0.08 per cent of the world population and 0.3 per cent of the world's gross domestic product.

Evidence of Ireland's export successes is the fact that Irish artists have been consistently represented in almost 30 per cent of the top ten albums on a worldwide basis. It is significant, also, that over the period 1996–2001, Irish artists have won 48 Platinum Awards, putting them in fourth place alongside much larger nations like the US, the UK and Canada. From an employment perspective, music is, by far, the most significant employer of all the creative industries segments in Ireland, although accurate estimates of employment are difficult to obtain. However, the Goodbody report (2003) has put the figure close to 10 000 full-time equivalent employees in the sector, the majority of whom relate to Dublin.

Tracing the Origins of *Riverdance*

The Irish music and dance sector is attempting to take advantage of the growing popularity, throughout the world, of 'all things Irish'. An oft quoted example of this is *Riverdance* which, although originally conceived as only a short interlude for the Eurovision Song Contest, was developed into a full-length theatrical show, with video and audio spin-offs (Henry et al., 2004).

Ireland has had legendary success in the Eurovision Song Contest, winning four times in the period 1992–96, inclusive. Undoubtedly, the most enduring achievement in this has been *Riverdance*, an upbeat and vibrant spectacle of reinvented traditional Irish dance and music which has grown to become a national and international success. A music and dance sequence of less than seven minutes, *Riverdance* was specially commissioned by RTÉ, the Irish public broadcasting authority, as the intermission feature for the 39th annual Eurovision Song Contest held at the Point Theatre, Dublin, Ireland in April 1994. As it happened, this interlude item, now known as *Riverdance – The Original*, overshadowed the result of the song contest – the winning of the award by an Irish entry for an unprecedented third time in succession (Ó Cinnéide, 1995). The 1994 Eurovision Song Contest was claimed by broadcasting authorities to have reached, at some point during its three-hours transmission, an estimated audience of 300 million worldwide. Once the Eurovision programme was broadcast there was spontaneous reaction in Ireland to the intermission piece with an unrelenting demand for more (Ó Cinnéide, 2005a).

As an illustration of its initial commercial impact, *Riverdance* audio and video cassettes featured prominently in the Irish music charts for well over a year after the Eurovision performance, retaining the number one position for over seven months, while the audio single distinguished itself in the UK *Top of the Pops*, reaching the top ten in early 1995. The original *Riverdance* interval act was expanded into a full-blown stage show in February 1995. The impact of *The Show* was dramatic and immediate, breaking all Irish box office records. Originally planned for a one-month run, the show at the Point Theatre, Dublin (with a 3500-plus seat capacity) played nightly to full houses and ran for over eight weeks. It is estimated that over 170 000 people attended the show at the Point Theatre by the end of its initial run. This was equivalent to 10 per cent of the Irish population aged 15–64 years.

Riverdance developed from a unique synergy between the management team and the performers. This involved Moya Doherty as producer, Bill Whelan as composer and Michael Flatley as choreographer and lead dancer. Flatley was essential to *Riverdance*'s genesis. Although American, he had been dancing with Irish traditional music group, The Chieftains, for nearly a decade, so it could be argued that, in many arenas throughout the world, particularly in Japan and North America, an embryonic form of *Riverdance* had already happened (Ó Cinnéide, 2002). Yet, *Riverdance* provided a complete shock to the system.

As a result of contractual disagreements, Michael Flatley was dismissed from *Riverdance – The Show* a day before its return to London in October 1995. After the parting of ways with *Riverdance*, Flatley felt that he had everything to prove, so, in *Lord of the Dance*, the choreography format of *Riverdance* was released in full flood, with more thunderous chorus lines, more insistent hard shoe hammering and more noise.

The *Riverdance* Eurovision interlude sparked a national debate on its likely long-term impact on the future development of Irish culture, particularly dance. From a management perspective, it has been interesting to see parallels emerge between the combative strategies of *Riverdance* and *Lord of the Dance* vis-à-vis Coke and Pepsi, mirroring the 'beverage battle' between the latter two worldwide brands, with one being identified as the 'originator' and the other as the 'challenger'.

Irrespective of the Coke versus Pepsi management analogies, there is no denying that both shows, *Riverdance* and *Lord of the Dance*, in addition to serving as fascinating case-studies of entrepreneurship, have been responsible for awakening a worldwide interest in Irish dancing.

Entrepreneurial Development and Spin-offs

The cultural renaissance embracing Irish traditional music and dance has not just been the result of a sudden explosion of interest following the Eurovision Song Contest in 1994. Rather, the show came at a time when there was an upsurge in indigenous performing arts and entertainment.

This created a new opportunity for producers, performers and audiences both in Ireland and in the worldwide 'Irish Diaspora' (Ó Cinnéide, 1998). This consists of up to 80 million people who claim Irish descent or affinity, mostly in the English-speaking world. Inevitably, many 'me-too' shows followed, the most successful of which, of course, was *Lord of the Dance*, but also including *Dancing on Dangerous Ground* (developed by ex-*Riverdance* lead dancers, Jean Butler and Colin Dunne), *Spirit of the Dance* (UK based), *Shelallion* (Scottish based) and *Gael Force* (Australian in origin).

However, the flourishing musical culture in Ireland can be said, on two planes, to be more apparent than real, since, firstly, international Irish stars such as The Corrs, Enya, The Chieftains and The Cranberries are signed up to British or US divisions of global record corporations. Consequently, their success will not sustain the Irish record industry to any significant extent. Hence, a major weakness in the current model is that considerably more effort is required to indigenise the industry so that further economic benefits can be achieved from native talent.

Secondly, the economic success of the Irish music sector, unlike most of its European counterparts, is not reflected in high sales levels from the domestic market, since the work of Irish artists represents only approximately a quarter of the domestic market by value. This is low by international standards and indicates that there is considerable scope to expand. From a positive perspective, there still remains a potentially large ethnic Irish pool of prospective customers for the Irish dance shows and their derivatives. One of the major challenges facing the *Riverdance* promoters in particular was how best to network further into the 'Great Irish Diaspora' (Ó Cinnéide et al., 2004). Through publishing a series of studies on *Riverdance* and *Lord of the Dance* (Ó Cinnéide, 2005b), it has been possible to demonstrate that the evolution of 'new age' Irish dance, with its unprecedented success abroad, can provide an important role model for both the arts and culture sector and the Irish business community in general.

CONCLUSION

Music and dance constitute a key part of the creative industries, becoming an international multi-billion-dollar sector during recent decades, so it is considered timely that attention be given to the industry's economic impact and its entrepreneurial development.

While policymakers around the world have become increasingly aware of the potential that individual segments and the creative industries as a whole can make, core support and research in relation to this sector of the economy have been limited to date. While a number of recent studies have provided important insights into creative entrepreneurs, the research has been particularly limited by comparison with other domains.

This chapter has attempted to illustrate how creative industries, and the music and dance sector in particular, have accumulated a significant amount of artistic and entrepreneurial knowledge. Despite a high level of uncertainty about the commercial response to the commodification of art products, the creative industries have generated economic yields in various ways through innovation and initiatives by art-entrepreneurs. Politicians have adopted a new perspective on these industries and are now beginning to treat them as 'the new mass manufacturers, situated at the very heart of the knowledge economy' (Creative Clusters Ltd, 2002), as indeed they should be. However, while opportunities abound for developing entrepreneurial ventures within the music sector, to date, the creative domain has developed organically, with comparatively few support structures.

Two key concepts in need of further debate emerge from this chapter:

- creative enterprises can be a powerful economic and social force in any economy; and
- creative entrepreneurs face a number of particular constraints in terms of access to appropriate education and training, and funding.

In relation to the latter issue, NESTA (2004) has clearly identified lack of funding options as a key issue for the creative industries. The NESTA report cites reluctance on the part of venture capitalists and other funding sources to invest, since ventures in the arts and entertainment fields are generally considered 'non-conventional' and, thereby, 'outside the box' in investment terms.

In addition, this chapter has taken a tentative step towards understanding the delicate symbiotic relationship that exists between entrepreneurial flair and management on the one hand, and artistic knowledge and talent on the other, in Irish society. Entrepreneurship has the potential to be an integrator in an artist's education through facilitating communication across disciplinary boundaries (Ray, 1990). However, when tailoring entrepreneurship courses towards the creative industries, business school faculty should be conscious of commendations in the academic literature on 'best practice' (see, for example, Ray, 1990; Bagby and Stetz, 1994; and Welsch and Kickul, 2001). By presenting the example of Ireland's highly successful music and dance sector, it is hoped that this chapter will be seen to represent another instance of best practice in the creative domain.

REFERENCES

Arts Council (1994), *The Arts Plan, 1995–1997*, Dublin: Criterion Press.
Bagby, D.R. and Stetz, P. (1994), *Can Entrepreneurs be Taught? The Art and Science of Entrepreneurship Education*, vol 1, 22–31.
Baines, S. and Robson, L. (2001), Being self-employed or being enterprising? The case of creative work for the media industries, *Journal of Small Business and Enterprise Development*, 8, 349–362.
Blair, H., Grey, S. and Randle, K. (2001), Working in film: employment in a project based industry, Personnel Review, **30** (2), 170–185.
Block, Z. and MacMillan, I. (1993), *Corporate Venturing*, Boston, MA: Harvard Business School Press.
Boden, M. O'Connor, A. and Raffo, C. (2000), Risk and trust in the cultural industries, Geoforum, 31, 453–464.
Carey, C. and Naudin, A. (2006), Enterprise curriculum for creative industry students, *Education and Training*, 48 (7), 518–31.
Coopers & Lybrand (1994), The employment and economic significance of the cultural industries in Ireland, Dublin: Cooper Lybrand.
Creative Clusters Ltd (2002), www.creativeclusters.co.uk/bi_creativeindustries.asp.
Drucker, P.F. (1988), The coming of the new organisation, *Harvard Business Review*, January/February, pp. 45–53.
Drucker, P.F. (1993), *Post-Capitalist Society*, New York: Harper Business.
Dubek, S.Z., Berneche, R., Berube, H. and Royer, S. (1991), Personality determinants of the commitment to the profession of art, *Creativity Research Journal*, 4 (4), 367–389.
Durkan, J. (1994), *The Economics of the Arts in Ireland*, Dublin: Arts Council, Criterion Press.
Florida, R. (2002), *The Rise of the Creative Class*, New York: Basic Books.
Forte Report on Music (1996), 'Access all areas: Irish Music – an international industry', Report to the Minister for Arts, Culture and the Gaeltacht. Dublin: Stationery Office.
Fussell, P. (1983), Class: a guide through the American Status System, Summit, New York.
Goodbody Economic Consultants (2003), The economic significance of the Irish Music Industry, Dublin.
Grant, D. (1994), *The Artist's Resource Handbook*, New York: Allworth Press.
Griffin, J. (1996), An examination of entrepreneurship in the arts and its role in local government. Unpublished MBS dissertation, University of Limerick.
Groth and Peters (1999), What blocks creativity? A managerial perspective, Creativity and Innovation Management, 8, 179–87.
Henry, C., Johnston, K., Ó Cinnéide, B. and Aggestam, M. (2004), Where Art meets the Science of Entrepreneurship: a study of the creative industries sector and the case of the music industry, IAM, Irish Academy of Management, 2–3 September, Dublin.
Hill, B. (1996), 'Income statistics for the agricultural household sector'. Proceedings of the Eurostat Seminar, Luxembourg, 10–11 January 1996.
Hisrich, R.H. and Peters, M.P. (1989), *Entrepreneurship: Starting, Developing and Managing a Successful New Enterprise*, Homewood, JL: BPI/Irwin.
Jack, S.L. and Anderson, A.R. (1998), 'Entrepreneurship Education within the

Condition of Entreprenolog', Proceedings of the Conference on Enterprise and Learning, Aberdeen.

Johannisson, B. (1990), Between territory and function: on the interfaces between small business, large business and communities, in R. Donckels and A. Miettinen (eds), *New Findings and Perspectives in Entrepreneurship*, Avebury, Aldershot.

Livesay, H.C. (1982), Entrepreneurial history, *Encyclopedia of Entrepreneurship*, Englewood Cliffs, NJ: Prentice-Hall.

M2 Presswire (2001), The British 'Credit Underclass' is Decreasing in Size, M2 Communications, 3 October.

Mitchell, C.J. and Wall, G. (1989), The arts and employment: a case study of the Stratford Festival, *Growth and Change*, **20** (4), 31–40.

Moore, M. and Fairhurst, A. (2003), Marketing capabilities and firm performance in fashion retailing, *Journal of Fashion Marketing and Management*, **7** (4), 386–397.

Murray, J. (2003), *Women's Hour*, interview with Kay de Lange and Tony Bennett, BBC Radio 4, 25 June.

NESTA – National Endowment for Science, Technology and the Arts (2004), 'New solutions to old problems: investing in the creative industries'.

Ní hAodha, Niamh (1997), The potential for Enterprise Development in the traditional Irish music sector. Unpublished MBS dissertation, University of Limerick.

Ó Cinnéide, B. (1995), *Riverdance Case Study*, Cranfield, UK: European Case Clearing House.

Ó Cinnéide, B. (1997), Branding Culture – Ireland's opportunities: music and dance, 'ECTARC', European Centre for Traditional and Regional Conference, Bunratty, Co. Clare.

Ó Cinnéide, B. (1998), The non-profit origins and impact of 'Riverdance: The Show' that became more than an enterprise, *Non-Profit Management and Leadership*, **8** (4), Summer, 40.

Ó Cinnéide, B. (2002), *Riverdance: The Phenomenon*, Dublin: Blackhall Publishing.

Ó Cinnéide, B. (2005a), 'Creative entrepreneurship in the arts: transforming old into "new" – Irish dance and music test cases such as "Riverdance" and "Lord of the Dance"', *Entrepreneurship and Innovation*, August, 153.

Ó Cinnéide, B. (2005b), 'The Case Method: its Role in Entrepreneurship Education and Training', Int-Ent, Internationalising Entrepreneurship Education and Training, University of Surrey.

Ó Cinnéide, B., Henry, C. and Johnston, K. (2004), 'Entrepreneurship in Irish Creative Industries: "Riverdance" and other exemplars in Music/Dance', Int-Ent, Internationalising Entrepreneurship Education and Training, Napoli.

Parkinson, M. (2004), Interview with George Michael, 13 March, BBC1.

Pufal-Struzik, K.I. (1992), Differences in personality and self-knowledge of creative persons at different ages, *Gerontology and Geriatrics Education*, **13** (1–2), 71–90.

Ray, D. (1990), Liberal arts for entrepreneurs, *Entrepreneurship Theory and Practice*, Winter, 79–90.

Schumpeter, J.A. (1934), The Theory of Economic Development, Cambridge, MA: Harvard University.

Welsch, H.P. and Kickul, J.R. (2001), Training for successful Entrepreneurship careers in the Creative Arts, in Brockhaus, R., Hills, G., Klandt, H. and Welsch, H. (eds), *Entrepreneurship Education: A Global View*, Aldershot: Ashgate, pp. 167–183.

Wolf, M.J. (1999), *The Entertainment Economy*, London: Penguin.

6. Building the film industry in New Zealand: an entrepreneurship continuum

Anne de Bruin

INTRODUCTION

The film industry in New Zealand (NZ) has moved rapidly from relative obscurity in the late 1970s, to an industry with global visibility as well as acclaim (Shelton, 2005). Most recently, NZ has been home to the creation of major blockbuster movies directed by New Zealanders. For example, Peter Jackson's *The Lord of the Rings* trilogy (2001–03) and the remake of *King Kong* (2005) have had outstanding international impact. New Zealander Andrew Adamson's *The Chronicles of Narnia: The Lion, the Witch and the Wardrobe* (2005) is similarly noteworthy. However, recent successes have not been confined to big-budget films. Lower-cost feature films, such as the Oscar-nominated, NZ story content film *Whale Rider* (2002), are also among recent success stories. Furthermore, NZ short films too have contributed to film industry achievement. Included among the latest acclaimed short films is multiple award-winning and Oscar-nominated *Two Cars, One Night* (2003) directed and written by Taika Waititi (Taika Cohen) and Welby Ing's *Boy* (2004), which won the Best Short Narrative Film Award at the 2005 Cinequest Film Festival. International filmmakers have also increasingly acknowledged NZ as an excellent location and a source of expertise and talent. For instance, NZ was the backdrop of nineteenth-century Japan for the Hollywood-directed blockbuster movie *The Last Samurai* (2004) starring Tom Cruise. Additionally, visual and physical effects production companies in NZ have been engaged to work on increasing numbers of international films including *I, Robot* (2004) and *The Legend of Zorro* (2005). Measured in terms of international recognition and acclaim, therefore, the NZ film industry has achieved success and strength in a relatively short period of around a couple of decades.

In this chapter, an explanation for the success of the film industry in NZ is sought in terms of a continuum of entrepreneurial activity at multiple levels: at the national and regional levels, and then moving down to the more micro, individual level. It is argued that, particularly for late-start, small-population (just over 4 million people) countries like NZ, building the project-based, capital-intensive film industry involves multi-level entrepreneurship. However, at the outset it must be emphasized that, while the focus of this discussion is on the growth of the film industry, it is situated within the wider specific context of the country's screen production industry (SPI).

The first section of this chapter sets the scene, providing background to the distinctive features of the global operation of the film industry. The subsequent section builds on this backdrop with a brief run-down of the NZ industry. The nature of entrepreneurship in the creative industry sector is then explored, followed by a discussion of the various aspects that constitute entrepreneurship along a multi-level continuum of activity. The subsequent sections illustrate each level of entrepreneurial activity within the NZ context, with the conclusion drawing the chapter threads together.

THE GLOBAL CONTEXT

In the first half of the twentieth century, the world of film-making and distribution was dominated by the Hollywood 'studio system' (Epstein, 2005, p. 4). The organization of this system corresponded to the standard Fordist, more localized, assembly-line mass production model (Rothman, 2004). Today, however, 'vertical disintegration' has led to a global, project-based, movie-by-movie subcontracting approach in keeping with the move from mass production to flexible specialization (Christopherson and Storper, 1986, 1989). There is a 'new map of Hollywood' (Scott, 2002) comprising two segments: the majors and their allied firms on the one hand, and a host of independent companies on the other. Hollywood, however, continues to be the main economic power and major player in the international film world, and also represents a valued 'regional cluster of competencies' (DeFillippi and Arthur, 1998, p. 133).

Running parallel to the charting of Hollywood's new map and the accelerating global outreach and mobility of the US film industry, is the rising tide of new clusters of creative and cultural industries across the globe and specialized industrial districts (Wu, 2005; Scott, 2004; Bassett et al., 2002). Commencing in the 1980s, fostering the creative industries as part of national strategies for structural redirection toward a new knowledge economy became increasingly common. Similarly, enabling production agglomerations of particular creative industries have become a fashionable component of urban regional and local development strategies (see, for example, Wu, 2005; Indergaard, 2003). It is worth reiterating here, however, that in many countries and regions it is not possible to divorce the strategic development of the film industry from its more allied context of promotion of the SPI, as well as the wider context of the general promotion of the creative industries, including digital media and computer gaming, music, design and advertising. For instance, some East Asian countries, notably Singapore, South Korea and Malaysia, have joined Hong Kong which already has a vigorous film and music industry, in a bid to actively grow their creative industries. Thus, Singapore has identified in Media 21 a potential cluster development for 'the full range of media industries, from print, broadcasting, film and new areas of convergent media such as digital and online media' (MDA Singapore, 2003, p. 1). Likewise, the Seoul Metropolitan Government is developing Seoul Digital Media City as an incubator for the creation of a world-class complex for digital media industries.

The enhanced scope for the decentralization of the film industry offered by the global economy also involves heightened competition between the various globally dispersed production centres. Anecdotes of one centre losing out to another often hit the popular press or are even included in more academic writing. For example, the story of the making of *The Matrix* (1999) in Australia, and the British film industry losing out as a production location for its sequels *The Matrix Reloaded or 'The Matrix 2'* (2003) and *The Matrix Revolutions or 'The Matrix 3'* (2003), has been mentioned in a Masters dissertation (Smith, 2002). On the pessimistic side, therefore, a consequence of such intense competition, particularly for blockbuster budget film projects, could mean that some of the emergent production centres are destined to die or shrink on account of the harsh climate of competition and inherent risk that characterizes the industry. More optimistically, however, some of these centres 'will conceivably carve out stable niches for themselves in world markets' (Scott, 2004, p. 475). Furthermore, some film-making local agglomerations can become self-sustaining on the basis of 'favourable local conditions that cannot be easily replicated elsewhere' (Bassett et al., 2002, p. 177). It is the contention of this chapter, therefore, that NZ is a centre that is moving rapidly forward to build a sustainable niche for itself within the globalized film industry. The factors contributing to this positioning are discussed in subsequent sections.

THE NEW ZEALAND FILM INDUSTRY: BACKGROUND

The recent rapid growth of the film industry and the larger NZ screen production industry (SPI) agglomeration (comprising film, television, commercials, animation and post-production in the sector) epitomises the centrifugal forces that have characterized the global industry. Chronologically, the NZ film industry is very youthful. Nicolaidi (1991) sets the inception of NZ cinema at 1977. Although NZ's first feature film was completed in 1914 there was no continuity of production before the establishment of the NZ Film Commission (NZFC) in 1978 and dedicated government funding for film production through the Commission (see New Zealand Screen Council, 2005, pp. 4–6, for SPI milestones). The rise of the industry is strongly correlated with activity of the NZFC (Waller, 1996), which provides the majority of NZ production funds. Other sources of government funds are also available to the industry, for example, the Screen Innovation Production Fund, a partnership with NZFC and Creative New Zealand, which is devoted to the financing of innovative moving-image productions. There is limited private investment available domestically and government funding has been critical to industry growth.

Currently, support for screen production is part of the government's broader commitment to building knowledge-intensive industries. The formation of the first Labour-led centre resulted in a coalition government in 1999, commencing a new era in policy configuration. Active industry policy and dedicated regional development is firmly on the agenda. Planning and public–private partnership form the core of industry and regional development practice. The national policy of the Growth and Innovation Framework, released in February 2002, intends systematically to bring NZ back into the top ranks of the OECD group of countries by strategically focusing government resources on key industry sectors. The creative industries is one of the three key industries selected (information and communications technology, and biotechnology are the other two).

Within the creative industries, screen production is targeted as an industry with significant potential. The Screen Production Industry (SPI) Taskforce was appointed in May 2002 to consider how the industry and government could work together to reap this potential. In March 2003, the Taskforce set out its recommendations and framework for sustainable growth of the industry (SPI Taskforce, 2003). Setting up a Screen Council was a key recommendation, and the New Zealand Screen Council, an independent industry organization charged with the responsibility of facilitating growth within the New Zealand screen production sector, has since been established (www.nzscreencouncil.co.nz). The Council has taken ownership of the growth targets set by the Taskforce (Anderton, 2004): to achieve foreign exchange earnings of NZ$400 million a year within five years; to have ten companies each with a turnover of at least NZ$50 million a year, and to have at least another 20 achieving annual turnovers of NZ$10 million.

Screen production is identified as a major contributor, not only to economic well-being, but also to cultural development, by defining and raising the profile of NZ's cultural identity. Among the various government measures to support screen production has been the establishment, in 2000, of the New Zealand Film Production Fund with an injection of government funding of $22 million to invest in larger-budget NZ films. An important feature of the fund is that funding eligibility requires at least 40 per cent of the budget to come from offshore sources. This public–private partnership model is proving to be a very successful one. The fund's first investment, *Whale Rider* (2002), has set box office records for a NZ feature and received acclaim with international awards. Subsequent investments have included *The World's Fastest Indian* (2005) starring the Oscar-winning actor Sir Anthony Hopkins as the NZ motor cycle legend Burt Munro, and *River Queen* (2005). The latter has received funding from the NZFC, the Film Production Fund and the UK Film Council.

In keeping with a worldwide trend, mainly for financial but also for creative reasons, an increasing number of films are being developed as international co-productions. This partnership model of entrepreneurship is now alive and well in the NZ film industry. If a co-production is appropriately structured, it is eligible for certification as a NZ film and may be able to attract production funding from the NZFC and also be eligible to receive the benefits of any tax incentives.

There is an ongoing promise of explicit and implicit government support of the SPI. A prominent initiative in the explicit support package is the Large Budget Screen Production Grant Scheme. Under this scheme set up in 2003, eligible film and television productions are granted a sum totalling 12.5 per cent of 'qualifying' NZ production expenditure.

New Zealand Trade and Enterprise (NZTE), as the central government economic development agency and a lead agency in the Growth and Innovation Framework, has dedicated resources for strategic initiatives in key industry sectors. It has a special focus on assisting companies in these sectors to identify and take advantage of global opportunities. A recent example of the support offered by NZTE in relation to the SPI sector is the 'sewing up' of a deal for a small computer animation studio in the Auckland region – Huhu – with Hollywood producer Promenade Pictures. This animation project – *The Ten Commandments*, based on the 1950s epic starring Charlton Heston – is worth over NZ$5.6 million but also includes another five pictures to follow up until 2008. NZTE provided mentoring, research and funding for Huhu, some of which enabled specialist training for its team of animators (NZTE, 2005).

In addition to central and local government agencies, the institutional infrastructural support of the industry includes industry-led bodies such as Film New Zealand. With a large slice of government funding and some industry sponsorship, Film New Zealand is NZ's national film locations office, responsible for information provision and overall responsibility for the facilitation of screen productions. It also leads and works collaboratively with regional film offices and local government to build a 'film-friendly' environment (Film New Zealand, 2005).

The specific examples and initiatives mentioned so far in this section point to the current favourable national climate for the SPI. This climate has contributed to significant industry growth and dynamism. In the period 1997–2001, the creative industries grew in nominal terms at an average of 8.7 per cent per annum, compared to 3.7 per cent for the rest of the NZ economy (NZIER, 2002a). Within the creative industry sector, film and television were the fastest-growing industries, although the significant impact of the *Lord of the Rings* (*LOTR*) production in 2000 and 2001 must be taken into account here. However, the relative size of the NZ creative sector is small, with the gross domestic product (GDP) contribution for the creative sector estimated at 3.1 per cent in March 2001 (NZIER, 2002a). In contrast, in the UK for example, the economic contribution of the creative industries is much higher and their estimated GDP share is over 5 per cent (Department for Culture, Media and Sport, 2001, p. 8). Cross-country comparisons are not, however, always easy or relevant, due to differences in the definition of 'creative industries'.

Employment levels in the SPI are a gauge of industry activity and scale. From 1999, these levels, especially the engagements of independent contractors (which can represent multiple engagements for each contractor), have been subject to noticeable fluctuations. This is in line with changes in the number and size of projects under way in the country. Thus, total screen production employment (based on Screen Production and Development Association of NZ survey data) peaked in March 2001 at 31 266, due to a high number (29 589) of independent contractor engagements (New Zealand Screen Council, 2005, p. 10), and once again, strongly influenced by the *LOTR* phenomenon. By March 2004, these numbers had fallen dramatically to a total employment level of 5511, and independent contractor engagements of 4637. Encouragingly, full-time equivalent employees in film and video production, however, have remained relatively stable over the past six years. Nevertheless, the sharply fluctuating employment numbers highlight the need for entrepreneurial activity to grow the industry, not only to expand the skills base, but also to retain this talent in the country and within the industry. As de Bruin and Hanrahan (2003) point out, the small scale of NZ's industry poses particular skills problems. Due to the lack of assured continuity of work there is an outflow of skilled people overseas, since the overseas labour market is an integral part of the industry's labour flows. Additionally, given the high degree of inter-occupational mobility of SPI skills, there is also a drain to other occupations during slump times.

DELINEATING ENTREPRENEURSHIP IN THE CREATIVE INDUSTRIES

There is no consensus definition of entrepreneurship, with the terms 'entrepreneur' and 'entrepreneurship' often being applied within a range of settings and used with marked variations in meaning (de Bruin and Dupuis, 2003). This divergence of views complicates the task of identifying the entrepreneur and delineating the nature of entrepreneurship within the creative industries – an area which has received limited academic attention. This task becomes all the more thorny when we consider that segments of the creative industries, such as the film industry, are organized in a complex way and centre on project-based activity.

A straightforward definition proffered by de Bruin envisages entrepreneurship in the creative industries as: 'The process of adding value to creative inputs / creativity' (2005, p. 145). Since the term 'creativity' is used in a variety of ways with different meanings, it is necessary, however, to elaborate that creativity in this subject-specific context is used to denote an artistic driving force as distinct from creativity of, say, scientific and engineering insights. Creative inputs emanate from the inspiration of artists and are dissimilar to what Caves describes as 'humdrum inputs that respond to ordinary economic incentives' (2003, p. 73). The value-adding process entails combining creative or artistic input(s) (some creative endeavours, such as a feature film, require not a single but several creative inputs) with humdrum inputs. It might also involve an 'entrepreneurial value chain' (de Bruin, 2003a). To take an example from the music industry: the artist composes the music but this initial creative input must then be turned into a commercial product that can be marketed. The artist might do this herself or himself, by burning some CDs that are personally marketed – this would be a link in the chain of adding value to the music, with the artist being entrepreneurial. Another link in the value chain might eventuate when an intermediary or agent enters the picture who then promotes the CD to a record label, and this agent is thus contributing further to the process of adding value. When the artist is signed to the record label through the agent and other promotional and marketing activity ensues, there is a further link in the chain and further value added.

The following sub-sections attempt to further our understanding of entrepreneurship in the creative industries by providing decomposition into distinct levels of entrepreneurship: the individual level; and two more collective forms of entrepreneurship – at the central government level, and at the more regional, local government level. Typically, entrepreneurial focus has been on the individual and the firm. Recent research, however, has pointed to the need to consider the external context or a creative milieu as being of importance to innovation (see, for example, Kresl and Singh, 1999; Porter and Stern, 2001). With the incorporation of the broader context to take into account entrepreneurial activity beyond simply the individual and firm level, a more comprehensive framework for examining entrepreneurship and the working of the process of value-adding in the creative industries is suggested.

The Individual Level: Artist Versus Creative Entrepreneur

It might be argued that artists and traditional entrepreneurs have similar traits (Welsch and Kickul, 2001), thus providing some justification for using the term 'artist' interchangeably with that of 'creative entrepreneur'. In furthering the understanding of creative industry entrepreneurship at the level of the individual, it is useful, nevertheless, to distinguish between notions of artist versus creative entrepreneur.[1]

According to Howkins (2002) 'creative entrepreneurs' are one of ten levers affecting the creativity process. They 'use creativity to unlock the wealth that lies within themselves' (2002, p. 129). This perspective, therefore, recognizes that the creative energy of the entrepreneur releases an inner element. There is, however, no explicit recognition of the impact of the external context on entrepreneurial activity. This facet is captured in a broader notion of 'art entrepreneurs' suggested by Henry et al. (2004). They combine the extrinsic with the intrinsic, defining art entrepreneurs as:

> individuals who use creative mindsets in response to two triggers for their entrepreneurial acts: *extrinsic*, that which is contextual and business-driven; and *intrinsic*, that which involves the internal desire to create something and a personal sense of challenge (Henry et al., 2004).

Schumpeter's distinction between 'entrepreneur' and 'inventor' can provide further illumination on the difference between the creative entrepreneur and the artist. For Schumpeter, 'the inventor produces ideas' while it is the entrepreneur who 'gets things done' (Schumpeter, 1991, p. 413). Schumpeter makes clear that it is the entrepreneur, rather than the inventor, who perceives opportunity, namely the possibilities for making profit, and is the catalyst in the utilization of scientific discovery and invention toward this end (de Bruin, 1998).

An artist may be said to be a person who draws on their inspiration and inherent artistic bent to fabricate and create an embodiment of their ideas. The artist, like the Schumpeterian inventor in the arena of scientific discovery and invention, is the originator and gives birth to the artistic expression or creative impulse which can take a variety of forms, for example music, painting, literature – the musician, songwriter, storywriter, painter and similar. Yet this initial creative input has to be commercialized and turned to profit, or to borrow from Caves (2000, 2003), art must meet commerce. It is only when the artist is, in the words of Schumpeter, the one who 'gets things done' that he or she corresponds to the creative entrepreneur.

The National Level: Role of the State and State Entrepreneurship

Schumpeter, when updating his earlier theory of the entrepreneur in the 1940s, stressed that the 'entrepreneurial function need not be embodied in a physical person and, in particular, in a single physical person. Every social environment has its own way of filling the entrepreneurial function' (Schumpeter, cited in Swedberg, 1991, p. 173). Drawing inspiration from Schumpeter, it is maintained here that entrepreneurship in the creative sector needs also to encompass activities at the national, and at regional and local community levels. The latter is discussed within the notion of 'municipal–community entrepreneurship' in the following sub-section.

The state has a fundamental role in the new knowledge economy. De Bruin (2003b) argues the need for new terminology better to convey the nature of the state and conceptualize the reconfiguration of the role of the state in this new economy. She offers the concept of the 'strategic state' as one which also fits with the entrepreneurship perspective of the global age, which as Audretsch and Thurik (1999) observe, has changed from the 'managerial economy' of the previous industrial era to a knowledge-based 'entrepreneurial economy'. Whatever the terminology used, however, this should not cloud core points: that the state has a role in creating and facilitating a broader environment of entrepreneurship and innovation, and that the state can be entrepreneurial in its own right. The latter point offers scope for the state to be a profit-seeking entrepreneur or an entrepreneurial actor within an industry, either in its own right or through its state-owned enterprises or state-funded agencies.

Innovation is recognized as an integral aspect of entrepreneurship and was an important feature of Schumpeter's (1934) highly influential work. Sustaining an innovative edge is crucial to both the continued success of entrepreneurs (Glancey and McQuaid, 2000) and the competitive advantage of the nation. In this new global era, however, innovation does not revolve around the activity of a single firm, but requires an active search for new knowledge and technology involving various actors – firms and institutions (OECD, 1999). The strategic state is a key driver of innovation in the national economy and is seen as a catalyst in the creation of favourable systemic conditions for knowledge creation and an important actor within the National Innovation Systems framework and regional systems of innovation.

Given the importance of the creative class (Florida, 2002, 2004), action on the education and skills front to grow employment in the creative job categories would also be included within the purview of the state's role of enhancing innovation and growing a knowledge economy. Thus tertiary education sector reforms make up part of NZ's efforts to grow the creative class.[2] According to The Global Creative-Class Index, which is based on the calculation of the proportion of people employed in creative job categories to the country's total number of workers, NZ ranks fifth, with 27.1 per cent of workers in the creative class, and Ireland, a country with a similar population size to NZ, ranks at the top, with 33.5 per cent of workers in the creative class (Florida, 2004).

The Regional Level: Municipal–Community Entrepreneurship

Greater activism at the local and regional government level to promote economic development and employment growth has been a common trend in the developed countries, particularly since the 1980s. The concept of 'municipal–community entrepreneurship' has been put forward to convey this local activism which involves dynamic community (includes private sector businesses and industry bodies) participation, though explicit and leading support is provided at the local governmental level (Cremer et al., 2001; Dupuis et al., 2003). The construct also captures the partnership element that often characterizes sustainable regional development. This chapter contends that municipal–community entrepreneurship is a significant element in building NZ's creative industries, especially the SPI. The case of the Wellington and Auckland regions is presented later, to illustrate this level of action.

THE NEW ZEALAND FILM COMMISSION: STATE ENTREPRENEURSHIP

Since its launch in 1978, the state-funded NZ Film Commission (NZFC) has been dedicated to supporting and fostering talented NZ film-makers by financing the development and production of NZ feature films. For example, Peter Jackson, currently NZ's most widely acclaimed director, acknowledges: 'My own development as a filmmaker was strongly assisted by the New Zealand Government through the NZ Film Commission' (NZIER, 2002b, p. iii).

The Commission 'began as a cultural endeavour. The government was persuaded that it was unhealthy for New Zealanders only to see other people's images, only to hear other people's voices, only to experience other people's stories' (Harley, 2002). Over the years, however, as the film industry has become important for economic growth, regional development and employment, government funding to the NZFC has significantly increased. The Commission has also become an important component of the entrepreneurial efforts to build the industry. It invests in the development and production of NZ feature films, but also promotes and sells them. Its Sales Agency is active in the overseas promotion of short films and features by young and emerging NZ talent. The Commission engages in professional development and upskilling activities. Importantly, it provides early support for those in the film industry and, in this respect, some of its activities are akin to assisting early start-up companies.

Although it is asserted that public entrepreneurship should involve more opportunity-seeking than risk-taking (Osborne and Gaebler, 1993; Dupuis et al., 2003), risk-taking is inherent and endemic in the film industry. Thus, the NZFC is necessarily a risk-taker. Only 10 per cent of the hundreds of writers and short film makers it supports make it through to the actual production of features, and of these, only around 10 per cent again are successful (Harley, 2002). While the NZFC might be described as entrepreneurial in its own right – seeking out new opportunities and risk-taking – features commonly associated with entrepreneurship, the Commission is only one facet, albeit a key one, of state entrepreneurship in the film industry. Other central government agencies and bodies also contribute to entrepreneurial activity, with the Commission often collaborating and cooperating with them. For example, under the auspices of an Audio Visual Agreement between NZ and Singapore in July 2004, the first feature film co-production agreement between NZ and Singapore companies was signed in June 2006.[3] The NZFC and New Zealand Trade and Enterprise (NZTE), together with Singapore's Media Development Authority, were instrumental in bringing these companies together. The entrepreneurial activity of the NZFC must also be set within the broader NZ politics and policy context. As the earlier section backgrounding the NZ film industry highlighted, the policy climate is favourable to the SPI and policy-wise to keep within the preceding example. The Singaporean and NZ governments have close ties and a Closer Economic Partnership/Free Trade Agreement operates between the two countries.

BUILDING REGIONAL SCREEN PRODUCTION CAPACITY: AUCKLAND AND WELLINGTON

The screen production and film industry is regarded as an important element of local development strategy in several regions of NZ. The regions that lead the 'SPI-friendly' approach are Auckland and Wellington. Auckland leads with around 70 per cent of SPI activity, though perhaps internationally the better-known region for film in NZ is Wellington, largely due to the fame of Peter Jackson's empire that is located there. Dedicated emphasis on screen production as a key industry has resulted in NZ$2 million funding under its Major Regional Initiatives (MRI) scheme for each of the regions to enhance their SPI.

Creative industry cluster development and incubators have become a popular means of building regional screen production industry capacity. These developments are driven by the economic agency arms of local and regional government and involve partnerships with central government and the private sector. For instance, Positively Wellington Business (PWB), Wellington region's official economic development agency, ensures the region is film-friendly.[4] It also supports the Creative Capital cluster of multi-media companies. Many of these SPI-related activities of PWB, however, had origins in the initial support of the film industry and promotional and cluster activities of Wellington City, and the term 'Wellywood' was coined to 'sell' the city's place in film (Jones et al., 2003).

Since 2000 a 'film-friendly approach' has been a feature of the Auckland region,[5] though in 2003, there was a big push to focus efforts to build the industry. The main thrust was to establish Film Auckland as the first point of contact for Auckland's SPI and to attract a share of central government funding under the MRI scheme. Supported by all of the region's city and district councils, Film Auckland is now established, MRI funding has been obtained and will match up with private sector funds; all forming part of the strategic building of the region's industry. Within the broader grouping of the loose regional cluster, other more geographically concentrated city- or district-focused cluster strategies to foster the industry are also in operation. Efforts of Waitakere City stand out in this respect and demonstrate entrepreneurship at the more micro city level. Developing strong industry clusters in lead sectors such as marine, organics, film and tourism through Enterprise Waitakere (the city's economic development agency) is now an important aspect of the city's economic development strategy. Diverse locations, three studio facilities and accessible suppliers, give the city a strong competitive advantage in film. The City Council itself is also an entrepreneur in its own right, with ownership of the Henderson Valley Studios. Formerly a coolstore facility, it has the added advantage that studio spaces can be temperature-controlled to below freezing (http://www. hendersonvalleystudios.com/). Importantly, by providing studio facilities, the council has ensured infrastructure to complement the natural advantages of the city.

A MERGING OF ARTIST AND ENTREPRENEUR: PETER JACKSON

With several blockbusters – *The Lord of the Rings* (*LOTR*) trilogy and *King Kong* (2005) – to his credit, together with formal movie world accolades including Oscars, Peter Jackson is NZ's best-known film director. His artistic imagination and prowess is undoubtedly a vital ingredient in the success of his film projects. By many yardsticks, as outlined below, Jackson is not only an artist but also an entrepreneur par excellence.

A broad perspective on entrepreneurship emphasizes the entrepreneur as an organizer of factors of production, as first highlighted by economist J.B. Say in the early nineteenth century (Glancey and McQuaid, 2000). Film production requires the organization and coordination of a wide range of creative inputs (associated with the artists – actors, scriptwriters, directors, cinematographers, costume designers, special-effects specialists, make-up artists, sound-track and music composers, editors and so on). This creative mix has to be combined with the humdrum inputs like finance for the project – functions encompassed in the role undertaken by film producers. Jackson has engaged in movie financing and involved himself in other organizational and coordination roles besides creative directing. His filmography reveals that he is director as well as producer or co-producer for all of his recent projects – *King Kong* (2005), *LOTR* trilogy, *The Frighteners* (1996) and *Heavenly Creatures* (1994). Many successful directors do not usually combine these functions. For instance, another of NZ's recent successful award-winning directors, Niki Caro (*Whale Rider*, 2002; *North Country*, 2005) has not combined the director and producer roles.

The entrepreneurial character of Jackson is evident in the start-up and ownership of several SPI companies. He has been described as a 'self-made industry in himself, with a production company (Wingnut Films), an effects company (Weta Ltd) and a studio (Three Foot Six) in Wellington' (Errigo, 2003, p. 121). Park Road Post is his more recent venture. It is a high-tech post-production facility described as 'a massive film-making enterprise' that is Jackson's 'love child' and contains the 'best cinema mix rooms in the world' (Stewart, 2004).

Innovation, often seen as an integral facet of entrepreneurship, lies at the heart of Jackson's movie-making art. His use of digital technological advancements and cutting-edge motion picture technology have been the hallmarks of *LOTR* and *King Kong*. The innovation associated with his films has also led to spin-off companies for other entrepreneurs. For example, Virtual Katy Development Limited has been set up to exploit the technology which was developed when working on *LOTR* and which enabled the sound department to keep pace with the ever-changing picture edit.

CONCLUSION

A main aim of this chapter has been to contend that entrepreneurship in the film industry, particularly for 'late-start' countries, involves a continuum of action – at an individual and firm level (noting here the possible dichotomy between artist and entrepreneur), as well as at the overarching national level and the regional and local levels. Together these multiple levels of entrepreneurial activity form an integrative framework for examining entrepreneurship and the working of the process of value adding. Although treated separately in this discussion, it must be noted, nevertheless, that there is often dynamic interaction and symbiotic interdependence at the various levels of entrepreneurship. A striking example of such interrelationships is that of the creative entrepreneurship of Peter Jackson, which was founded on and linked to the initial support of his career by the NZ Film Commission.

Another possible interpretation of what has been put forward in this chapter as the national and regional levels of entrepreneurship, is to argue that this is simply central and local government proactiveness and targeting of economic development resources to build selected industries. Whatever the interpretation, however, a prerequisite for growing a project-based creative industry, such as film and the SPI in a small domestic market like NZ, is a comprehensive framework conducive to building the pool of industry skills and adding value to creative inputs. This involves ongoing efforts to ensure a continuous flow of projects to the country and carving out a NZ niche in the intensely competitive global marketplace. These efforts may be viewed as a continuum of entrepreneurial activity, vital for the self-sustaining growth of complex and capital-intensive creative industries such as film.

NOTES

1. Interestingly the social philosopher Arthur Koestler (1964) distinguishes between three types of creative individual – the Artist, the Sage and the Jester. The artist is involved with the creation of aesthetic beauty, the sage creates ideas or solutions, and humour is an act of creativity for the jester.
2. The creative class comprises a broader occupational grouping than those classified in the creative industries – for example arts, architecture, design, and entertainment. It also includes those in science and engineering and includes all those in jobs that create new ideas, new technology and new creative content.
3. Under this deal, Singapore-based MediaCorp Raintree Pictures and New Zealand's Eyeworks Touchdown intend to co-produce two films – the New Zealand-based *Tattooist* and Singapore-based *Altar* (Executive Government e-mail announcement 18 June 2005, 'Rt. Hon Helen Clark: NZ- Singapore film co-production agreement welcomed').
4. The Wellington region is made up of five cities: Wellington City, Hutt City, Upper Hutt, Porirua and Kapiti.

5. The Auckland Region comprises the four cities of Auckland, North Shore, Waitakere and Manukau as well as three districts (Rodney, Papakura and part of Franklin District). The region is NZ's most populous. At the last 2001 National Census, the region was home to 1.2 million people, representing approximately 31 per cent of NZ's total population.

REFERENCES

Anderton, J. (2004), Speech at the SPADA Conference, 19 November.

Audretsch, D. and Thurik, R. (1999), Capitalism and democracy in the 21st century: from the managed to the entrepreneurial economy, *Journal of Evolutionary Economics*, 10, 17–34.

Bassett, K. Griffiths, R. and Smith, I. (2002), Cultural industries, cultural clusters and the city: the example of natural history film-making in Bristol, *Geoforum*, **33** (2), 165–177.

Caves, R. (2000), Creative Industries: Contracts between Art and Commerce, Cambridge, MA: Harvard University Press.

Caves, R. (2003), Contracts between art and commerce, *Journal of Economic Perspectives*, **17** (2), 73–83.

Christopherson, S. and Storper, M. (1986), The city as studio; the world as back lot: the impact of vertical disintegration on the motion picture industry, *Environment and Planning. D*, **4** (3), 305–320.

Christopherson, S. and Storper, M. (1989), The effects of flexible specialization on industrial politics and the labor market: the motion picture industry, *Industrial and Labor Relations Review*, **42** (3), 331–347.

Cremer, R.D., de Bruin, A. and Dupuis, A. (2001), International sister-cities: bridging the global–local divide, *American Journal of Economics and Sociology*, **60** (1), 377–402.

de Bruin, A. (1998), Entrepreneurship in a new phase of capitalist development, *Journal of Interdisciplinary Economics*, **9** (3), 185–200.

de Bruin, A. (2003a), Electronic entrepreneurship, in de Bruin, A. and Dupuis, A. (eds), *Entrepreneurship: New Perspectives in a Global Age*, Aldershot: Ashgate, pp. 76–91.

de Bruin, A. (2003b), State entrepreneurship, in de Bruin, A. and Dupuis, A. (eds), *Entrepreneurship: New Perspectives in a Global Age*, Aldershot: Ashgate, pp. 148–168.

de Bruin, A. (2005), Multi-level entrepreneurship in the creative industries: New Zealand's screen production industry, *International Journal of Entrepreneurship and Innovation*, **6** (3), 143–150.

de Bruin, A. and Dupuis, A. (2003), Introduction: Concepts and Themes, in de Bruin, A. and Dupuis, A. (eds), *Entrepreneurship: New Perspectives in a Global Age*, Aldershot: Ashgate, pp. 1–24.

de Bruin, A. and Hanrahan, S. (2003), The Screen Production Industry in The Auckland Region: Towards Understanding Human Capacity Issues. A report prepared for the Auckland Regional Economic Development Strategy.

DeFillippi, R.J. and Arthur, M.B. (1998), Paradox in project-based enterprise: the case of film making, *California Management Review*, **40** (2), 1–15.

Department for Culture, Media and Sport, UK (2001), Creative industries mapping document 2001, available from http://www.culture.gov.uk/global/publications/archive_2001/ci_mapping_doc_2001.htm

Dupuis, A., de Bruin, A. and Cremer, R. (2003), Municipal–Community Entrepreneurship, in de Bruin, A. and Dupuis, A. (eds), *Entrepreneurship: New Perspectives in a Global Age*, Aldershot: Ashgate, pp. 128–147.

Epstein, E.J. (2005), *The Big Picture*, New York: Random House.

Errigo, A. (2003), *The Rough Guide to The Lord of the Rings*, London: Haymarket Customer Publishing for Rough Guides Ltd.

Film New Zealand (2005), *Annual Report 2005*, Wellington: Film New Zealand.

Florida, R. (2002), *The Rise of the Creative Class*, New York: Basic Books.

Florida, R. (2004), America's looming creativity crisis, *Harvard Business Review*, 82 (10), 122–130.

Glancey, K. and McQuaid, R. (2000), *Entrepreneurial Economics*, London: MacMillan.

Harley, R. (2002), How we created world class performance, Speech, 11am Showcase Session Wednesday 6 March, Innovate Conference, 5–7 March, New Zealand.

Henry, C., Johnston, K., Ó Cinnéide, B. and Aggestam, M. (2004), Where art meets the science of entrepreneurship: a study of the creative industries sector and the case of the music industry. Paper presented at the Irish Academy of Management Conference, 2–3 September.

Howkins, J. (2002), *The Creative Economy: How People Make Money From Ideas*, London: Penguin Books.

Indergaard, M. (2003), The webs they weave: Malaysia's multimedia super-corridor and New York City's Silicon Alley', *Urban Studies*, **40** (2), 379–401.

Jones, D., Barlow, J., Finlay, S. and Savage, H. (2003), *NZfilm: A Case Study of the New Zealand Film Industry*, Wellington: CANZ – Competitive Advantage New Zealand.

Koestler, A. (1964), *Act of Creation*, London: Hutchinson.

Kresl, P. and Singh, B. (1999), Competitiveness and the urban economy: twenty-four large US metropolitan areas, *Urban Studies*, **36** (5–6), 1017–1027.

Media Development Authority – MDA – Singapore (2003), Media 21: Transforming Singapore into a Global Media City, available from http://www.mda.gov.sg/wms.ftp/media21.pdf, accessed 26 June 2005.

New Zealand Screen Council (2005), Overview of the New Zealand Screen Production Sector, Wellington: New Zealand Screen Council.

Nicolaidi, M. (1991), New Zealand cinema now, in P. Cowie (ed.), International Film Guide, Los Angeles, CA: Silman-James Press, pp. 18–50.

NZIER (2002a), The Creative Industries in New Zealand: Economic Contribution, NZ Institute of Economic Research, May.

NZIER (2002b), Scoping the Lasting Effects of The Lord of the Rings. Report to the New Zealand Film Commission, NZ Institute of Economic Research, April.

NZTE (2005), From Snells Beach to Hollywood, October 26, available from http://www.nzte.govt.nz/section/11894/14641.aspx, accessed 14 December 2005.

OECD (1999), *Managing Innovation Systems*, Paris: Organisation for Economic Co-operation and Development.

Osborne, D. and Gaebler, T. (1993), *Reinventing Government: How the Entrepreneurial Spirit is Transforming the Public Sector*, New York: Plume.

Porter, M. and Stern, S. (2001), Innovation: location matters, *MIT Sloan Management Review*, Summer, 28–36.

Rothman, J. (2004), *Hollywood in Wide Angle*, Lanham, MD: Scarecrow Press.

Schumpeter, J. (1934), *The Theory of Economic Development*, Cambridge, MA: Harvard University Press.

Schumpeter, J. (1991/1946), Comments on a plan for a study of entrepreneurship in Swedberg, R. (ed.), *Joseph A. Schumpeter*, Princeton, NJ: Princeton University Press, pp. 406–428.

Scott, A. (2002), A new map of Hollywood: the production and distribution of American motion pictures, *Regional Studies*, **36** (9), 957–975.

Scott, A. (2004), Cultural-products industries and urban economic development: prospects for growth and market contestation in global context, *Urban Affairs Review*, **39** (4), 461–490.

Shelton, L. (2005), *The selling of New Zealand Movies*, Wellington, NZ: Awa Press.

Smith, D. (2002), The state of the UK film industry in a global market. Dissertation for the University of Hertfordshire Business School, Executive MBA.

SPI (Screen Production Industry) Taskforce (2003), 'Taking on the World: The Report of the Screen Production Industry Taskforce', March.

Stewart, A. (2004), A visit to Park Road Post, available from http://www.onfilm.co.nz/editable/PostProdSound_Spotlight_Nov_04.pdf, accessed 17 November 2005.

Swedberg, R. (1991), *Joseph A. Schumpeter: His Life and Work*, Cambridge: Polity Press.

Waller, G.A. (1996), The New Zealand Film Commission: promoting an industry, forging a national identity, *Historical Journal of Film, Radio and Television*, **16** (2), 243–263.

Welsch, H.P. and Kickul, J.R. (2001), 'Training for successful entrepreneurship careers in the creative arts', in Brockhaus, R., Hills, G., Klandt, H. and Welsch, H. (eds), *Entrepreneurship Education: a Global View*, Aldershot: Ashgate, pp. 167–183.

Wu, W. (2005), Dynamic Cities and Creative Clusters, World Bank Policy Research Working Paper 3509, February.

PART II

Supporting the creative industries sector

7. Investment and funding for creative enterprises in the UK

Tom Fleming

INTRODUCTION

This chapter introduces the challenges faced by a public sector that is seeking ways forward for supporting, undertaking and levering investment for start-up and early-stage creative industries businesses. It builds on research undertaken by the UK's National Endowment for Science, Technology and the Arts (NESTA, 2005) as it seeks to lead strategic approaches to creative industries investment for a range of English Regional Development Agencies as they seek to introduce targeted investment and support initiatives for the sector. The research was based upon a mixed methodology that included over 50 interviews with policymakers, intermediaries, investors and creative businesses.

The chapter introduces the multiple barriers to creative industries investment and provides an overview of the range of intervention opportunities for overcoming these barriers – including dedicated creative industries funds and investment readiness initiatives.

The chapter shows that, rather than create a landscape of initiatives, the public sector too often adopts a piecemeal approach to creative industries investment that lacks clarity and partnership in both focus and form. In addition, the public sector often adopts 'catch-all' approaches to creative industries investment, without attending to the multiple opportunities and barriers faced by creative businesses that occupy different parts of a complex value-chain (Pratt, 1997, 2004a).

Five intervention dilemmas are introduced in the chapter as essential points of engagement for the public sector as it conceptualizes how to establish a landscape of investment initiatives that support different parts of the creative industries value chain in a coordinated way. Thus, the chapter provides a starting point for reconceptualizing the creative industries as a 'support proposition' and for configuring how a coherent creative industries landscape – based on partnership, commitment, specialism and genericism – may be formed.

A POLICY CONTEXT

Approaches to public sector-led intervention in creative industries investment operate as part of a much broader approach to sector support and development on all scales. The convergence of culture and economics has allowed policymakers and intermediaries across the UK to make the case for increased intervention in a sector that previously lacked an 'economic profile' and was often categorized by economists as a 'consumption industry' – mere entertainment rather than a significant production-orientated economic driver (Pratt, 2004b). In 1998, the Department of Culture, Media and Sport (DCMS), through a high-profile mapping document and the establishment of a Creative Industries Task Force, raised the stakes, presenting a group of what might be termed 'creative disciplines' as one of the fastest-growing sectors of the UK economy. According to DCMS (2003), the sector accounted for 1.9 million jobs, generated revenues of over £110 million, and would become increasingly significant as a key ingredient of global competitiveness (Cash and Hughes, 2000; Cox, 2005).

It is at a regional level that the public sector has therefore sought, through a variety of means, to support the development of the creative industries sector, often through a focus on specific cities or districts within the region, and sometimes on a sub-sectoral basis (Rifkin, 2000). The creative industries are increasingly appreciated at the regional level for their growth potential, for the 'added value' they offer other sectors, and for their role as a transforming influence on regional identity (Scott, 1997; O'Connor, 2006). A sector important in its own right, the creative industries are understood as a 'catalysing sector', where to have a strong and distinctive creative industries sector is to develop a 'honey pot' that attracts other sectors and a highly qualified workforce (see, for example, Kelly, 1998; Sandercock, 1998; Florida, 2002; Pratt, 2002). Utilizing central government funds and a range of funds derived from the European Union, regional strategies and subsequent interventions include:

- The heavily instructive – through the development of physical workspace (including incubation) or broadband facilities for creative businesses, perhaps as part of a Creative Quarter or Cluster Strategy.
- The soft(er) approach – through marketing and cultural tourism initiatives, creative networks and showcase events.
- The highly specialized – through dedicated intermediary and business support services (including advice), targeted training, export support and investment initiatives.

These approaches to creative industries intervention, and especially the latter, are based on an understanding that the sector requires specialist attention and that it provides special opportunities for the region or a part of the region.

INVESTMENT INTERVENTIONS

In the UK, creative industries policy development with an investment focus can be linked to an increasing appreciation of the barriers faced by start-up and early-stage creative businesses seeking investment, plus of course the value of having a strong creative industries sector in a given locality (NESTA, 2006):

- Early-stage and start-up creative industries businesses struggle more than businesses from most other sectors to raise finance, which has a tangible impact on business growth. The creative industries are relatively 'under-invested' (Finance South-East, 2005). This is despite the significant growth of the sector in recent years and the proliferation of national to local creative industries policy and support. This is an issue of market failure: there is a recognized finance gap for creative businesses.

- Additional reasons for this underinvestment can be attributed to generic 'small business and start-up issues', plus very specific structural and cultural barriers that stand in the way of creative industries investment. These are built upon a combination of investee and investor factors. These range from a lack of knowledge of opportunities, to the relative significance of people rather than products as the 'object of investment', to inappropriate provision of opportunities, to a perception by many investors that creative businesses depend too acutely on unpredictable movements of 'taste' (Hesmondalgh, 2002; Pratt, 2004a). These factors can be reduced – in simple terms – to deficiencies in investment and investor readiness. Problems in supply and demand combine to exaggerate market failure.

- Variations in context and sub-sector mean that, in many cases, improved investment and investor readiness are not sufficient to lever required investment. This is because current investment support and provision in many places is insufficiently flexible to respond to the distinctiveness of some types of creative business (NESTA, 2005). Existing investment tools do not have the flexibility and intelligence resources to identify and extract the often very specific value of a creative business.

In the UK, public sector responses to an increasing 'creative industries investment agenda', have focused predominantly on the need to establish dedicated creative industries investment readiness initiatives to advance the capacity of creative businesses, assist them in identifying growth potential, and ensure that their profiles are at least satisfactory for target investors. These include a focus on advancing business skills, developing management teams, identifying value, protecting this value as intellectual property rights (IPR), and preparing IPR for suitable markets that offer opportunities for marked business growth. Interventions include the support services offered by creative development agencies such as CIDS[1] and CIDA,[2] intensive programmes such as the Creative Seed Fund in Scotland, and IPR information and support programmes such as Own It in London.[3]

An additional focus is based on the need for parallel investor readiness initiatives – to demystify the creative industries, establish a working relationship between creatives, intermediaries and investors, and build in new metrics that suit the changing business profiles of creative businesses. This requires an attention to building in-depth intelligence of different creative investment propositions, including a detailed understanding of where each business is located in the value chain, and thus, where its 'value' lies – whether in a service, product, project or a range of features. Interventions include the advocacy work of Culture Finance North West[4] and the specialist Creative Industries Officer of the Prince's Trust East Midlands. Significant here is the requirement of building strong networks of public and private sector intermediaries – such as business advisors, lawyers and accountants – to operate as 'gatekeepers', brokers and generators of ongoing partnership. Such actors can help to make the investment landscape navigable and demonstrate investment opportunities to each party.

Yet in some locations, there is a recognized need and related political and strategic will to move beyond encouraging and facilitating investment to introduce new dedicated funds. These are deemed necessary to fill gaps in the market, operate as a lever to existing investment sources, and act as a vehicle to build strong partnerships between investment communities, intermediaries and the creative industries sector. These range from micro finance (such as Culture Finance North West) to venture capital (such as the Advantage Creative Fund in the West Midlands).[5] Most approaches operate at a regional level, managed through the resources of Regional Development Agencies or equivalents. They operate as strategic funds rather than total solutions because even if the public sector increased investment in the creative industries many times over, it would still occupy a tiny proportion of the overall investment market. The funds, therefore, operate as tools of facilitation, advocacy and brokerage, and they work most effectively as part of a broader landscape of support that includes a focus on investment and investor readiness. The level of cohesiveness of this landscape depends to a large extent on the commitment of public sector partners to engage with the questions introduced below.

FIVE INTERVENTION DILEMMAS FOR THE PUBLIC SECTOR

Rightly, the public sector in the UK feels compelled to intervene: to push positively towards supporting a high-growth and value-adding sector, and to respond to negative forces that artificially suppress growth potential. Many of the latter can be linked to issues of under investment or inappropriate investment. However, the public sector too often develops policies and interventions without due consideration of the focus, strategic position and potential outcomes. Research undertaken for NESTA (2005) has uncovered five complex, inconsistent and, in some instances, irresolvable dilemmas faced by policymakers and intermediaries when considering whether to intervene, how to intervene and where to intervene through creative industries investment and support.[6] Each of these is linked to the following questions: How to deal with the creative industries? and, What is meant by creative industries investment.

Dilemma 1. Creative Industries: A Special Case?

A misplaced assertion is often made that start-up and early-stage creative businesses are, for the most part, significantly different from businesses in any other sector which are at a similar stage in the life cycle. Such businesses in any sector often have underdeveloped markets, poor business skills, a lack of equity, a project mentality, reluctance to cede control, suspicion of mentors, and so on (ACCA, 1996). Investment opportunities for many creative businesses do not, therefore, always differ greatly from those available to any start-up or early-stage firm in the UK.

However, in certain locations and for specific parts of the creative industries value chain, creative businesses face very different investment challenges to businesses in other sectors. This is due to relatively poor business and management skills (NESTA, 2004), the absolute dependence on 'people as assets' (O'Connor and Wynne, 1996), the long lag times between idea creation and commercialization (Pratt, 2004a), a project dependency (Hesmondalgh, 2002), and low levels of recognition from potential investment communities (see, for example, NWAB, 2000; CIM, 2004). Indeed, problems of underprovision and barriers to that provision are evident in the North West region of England: recent research undertaken for Culture

Finance North West found that 67 per cent of creative businesses consider the provision of financing insufficient, 62 per cent had difficulty accessing public sector financing, and 80 per cent found private sector finance either fairly difficult or very difficult to access (CFNW, 2004a, p. 2).

Dilemma 2. Start-up and Early-Stage Businesses: Underinvested?

It is widely accepted that a finance gap exists for those SMEs seeking investment in the range of £250 000 to £1 million (the space between the upper limit of business angel investment and the lower limit of the desired deal size for venture capital) (Small Business Service – SBS, 2003). However, very few start-up and early-stage businesses require investment of that magnitude for the first three years of trading (ACCA, 2003). Indeed, just 35 per cent of SMEs currently use external investment (mostly from high street banks), with 61 per cent utilizing cash from friends, family and that generated by turnover (Envestors, 2004a). Indeed, despite the array of public sector investment vehicles, their reach and uptake is minor in the context of a market dominated by banks and 'owner finance'. Therefore, some argue that the investment market for start-up and early-stage businesses is active, dynamic and, for the most part, responsive to investment requirements: '(G)enerally speaking businesses should not find it too difficult to access capital' (IOD, 2004, p. 15).

However, it is clear that in many cases, start-up and early-stage businesses – and especially those that are ideas-based and content generating – face significant difficulty in raising investment to develop the business or a product or project within the business. This is due to:

- Risk factors: banks and equity investors are risk averse. They undertake a security-based lending protocol referred to as the 'gone concern approach', as opposed to a 'going concern approach'. This favours businesses with a strong track record, a definable market, and established distribution arrangements to reach that market (ACCA, 2003). Businesses seeking to develop a product or project or prove a concept are rarely supported with a 'gone concern approach', thus making it difficult to invest in new ideas, products and processes unless they are already proven as commercial propositions.
- Market factors: equity markets are not performing strongly. A general reduction in deal flow causes a reduction in seed and start-up deals (Envestors, 2004b). Most start-up and early-stage businesses will not require the scale of investment provided by equity deals. Yet for a minority of high-growth, scalable propositions, the downturn in the equity market places limitations on their immediate growth potential.

- Intelligence factors: despite increases in available business advice and support (much of it specialist), management techniques and systems have not significantly improved (ACCA, 1996). This is certainly the case for the creative industries (NESTA, 2005). In addition, there is little sign that investment communities are better informed of the distinct business profiles and investment opportunities of many small businesses. Since most early-stage creative businesses are small and some are very distinctive, investment is unlikely to be forthcoming.
- Policy precedent: evidence exists of where the public sector has worked effectively to 'pump-prime' private investment markets by introducing dedicated sector-specific, investment-focused initiatives (including both funds and support services). For example, the considerable commitment to investing in technology-focused research and development by the Finnish government (including partnerships with the higher education sector and private technology investors) operated initially as a loss leader, but it provided the stimulus for the very high growth of the knowledge economy that has accelerated Finland into a world leader amongst smaller nations (see, for example, Bell and Hietala, 2002; Routti, 2003; CIM, 2004).[7] The expanding technology market requires content, so parallel investment in the creative industries seems a logical next step (CIM, 2001).

Dilemma 3. Start-up and Early-Stage Creative Businesses: High Growth or 'Ideal Size'?

It is only ever likely that a small minority of creative businesses will show the high growth – and continue to grow – to a scale that attracts, for example, equity investment. At best, certain sub-sectors such as film might expect to raise equity investment on a project basis, such as towards the production of a film. In short, the creative industries sector, wherever the locale, is a small-business and low-scalability sector. The sector gains its scale and high growth rates in aggregation and often through the disproportionately large contributions of specific businesses located in particular creative sub-sectors.

Creative businesses in most cases remain small because, for example:

- Many produce content on a project-by-project basis, working with a key set of clients, rarely producing content that can be distributed more widely (Crewe and Forster, 1993). They are, thus, locally embedded and globally limited.[8]
- Owner-managers of creative businesses (most creative businesses are very small, often operating as freelancers or sole traders)[9] are

characterized by strong degrees of protectiveness and a reticence to build partnerships that require a ceding of control. Many such businesses have strong inclinations towards retaining a strong ownership role – of both products and businesses. This enforces a perceived 'ideal size' on a business (ACCA, 2003, p. 1), expressed through a disinclination to expand. Investment that enables expansion may, therefore, be undesirable for a micro creative business.

● Many creative businesses pursue commercial objectives as complimentary to lifestyle objectives. This is an entirely worthy, pragmatic approach to creative development and income generation and should not be discouraged or denigrated. However, it places limitations on the growth capacity of creative businesses because, for growth to be made possible, allied with investment, requires significant resource development in, for example, management, administration and legal infrastructure. This requires in turn a dilution of the 'lifestyle benefits' and a strong focus on the perhaps less culturally gratifying mechanics of running a high-growth business (at least until investment has enabled the resourcing of management and legal teams).

Public sector policymakers and intermediaries might, therefore, be mistaken if an exclusively high-growth approach to investment support and provision is pursued. Most creative businesses have neither the capacity nor inclination to grow big and fast; and many creative businesses require low levels of investment to enable them to grow to an 'ideal size' that satisfies both themselves and mutually dependent businesses situated up and down the creative value chain.

However, the notion that creative businesses operate within the boundaries of a self-imposed 'ideal size' is to overlook the possibility that many creative entrepreneurs are unaware of their growth potential, misguided if they consider investment to equate to significant loss of control, and inaccurate to consider growth to be inimical to a creative lifestyle. For example, much digitally-derived creative content is scalable as product without requiring a significant overhaul and expansion of business and management resources. Appropriate licensing agreements and supporting investment can enable specialist services to be bought in on a project-by-project basis. This enables creative businesses to have very high turnovers while remaining small.

Indeed, improvements in digital technologies, expanding markets for 'distinctive goods' and increasing trade-focused support for the creative industries, are presenting new growth opportunities for a wider range of creative businesses.[10] The key challenges for the businesses, public sector support services and interested investors are to: identify growth potential on a business-to-business basis; isolate the parts of the business that offer growth (that is, find out where the 'value' lies); seek ways to protect that value (that is, make it more valuable); identify market opportunities for these valuable products or services; build a business plan that articulates growth potential; and identify appropriate investment vehicles to assist and add value to that growth.

It is clear that the public sector can play a role in identifying patterns and profiles for specific types of creative business, building partnerships with different types of investment community to assist them in developing creative industries' intelligence, and brokering relationships between investors and investees to allow for a partnership-based approach to creative business growth. It is also clear that the public sector might play a role in proof-of-concept and seed investment that enables creative entrepreneurs to test the value of their previously undervalued ideas. This is an approach to dedicated investment and support that does not subscribe to the 'forever small' construct of creative industries businesses.

Dilemma 4. Start-up and Early-Stage Creative Businesses: Local or Global?

As introduced above, the creative industries is a small business sector (Pratt, 2004a). Most regions are characterized by large numbers of small businesses and small numbers of large businesses (O'Connor, 2006). Most creative businesses are locally embedded, dependent on keenly networked local clusters that often have few or unpredictable links to global networks.[11] The most successful regions tend to have higher numbers of large businesses that operate through highly networked value-chain relationships with many strong, small creative business (Jeffcutt, 2004; O'Connor, 2004). Such regions are in the minority, operating as nodes in global creative markets (such as London and South East England, New York, Tokyo, Seoul) (Hesmondalgh, 2002).

This places a ceiling on the capacity of most regions to nurture many large creative businesses, which carries with it investment implications. For example, if the region is not a global node, start-up and early-stage creative businesses will, in most cases, struggle to provide the types of scalable, high-return propositions favoured by equity investment (especially if it is solely from the private sector). Also, it is possible that high growth will be focused on those start-ups and early-stage businesses that have built connections with markets and investors while being based elsewhere: they are 'returnee creatives'.[12] They are likely to be small in number, will have well-developed relations with investors (often as global capital), and/or will have keenly identified markets and strong management capacity. This will make them attractive to existing investment opportunities in a region before they need to consider approaching specialist investment packages. Therefore, the public sector might be more successful in encouraging creative industries growth if it strives to attract returnee creatives and their colleagues as a type of inward investment policy (see for example Crone, 2004).

To complicate matters further, increasing numbers of creative businesses have scalable, international growth opportunities, regardless of where they are located. This is because they mirror the growth potential of software and technology companies that are 'born global'.[13] Processes associated with digitalization enable businesses to enter international markets from the outset. This greatly increases their scalability and thus their potential to attract equity investment rather than locally distributed debt finance. The rise in born-global technology firms and their hunger for content has the potential to carry with it a rise in born-global content firms, introducing truly investable propositions to early-stage and start-up creative industries markets for the first time (CIM, 2001, 2004). This places an emphasis on the importance of the public sector role in nurturing innovation and creativity, seed investment and investment readiness support that focuses on IPR identification, valuation and protection.

Dilemma 5. Creative Businesses: Locked into a Traditional Arts Funding Mentality?

A significant proportion of start-up and early-stage creative businesses have entered business as a direct 'spin-out' from the relatively subsidy- or grant-dependent arts sector. Indeed, many operate across dual platforms, combining subsidy-dependent creative activity and project development with complimentary commercial activity. This is common practice in subsectors such as theatre and design. It has significant policy implications for institutions such as the Arts Council, which is increasingly interconnecting programmes of activity that have both an arts agenda (attending to issues of access, quality and diversity) and a creative industries agenda (attending to issues such as business support, professional development and export).

This intermingling of 'the commercial' and 'the cultural' is considered by many to symbolise the inability of creative businesses to relieve themselves of that which is interesting, evocative and fulfilling, and drive belligerently towards achieving purely commercial goals. Just as 'lifestyle business' is used as a pejorative term, creative industries businesses can be denigrated by 'industrialists' as interested more in process than product, and thus: less concerned with exploiting a product than experimenting further with process; distracted by texture and detail rather than market potential; expectant of financial support so long as it is project-focused grant 'investment';

and suspicious of commercial development if it detracts from creative and artistic values.

This presents a dilemma for public sector bodies – especially those charged with an economic development agenda: how to support creative businesses that operate as meaningful and valuable economic units, many of which have significant growth potential, without perpetuating a subsidy-dependent approach to creativity? The answer for some is to refrain from investment, seek to target those that aspire to commercialize and grow, and thus rely on traditional agents of arts development such as the Arts Council(s) to supply the creative industries with an ongoing source of 'R&D investment'.

CREATIVE INDUSTRIES INVESTMENT: UNDERSTANDING THE VALUE CHAIN

The five dilemmas introduced above reveal the deeply intertwined inconsistencies of the creative industries – both internally and in relation to or by comparison with other sectors. Such characteristics contribute to the exclusiveness or 'exceptionalism' of the creative industries (Pratt, 2004a, p. 10) and, therefore, provide the rationale for investment while still presenting complex challenges to the public sector as it endeavours to intervene.

To ensure that investment intervention is appropriate and effectively situated within a broader landscape requires a much-needed reconceptualization of the creative industries according to those types of business within a range of sub-sectors that offer relatively high commercial investment opportunities, as opposed to those that will rely on investment that requires less dramatic returns (mostly debt finance). The policy consequence for this is the need for specialist support services, as part of a more general drive towards 'investment-readiness' and 'investor-readiness', that advance understanding of both the location of a creative business (or type of business) in the value chain, and the composition and potential of the value of a business. This may require from the public sector specialist IPR investment readiness services (to compliment more general services that attend to features such as management capacity) and parallel investor briefings. It may require dedicated seed and proof-of-concept funds to allow a business to determine its value, and project investment to comply with the business profiles of many creative businesses. Alternatively or additionally, it may require a mix of other investment instruments – such as debt and mezzanine – to lever co-investment from a still nervous commercial investment market; plus a range of other investment readiness and, as a last resort, investment instruments, to ensure that smaller, less high-growth creative businesses are catered for within the broader investment landscape. To ignore the majority of creative businesses in the value chain would imperil those with commercially scalable IPR.

Crucial in assessing the value of a (local, regional, and so on) creative industries sector is understanding the value chain, which should in turn inform policymakers of where and how to intervene. Pratt (2004a) identifies a creative industries value chain (using the term 'production chain') as containing four key links:

- Creation and content origination: the multiple 'processes by which creative material and intellectual assets are originated and produced' (Pratt, 2004a, p. 12). This 'stage' includes all creative forms: the images, ideas, compositions, designs, games, titles and packages.
- Manufacture: 'the making of "one-offs", or prototypes, which may be reproduced later' (Pratt, 2004a, p. 12), plus specialist goods used towards creative production such as paint brushes, cameras and musical instruments.
- Distribution and mass production: activities that channel content and services to markets such as CD replication, shipping and (increasingly) digital delivery systems.
- Exchange: the exhibition of creative products (for example, venue-based activities undertaken in theatres, concert halls and cinemas), and the retailing of products (such as books, CDs, games, or even products sold on the basis of a brand).

Creative businesses located in specific parts of the value chain will require different approaches to investment and support. The two examples below explore this further.

Example 1: Creative Service Companies

Commonalities are clear between architecture, advertising and many design businesses: they share features of 'advanced producer services' such as management consultancy, working on a basis of 'money for time' (as a day rate or fixed fee) rather than through the exploitation of IPR (through licences or royalties) (Pratt, 2004a). This has implications for the 'scalability' of the business as well as the type of investment required, because 'there are limits to how much it is possible to "sweat the human assets" out of such service-based industries' (Pratt, 2004a, p. 16); and thus, return per unit of investment will be less than for a business that can expand at a lower cost (such as one that expands through the widespread distribution of products rather than increased capacity of teams).

Creative service companies such as design and architecture are thus less attractive to commercial investors seeking high returns through large-scale investment. This position is cemented by the likelihood that businesses in this part of the value chain hold a fragility in growth potential because they are so people-dependent and thus undercapitalized: changes in personnel incur high costs and possibly reduce the value of the brand. It is only when a business has a brand which is not people-dependent that a creative service company can be classified as 'truly scalable'.

Example 2: Scalable IPR-Led Creative Companies

Unlike most creative businesses that dedicate their energies to providing services, an increasing number of creative businesses are exploring new structures and value chains that provide access to rapidly internationalizing market opportunities. Businesses capable of identifying IPR that can be adequately protected, valued, packaged and connected at low cost through distributors to the consumer(s), are those that have the most scalable propositions and that – for the purposes of private equity investors – have the most 'value' (see, for example, Carpenter and Oetersen, 2002).[14] In this regard, products could include an idea, an image, a sound, a script, a combination of multiple media. Their scalability is vital. Deficits in management capacity or entrepreneurial panache can be overcome – albeit with difficulty and at a cost – so long as a business is able to identify and maximize the potential of its value:

> The digital revolution in radio, TV and especially the internet has transformed the Creative Industries. Today demand often exceeds supply. Some experts talk of distributors becoming subcontractors for content creators. (CIM, 2001, p. 3)

Add to the above platforms the ever-extending content-focused role of the mobile phone, and this change in the creative industries ecosystem brings with it potential investment opportunities that did not exist a few years ago. Moreover, it brings potential investment opportunities to a wider range of often smaller creative businesses, because smaller businesses that rapidly turn over new content can grow very quickly, mirroring in many ways the 'born globals' of the technology sector.[15] This is especially the case for English-speaking creatives, thus providing the UK creative economy with an initial comparative advantage.

In addition, while the proliferation of new content-hungry platforms is of obvious potential benefit to new generations of growth-focused digital media creatives, IPRs in traditional arts have the potential to gain value. Opportunities might be linked to the demand from new television channels for increased 'quality programming', an increasingly media-savvy consumer seeking to purchase visual art IPR through the Internet, or an opera, theatre or dance company building a protected portfolio for sale to television, radio and, by extension, through alternative commercial routes such as merchandizing.

CONCLUSION

This chapter calls for the coordination of a range of approaches that flexibly respond to the distinctive business profiles of different types of creative businesses. This is based on an acceptance that growth and investment opportunities vary from creative business to creative business, discipline to discipline, market to market and location to location. There is a need to establish far more clearly the rationale behind intervention and investment, making clear the objectives of any intervention or investment, and ensuring it is strategically and practically 'parcelled-up' with other interventions from both public and private sector sources.

Any new investment and support in the creative industries should, therefore, be positioned to complement existing initiatives and to join them together so that different types of creative business are faced with a coherent landscape of support and investment opportunities. In addition, private sector investors have called for more and better intelligence on the business profiles and growth potential of creative businesses, and they have requested that the use of private sector intermediaries be advanced to ensure they have confidence in the intelligence presented to them. It therefore follows that intervention in the creative investment landscape must be predefined by the intelligence and partnership provided by dedicated creative value-chain research. The interventions which gain most private investor respect and result in positive creative business responses are those that are appropriately located within the creative investment landscape and utilize intelligence innovatively to ensure that they involve the following features.

Account for Difference and Specialism

The creative industries are internally diverse. Start-up and early-stage creative businesses vary by discipline, motivation and market, and by content, aspiration and suppliers. Each business has different investment needs and divergent potential to identify and protect 'investable assets' (which of course vary by investment type). Many creative businesses have investment needs that are of little relevance to businesses in other sectors. This requires that either the investment vehicle (the 'type of money' and structure of the deal) be very bespoke, or the support services (the expertise of intermediaries, the quality of investment readiness) be sufficiently flexible to work the business towards fitting the money, or work the money towards fitting the business. In other instances, the support services may be good enough to work the business without requiring the money. Each of these scenarios requires an understanding of where a business is based in the creative value chain and how to maximize growth potential from that position. Investment should not be used to shunt a business artificially to a position it does not aspire to be in; there is no 'one size fits all' solution to creative industries investment.

Place IPR at the Centre of Investment Considerations

By viewing different creative businesses within this series of value-chain relationships, it is possible to begin plotting the growth potential and identifying where the value of the business may lie. Of course, many creative businesses simultaneously occupy multiple parts of the value chain. This introduces additional challenges in locating the 'investable value' – the IPR – of a business or groups of businesses according to the investment criteria of different types of finance. The closer the relationship between investor and investee, the better the intelligence, and thus, the greater the likelihood of the investment reaching the IPR and translating it into a scalable proposition.

Use Intermediaries

Private sector intermediaries (that is, lawyers, accountants, PR specialists, and so on) are underused in public sector creative industries intervention. This is despite their undeniable power to locate the value in creative businesses, broker investor–investee relations and impart expertise. Initiatives that can build partnerships with intermediaries to connect specific expertise to specific issues flexibly, and introduce free-flowing networks of intermediaries interfacing with investees and investors, will have a far greater impact.

Develop Complimentary Cluster or Agglomeration Strategies

Creative businesses in general like to cluster. They gain creatively and commercially through the encounters and exchanges provided by proximity and networking (Porter, 1998; Fleming, 2004). The public sector has responded to this by introducing an array of cluster strategies, workspace initiatives, network projects and, in partnership with the higher education sector, spin-out programmes, incubation facilities and knowledge-transfer interventions. However, few focus on the relationship between creative content development and investment.

In the UK, cluster-focused investment initiatives are exclusively targeted towards technology and health sectors. The relationship between technology innovation and the spiralling need for content has not as yet reached the strategic agendas of cluster managers or investors. Such clusters of ideas creation, research and development, and content to technology transfer, might offer significant opportunities for regional economies through flexible specialization as a basis for comparative advantage. They may also help to 'show the way' to investors by revealing how many creative content producers are complicit with high-growth technology producers.

Do not Have Overlapping Policy Agendas

The creative industries have multiple 'positive externalities' that prove irresistible to public policymakers – especially at a regional level (O'Connor, 2006). However, when establishing creative industries investment and support initiatives, these should be sidelined. Investment should focus solely on extracting value from creative businesses; on levering a commercial return from a growing economic unit. This is imperative if the private sector is to take the public sector seriously and if creative businesses are to relieve themselves of an endearment to public subsidy as a required recognition of their cultural value.

Invest as a Last Resort

Investment and investor readiness initiatives can advance the deal flow of investments in the creative industries, but in most cases, market failure will persist: the reach and influence of the initiative may not be sufficient to influence many investors; challenges in recognizing, valuing and protecting IPR will persist; and investors from 'across the market' will continue to exhibit reticence when faced with a creative industries proposition. This is why new money – money as co-investment, money to prove the concept, money to afford appropriate intermediaries, money to subsidise the deal flow – is needed. However, unless it can be proven that it is absolutely necessary, and that the 'need' is of sufficient importance for it to be 'satisfied', then the public sector should seek to make existing money work rather than spending new money. This applies to every type of creative industries intervention.

NOTES

1. The Creative Industries Development Service in Manchester. See www.cids.co.uk.
2. The Cultural Industries Development Association in East London. See www.cida.co.uk.
3. Own It provides a free IPR rapid response support mechanism and advice facility to creative people across London. The service relies upon an extensive network of sector-specific and legal experts, subsidised to offer their services. It is managed by a lead partner, London College of Communication (part of the University of the Arts). Services include online news and features, specialist seminars and one free legal advice or intervention session (maximum 45 minutes) with a lawyer from Own It's associated intellectual property law firm Briffa. See www.own-it.org.
4. Culture Finance North West (CFNW) was established as a two-year pilot project between January 2003 and December 2004, to test the potential market for micro credit for creative businesses and assess the viability and capacity of an agency that works to broker 'creative investment' from other sources. It is funded and supported through a partnership of the Arts Council of England (North West) (ACE) and the North West Development Agency (NWDA), and operates under the auspices of the ACE (with a possible future as a stand-alone agency or an agency operating within another appropriate organization). See www.culturefinance.co.uk.
5. A £5 million region-wide venture capital investment fund set up specifically to help creative businesses in the West Midlands to grow. See www.advantagecreativefund.co.uk.
6. This was based upon an intensive qualitative methodology, including over 50 interviews with public sector policymakers and intermediaries, fund managers, investors and growth-orientated creative businesses.
7. In Finland, R&D investments rose from 1.5 per cent of GNP to 3.2 per cent over a ten-year period from the 1990s to the new millennium. The subsequent increase of high-technology export share from 5 per cent to over 20 per cent of total exports is too considerable to be coincidental (see Routti, 2001).
8. See Pratt (2004a, 2004b) for an introduction to how this local embeddedness is crucial for distinctive creative industries cluster development. However, Pratt does not downplay the significance of global factors in local value chains. Indeed, he suggests that the local and global interact in different ways by location. For example, a global node in the creative industries such as London is more likely to have a creative industries sector with major capacity in content production. By contrast, a provincial location may rely more significantly on manufacturing and distribution of creative products and services.
9. For example, 36 per cent of creative businesses in Northern Ireland operate below the VAT threshold – in 2005 just under £60 000 gross turnover per annum (Jeffcutt, 2004).
10. See Dorset County Council (2006).
11. See for example Christorpherson and Storper (1986) and Mommaas (2004) for an exploration of the local and global dynamics of creative clusters.
12. See Saxenian (2000) for an example from Bangalore, India, on how emigration and return migration of skilled workers can play an important role in 'indigenous' business development and international knowledge transfer (see Crone 2004 to connect these processes to software start-ups in Ireland).
13. See Rialp-Criado et al. (2002), and Crone (2004) for an introduction.
14. Pratt (2004b) introduces this new age of opportunity for the creative industries through a focus on the influence of technological change on content development: 'Technological changes have created new organisational possibilities: digitisation of separate analogue forms creates a new possibility of convergence of technologies, art forms, and organisational structures, and critically, of producers and consumers' (p. 3).
15. However, it is not clear whether this 'small is beautiful' trend will continue. For example, in broadcasting it is possible that larger production companies will acquire smaller companies, leaving remaining smaller companies to provide highly specialized programming and associated services. Their 'investable value' might, therefore, be short-lived.

REFERENCES

ACCA (1996), The Financial Management of Small Firms: An Alternative Perspective. ACCA Research Report No. 49.

ACCA (2003), Can European Banks Plug the Finance Gap for UK SMEs? ACCA Research Report No. 81.

Bell, M. and Hietala, M. (2002), *Helsinki: The Innovative City*, Helsinki: Finish Literature Society and City of Helsinki Urban Facts.

Carpenter, R. and Oetersen, B. (2002), Capital market imperfections, high-tech investment and new equity financing, *Economic Journal* 112, 54–72.

Cash, A. and Hughes, A. (eds) (2000), British Enterprise in Transition 1994–1999, Swindon: ESRC Centre for Business Research.

Christorpherson, S. and Storper, M. (1986), The city as studio; the world as backlot: the impacts of vertical disintegration on the motion picture industry, *Society and Space*, 4 (3), 305–320.

Cox (2005), *Cox Review of Creativity in Business: Building on the UK's Strengths*, London: HM Treasury.

Creative Industries Management – CIM (2001), Content – Europe's New Growth Engine (CIM, Finland).

Creative Industries Management – CIM (2004), Venture Fund for Creative Industries and Creative Industries Markets (CIM, Helsinki).

Crewe, L. and Forster, Z. (1993), Markets, design and local agglomeration: the role of small independent retailers in the workings of the fashion system, *Environment and Planning D: Society and Space*, 11, 213–229.

Crone, M. (2004), Celtic Tiger Cubs: Ireland's VC-Funded Software Start-ups (Economic Research Institute of Northern Ireland, Belfast).

Dorset County Council (2006), Creative Dorset Strategy (DCC, Dorchester).

Envestors (2004a), A Fresh Approach to Raising Finance of up to £1m (Envestors, London).

Envestors (2004b), Bringing Entrepreneurs and Investors Together – Bridging the Funding Gap (Envestors, London).

Fleming, T. (2004), Supporting the Cultural Quarter? The Role of the Intermediary, in Jayne, M. and Bell, D. (eds), *Cultural Quarters*, Aldershot: Ashgate Publishing.

Florida, R. (2002), *The Rise of the Creative Class*, New York: Basic Books.

Hesmondhalgh, D. (2002), *The Cultural Industries*, London: Sage.

Institute of Directors – IOD (2004), Business Finance 2004 (IOD, London).

Jeffcutt, P. (2004), Knowledge Relationships and Transactions in a Cultural Economy: Analysing the Creative Industries Ecosystem (Media International, Australia).

Kelly, K. (1998), *New Rules for the New Economy: 10 Radical Strategies for a Connected World*, London: Fourth Estate.

Mommaas, H. (2004), Cultural Clusters and the Post-industrial City: Towards the Remapping of Urban Cultural Policy, *Urban Studies*, 41 (3), 507–532.

National Endowment for Science, Technology and the Arts – NESTA (2003), Forward Thinking – *New Solutions to Old Problems: Investing in the Creative Industries*, London: NESTA.

National Endowment for Science, Technology and the Arts – NESTA (2005), Creating value – How The UK Can Invest in New Creative Businesses (NESTA, London).

National Endowment for Science, Technology and the Arts – NESTA (2006), Creating growth: How The UK Can Develop World-class Creative Businesses (NESTA, London).

NWAB (2000), Banking on Culture: New Financial Instruments for Expanding the Cultural Sector in Europe.

O'Connor, J. (2004), 'A Special Kind of City Knowledge': Innovative Clusters, Tacit Knowledge and the 'Creative City'.

O'Connor, J. (2006), Creative Cities: The Role of Creative Industries in Regeneration (Renew North West, Manchester).

O'Connor, J. and Wynne, D. (eds) (1996), *From the Margins to the Centre: Cultural Production and Consumption in the Post-industrial City*, Aldershot: Ashgate Publishing.

Porter, M. (1998), Clusters and the New Economics of Competitiveness, *Harvard Business Review*, December, 78–90.

Pratt, A. (1997), The Cultural Industries Production System: A Case of Employment Change in Britain, 1984–1991, *Environment and Planning A*, **29** (11), 1953–1974.

Pratt, A. (2002), Hot jobs in cool places. The material cultures of new media product spaces: the case of south of the market, San Francisco, *Information, Communication Society*, **5** (1), 27–50.

Pratt, A. (2004a), Creative Clusters: Towards the Governance of the Creative Industries Production System? (Media International Australia).

Pratt, A. (2004b), *Cultural Industries: Beyond the Cluster Paradigm?*, London: LSE.

Rialp-Criado, A., Rialp-Criado, J., Knight, G.A. (2002), The phenomenon of international new ventures, global start-ups, and born-globals: what do we know after a decade of exhaustive scientific enquiry?, http://selene.uab.es/dep-economia-empresa/documents/02-11.pdf.

Rifkin, J. (2000), *The Age of Access: How the Shift From Ownership to Access is Transforming Capitalism*, London: Penguin.

Routti, J. (2001), *Creating Value Through Innovation and Applied Creativity*, Helsinki: CIM.

Routti, J. (2003), Research and Innovation in Finland – Transformation into a Knowledge Economy (Knowledge Economy Forum II, The World Bank and Finland, Helsinki).

Sandercock, L. (1998), *Cosmopolis*, Chichester: Wiley.

Small Business Service – SBS (2003), Bridging the Finance Gap: A Consultation on Improving Access to Growth Capital for Small Businesses.

Saxenian, A. (2000), The Bangalore Boom: From Brain Drain to Brain Circulation? in Kenniston, K. and Kumar, D. (eds), *Bridging the Digital Divide: Lessons from India*, Bangalore: National Institute of Advanced Study.

Scott, A.J. (1997), The cultural economy of cities, *International Journal of Urban and Regional Research*, **21** (2), 323–339.

8. Promoting entrepreneurship in arts education

Ralph Brown[1]

INTRODUCTION

The recent *Lambert Review of Business–University Collaboration* commented that employers from the creative industries were particularly concerned about the quality of courses in their subject areas and whether, in all cases, they were properly equipping students for careers in the creative industries (Lambert, 2003, p. 118). The Higher Education Funding Council for England (HEFCE) national study of employability in higher education also revealed significant differences between managerial assessments of the skills requirements for graduate jobs and graduates' own assessments of the skills they were able to use and the extent to which their university education had helped them to develop those skills (HEFCE, 2003, p. 78). The relationship of higher education to the labour market is bound to become more important because student numbers are rapidly expanding. There are currently 1.5 million students in UK higher education, with around 400 000 graduates entering the labour market each year, but there are only around 62 000 'graduate jobs' on offer in major household-name organizations. Brown and Hesketh (2004, p. 63) claim that there is 'no prospect of the graduate labour market expanding in line with the increased supply of graduates'. Up to 40 per cent of graduates are now in 'non-graduate' work, and that figure is likely to increase with further moves towards the 50 per cent target for participation in higher education (Brown and Hesketh, 2004, p. 216).

At the same time, the demand for performing arts courses at all levels is booming. For example, since 1996/97 student numbers in music have risen by 37.9 per cent, and in drama and dance by 45.3 per cent. Performing arts higher education is becoming increasingly concerned to look more closely at where students go after graduation, and at whether there is a fundamental 'dishonesty' about training so many potential performers when there are only a small number of employment opportunities available to them in performance and competition for the available opportunities is becoming more intense. Compared with 1991, there are 55 per cent more musicians and 40 per cent more actors now working in Britain (Leadbeater, 2004, p. 7).

There is often a stark contrast between graduate career paths in the arts sector and those in other industries. In the UK 13 per cent of the total labour force are self-employed. In the creative sector 34 per cent of individuals work on a self-employed basis, while in the music industry 68 per cent of workers are self-employed (Burns, 2000, p. 116). Freelancing and self-employment are, in fact, the most frequent types of employment in the creative sector, and there are particularly large concentrations of small enterprises and sole traders in music and the performing arts, film, TV and radio. Estimates have suggested that less than 50 per cent of employment in the arts sector involves a primary occupation – people doing one type of work (Summerton, 2001, pp. 8–9). Actors, dancers and musicians often typically work for several employers on temporary, short-term engagements on a non-exclusive basis (Menger, 2001; Towse, 2001, p. 85–102). They can have a variety of roles and forms of work, on a spectrum from paid to unpaid, permanent to part-time; seasonal jobs, freelance employment and self-employment. They frequently have other sources of income alongside, often supporting, their creative work, for example teaching work, which is particularly common among musicians and dancers.

This chapter considers the ways in which higher education institutions in the UK are working to raise the profile of entrepreneurship among arts students and graduates. It begins with a discussion of the importance and relevance of enterprise skills in preparing students for working in the creative sector. It then goes on to highlight the lack of enterprise teaching material appropriate to the needs of students aiming to find employment in this sector, and the work undertaken by the PACE Project to address this need. While the teaching of creative enterprise is still an emergent field of knowledge, with relatively little in the way of pedagogical research, the range of activities and approaches featured in this chapter demonstrates that there is now a growing body of effective practice starting to be developed in response to recent national and regional debates and initiatives.

PERFORMING ARTS ENTREPRENEURSHIP

If arts students are going into careers as professional performers, they will have to work on a freelance basis at some stage. For example, over 60 per cent of dance in England is delivered by freelance artists (Heeley and Pickard, 2002, p. 34). Freelance artists need to consider what their market is, how to value their time, how to be commercial in the arts sector and how to work collaboratively. So, unlike most arts subjects taught in higher education, where enterprise skills are often seen as a very marginal issue with little, if any, relevance to day-to-day teaching, the performing arts are powerfully placed to provide a context in which entrepreneurship thrives and which can provide exemplars of approaches and practice to other disciplines.

As performing arts students tend to define themselves as 'musicians' or 'dancers', rather than as 'students', it is easy to make the assumption that they are not thinking about profit and markets, but about realising their dreams. Yet the arts are a business, not just art forms, and students need to be commercially aware. Joining a band, for example, means legally being involved in a partnership, and students need to know the implications of that, as well as being able to work together musically. If students are serious about self-employment in the music industry, then they also need to understand the different income streams for publishing rights, recording and performing rights.

There seems to be considerable potential for self-employment among arts graduates. According to the recent review of graduate entrepreneurship conducted by the new National Council for Graduate Entrepreneurship (NCGE), 'more arts/cultural businesses than science-based businesses are started by graduates' and 'we don't really know if this is a sectoral or financial issue' (Hannon, 2004, p. 49). Of those graduates who left higher education in 2003 and were self-employed six months after leaving university, over a third (36.8 per cent) had studied creative arts or design subjects (Graduate Prospects, 2005, p. 4).

How do these statistics on graduate self-employment relate to the attitudes and ambitions of current students? The evidence seems to indicate that, in contrast with graduates from other academic disciplines, many performing arts graduates do not initially plan to start their own business after leaving university. Rather, they set up dance and theatre companies and bands because this is the only way they are able to work, a form of 'accidental entrepreneurship' (Wedgwood, 2005). Many performers, especially in music, become sole traders by default, operating on a series of short-term contracts with a range of different clients. Performers in this situation often lack the business training and commercial skills they require. The House of Commons Select Committee report on dance development found, for example, that 'many of the people employed or volunteering' in the dance sector 'do not necessarily have the administrative or other skills required to carry out much of the work involved in applying for funding or attracting sponsorship' (House of Commons, Culture, Media and Sport Committee, 2004, p. 28).

Practicing artists need to be innovative stylistically and also in organizing, producing and distributing their work. The 'artist's earnings, like those of any self-employed worker, depend' not only on 'skill, talent and effort', but also on performing 'the managerial and entrepreneurial functions' (Menger, 2001, p. 13). While there is always an oversupply of students, many of whom will never find employment as practitioners in their chosen art form, there is also a strong demand for creative people outside the arts sector who possess these transferable self-management, commercial awareness and business skills.

A main difficulty arts students have faced is that most of the generic enterprise teaching material is aimed at business students, much of which is not directly relevant to the work they want to do. These students often have little, if any, prior knowledge and understanding of business management. There is a clear need 'to develop programmes tailored to the specific needs of target markets, rather than providing generic courses' (Hannon, 2004, p. 41).

The pioneering Department for Education and Skills-funded Entrepreneurial Skills for Graduates initiative (2004–05) aimed to develop approaches to enterprise teaching that were compatible with a wide range of subject disciplines at undergraduate level. Under this scheme, Higher Education Academy Subject Centres adapted an established model for understanding the process of starting a small business focused on the personal entrepreneurial capacities of individuals (Gibb and Ritchie, 1982). As part of this programme PALATINE, the national Subject Centre for Dance, Drama and Music, ran the PACE (Performing Arts Creative Enterprise) Project, which investigated ways of further developing and enhancing the teaching of entrepreneurial skills in the performing arts.

PALATINE recently issued an invitation to all UK higher education performing arts departments to bid for small PACE Innovation Project grants (c. £1500–£2000) to fund new initiatives focused on effectively promoting or enhancing entrepreneurship within learning and teaching, in ways that would potentially be of significant future value to the wider higher education performing arts community. Six new learning and teaching projects were selected for funding. The focus of these PACE Innovation Projects was to produce new courses and teaching materials specifically for a performing arts context that staff and students can draw on in order to share and promote good practice.

CULTURAL ENTREPRENEURSHIP: CAN IT BE TAUGHT AND, IF SO, WHAT DOES EFFECTIVE PRACTICE LOOK LIKE?

New artistic enterprises may not always expose arts graduates to the same degree of personal financial risk as new small businesses in other commercial sectors where people often have to put their own money into starting a company. This is because national funding bodies or sponsors often take the financial risk in supporting new artistic ventures. Nonetheless, the personal emotional exposure confronting a creative entrepreneur could be as significant, or even greater, because of their emotional attachment to their own new creative idea. The nearest approximation to this degree of emotional exposure in an educational context is the linking of student academic work to 'real-life' project performance (Pittaway, 2004, pp. 12–17). Here, higher education has a vital role as it offers students a safe environment for creative experiment and innovation.

The element of personal risk in starting a creative business can also be offset by the artist's own critical 'sense of remaining cutting edge, culturally relevant' and 'creatively self-reflexive' (Banks et al., 2000, p. 458). Reflective practice can be developed through teaching based on situated learning and mentoring, work-based learning and context-specific training in practitioner-based environments. Another important element in teaching initiatives that reflect the way entrepreneurs learn is the active involvement of students in communities of practice, working with professional artists and companies, and of performing arts institutions and departments building communities of learning with relevant stakeholders (Gibb, 2002, p. 253; Raffo et al., 2000a, p. 363).A particular emphasis is placed upon the value of personal contact between students and mentors. This enables students to experiment with new ideas, 'learn by doing', and reflect on what they are doing, learning experientially in a supportive relationship. This process of interaction with professional practitioners in 'real-life' situations stimulates creative ideas and also helps students to develop an awareness of how and why their ideas may, or may not, work (Raffo et al., 2000a, p. 361).

A PACE Innovation Project based at the University of Sunderland, School of Arts, Design, Media and Culture – the Dance Apprentice Mentor Learning and Teaching Model – was a mentoring scheme that addressed the need for the ongoing education and training of dance artists, students and graduates. Mentors and apprentices worked together in the community and in challenging environments (such as working with pupils who have been excluded from mainstream school at Key Stage 3/4). The project developed ways to better enable level three dance students to understand how to apply their subject knowledge and skills within an artistic community and thus be more readily prepared for employment on graduation.

Students worked with dance tutors in-house as 'apprentices' in order to develop a range of material, skills and strategies that they later applied, mentored by their tutor. From 2007, the mentor scheme was developed further through links with the university's Hatchery enterprise incubation unit, focusing on dancers working as freelance practitioners and starting new companies. The project team are also looking to build on the project in a planned youth and community dance conference featuring the work of the mentor scheme in a broader context of community arts and social enterprise.

Trinity College of Music also developed a PACE-funded mentor scheme – Preparation for the Profession – for postgraduate students, working with musicians from a wide range of professional orchestras and ensembles. This new scheme – the first of its type within the music conservatoire sector – facilitated a vibrant interface between senior students and the music profession. The mentor scheme was developed into a new postgraduate course, beginning in September 2005. The work of the project may also be further developed in the longer term through more collaboration with dance companies, following the merger of Trinity College of Music and the Laban Conservatoire for contemporary dance.

Both the mentoring projects at Trinity and Sunderland exposed students to the challenges of performing and working in a range of contexts, requiring a variety of applications of entrepreneurial knowledge, acquired through 'learning by doing'. They used professional mentors to inspire, motivate and educate students in the demands of an entrepreneurial career. Mentor schemes can also set students particular challenges of 'real-life' uncertainty and ambiguity, and challenge their thinking, requiring them to apply their existing knowledge to new problems (Pittaway, 2004, p. 5). This process helps to develop the confidence and raise the aspirations of students by enabling them to understand how to apply their subject knowledge and skills in an artistic community, in a variety of professional contexts.

The Ideas Generation PACE Innovation Project, based at Leeds University, aimed to develop a greater understanding of the process of creativity, encouraging academic staff and students to explore creativity, innovation and risk. The project developed workshops that were delivered by experienced performers and companies who understand the processes and can impart their knowledge to students in an innovative way. The main aim of the workshops was to convey a greater understanding of the process of creativity and encourage participants to explore different ways of achieving innovation. In addition, the involvement of professional performers, arts companies and regional agencies enabled potential entrepreneurs to understand how the processes involved can be applied in the real world of performance. Participants from the workshops were also followed up individually or as a group by a business adviser to discuss their individual ideas confidentially.

Arts Graduates in Yorkshire: Flexible Entrepreneurs, based at York St John College, School of Arts, Literature and Theatre, was a PACE Innovation Project based on the experiences of alumni who have already become successful, professional, entrepreneurs. This project aimed to investigate and identify the aspects of current undergraduate programmes that inspire and enable performing arts and film and TV production graduates to build medium-risk creative professional careers, comprising a flexible and varying mix of entrepreneurial activities and conventional employment.

The following were some of the key issues that were investigated:

- When and why do students begin to move away from thinking in terms of a definite job and start to consider making their own work?
- How does this process relate to entrepreneurial teaching in the current curriculum?
- How do students' attitudes develop and change from first to third year?
- How does their interaction with industry change their aspirations?
- How is that change then met by the teaching provided?
- How can tutors develop the students' imaginative capacity about what they could do?
- How well are courses developing abilities to interact with employers, negotiate, develop client relationships and create sustainable work?
- How can students demonstrate they have done more than just get a degree, that is, generate portfolios, reflect on the making process in terms of what they are making and why?

A particular interest was in 'flexible entrepreneurs'; graduates who mix and match a variety of often part-time entrepreneurial arts activities with some conventional employment, a flexible 'portfolio' employment model. Graduates in the creative sector often adopt such 'portfolio' working patterns, managing multiple jobs or creative projects, often simultaneously (Ball, 2003, p. 15). It is frequently argued that the 'hands-on', problem-based learning, approaches of creative arts courses readily produce multi-skilled, flexible and adaptable entrepreneurs. Yet the processes and skills involved are rarely defined and articulated (Ball, 2003, p. 33). The York research investigated the variable and changing individual patterns of flexible entrepreneurship including responses to setbacks, creative solutions and decision-making.

The project team has also developed contacts with two entrepreneurs who have been working directly with staff and students: Mark Herman (a writer and director) and Alistair Griffin (the singer-songwriter and ex-York St John graduate). This has helped students to become more confident and proactive about what they do and also to look at ways in which the industry is changing and how to prepare for that. It is expected that the work of this project will now be taken forward in curriculum development of School of Arts programmes at York St John College, influencing foundation degrees in Creative Industries and Technologies. The project will also feed into the work of the new Centre for Excellence in Teaching and Learning in Collaboration for Creativity (C4C) in the Arts.

The PACE Innovation Project based at the University of Winchester produced a set of freely available and high-quality online pedagogical resources designed to help tutors teach enterprise to performing arts students. These resources were developed from a successful Higher Education Innovation Funded (HEIF) Enterprise in the Arts course currently being taught to students of dance and performing arts. Teaching materials from the HEIF project have now been introduced at undergraduate and Masters level, focusing on topics such as arts management, obtaining funding, sponsorship and marketing. Students work with local arts organizations, looking at how they work as businesses and how they operate in terms of management and communication. This then feeds into final-year projects in areas like community theatre, where students have to be entrepreneurial themselves in organizing productions, tours and drama workshops with local schools. The teaching website produced by the PACE-funded project will be an expanding resource that colleagues from different institutions could contribute to in order to share successful practice.

WHO SHOULD BE RESPONSIBLE FOR ENTERPRISE EDUCATION IN THE ARTS?

To what extent do university vice-chancellors and pro-vice-chancellors approach the teaching of enterprise in the arts as part of the drive to create more enterprising universities that are academic-led and in partnership with industry? There is still a widespread perception that little is being done to bring together the two cultures of art and science, and that the UK economy is lagging behind other parts of the world in these areas. More could also be done by universities to develop and promote a culture of entrepreneurship within arts higher education, linking arts projects with university business schools and incubation units to share expertise in developing experiential learning experiences and enterprise skills as part of the arts curriculum.

Traditionally, higher education institutions have not fully integrated arts practice with the arts working environment. Several of the newly established Centres of Excellence in Teaching and Learning will be focusing on the connections between culture and business and industry, including ways to support business development across the creative industries (HEFCE,

2005). The Department for Culture, Media and Sport (DCMS) has also been promoting closer links between higher education and the creative industry sector and has been working to develop a national policy framework for graduate entrepreneurship in the creative industries (Wedgwood, 2005). The creative industries are now seen as a sustainable sector for labour market growth, as a vital element in the new 'knowledge economy' and as important in urban regeneration and the re-imaging of cities and regions.

The UK creative industry sector grew by an average of 8 per cent between 1997 and 2001, compared to an average of 2.6 per cent for the whole economy during the same period (Department of Culture, Media and Sport, 2003, p. 2). Despite this strong rate of growth and the high political profile of the creative industries (Department of Culture, Media and Sport, 2001; Leadbeater and Oakley, 1999, pp. 31–40), investors can still tend to view new creative businesses as too non-conformist to risk putting money into. The degree of readiness of existing businesses in the creative sector to work with specialist higher education institutions has been another area of difficulty. Most publicly-funded arts organizations have lacked funds for development work, and grants from bodies like the Arts Councils rarely encourage links with higher education institutions as ways of pursuing common goals. Commercial organizations are generally unaware of the opportunities available and tend to view higher education institutions as lacking the expertise to work with them. Furthermore, it is often difficult for higher education institutions to invest time and money in order to raise the profile of what they could offer.

Nonetheless, the mapping exercises undertaken in different parts of the UK have demonstrated that creative businesses do tend to 'cluster' around centres of academic and creative excellence (Department of Culture, Media and Sport, 2001; Culture Northwest, 2004). Higher education has a vital role to play in maintaining the creativity base within the creative industries; the stimulation of new talent that continuously challenges existing notions, ideas and practices, fostering imagination and creativity, and the skills and knowledge to produce and innovate. The role of higher education in developing creative talent is being increasingly recognized as important at the regional planning level. It is reflected in initiatives to retain and develop creative graduate talent, enriching both local businesses and communities (Leadbeater and Oakley, 1999, p. 17).

The DCMS has established the Creative Industries Higher Education Forum (CIHEF) to increase the transfer of knowledge from universities to the commercial and public sector. Higher education institutions and individual performing arts departments have also been seeking to develop closer direct links with industry (Wedgwood, 2002; Greenlees, 2005). The new foundation degrees (two-year employment-related vocational courses) are also specifically intended 'to develop programmes that give students insights into the prospects of self-employment and develop entrepreneurial qualities' (HEFCE, 2000).

There are several ways in which arts students can be given insights into the world of self-employment. For example, a PACE Innovation Project based at the Nuffield Theatre, Lancaster University – Nuff Said: A Weekend of New Work by Up and Coming Artists – organized a three-day festival (4–6 February 2005) that focused on key areas crucial to the survival of new artists and companies and the role that higher education institutions might play in supporting emergent practice. The work of emerging artists was shown in the context of a number of debates, discussions, seminars and presentations. These focused on both the creative and administrative demands that setting up as an artist or a company involves. Other sessions discussed the various ways in which the established professional sphere can facilitate new artists. There were specific sessions run by training bodies (including the Arts Council and Independent Theatre Council) addressing best practice around how to set up a performing arts company.

A central concern was an investigation of the different demands that group- and solo-based work creates and the support structures that are currently available for these two different areas of practice. The festival also provided an opportunity for new artists to respond to each other's work, as well as 'talk back' to the professionals – focusing on the specific problems they have encountered in the arts industry so far and the ways in which the industry and their own educational institutions can respond to their various needs. In this way the event was intended to be a two-way teaching and learning process – in which the artists gain knowledge from the professionals, and vice versa.

CREATIVE ENTERPRISE IN HIGHER EDUCATION

Business and academia are often perceived to have a relationship of opposites. There is no risk culture in higher education, while a risk culture is inherent in many companies. Arts practice is, however, an area where risk is much more of a factor than in other academic disciplines. The arts are a risky business – you don't know what's going to sell. Unlike other businesses, where demand for a product usually predates manufacture, cultural entrepreneurs need to create a market which does not already exist. Creative businesses also have a higher rate of innovation and development than other sectors because new technology and new business models of creation, distribution and consumption are constantly transforming the way in which the creative industries operate.

While the creative industries are a natural cluster for innovation in products and services, enterprise and innovation funding in higher education is still predominantly focused on science, engineering and high-growth technology-based businesses. As there are only a handful of large companies in the creative sector, compared with sectors like manufacturing and retail, knowledge transfer potential in the arts seems to be more limited – universities are unable to sell their services because most arts companies are too small to afford to become involved.

There is also a perception that there is a problem of institutional focus – rewards are regarded as driven by the Research Assessment Exercise (RAE) and so knowledge transfer and cultural engagement are not regarded as a priority. Arts practitioners could, perhaps, do more to set a research agenda for universities to take up. In addition, there is still a considerable lack of knowledge about commercial investment and activity in the arts sector and the distinct role that higher education institutions could adopt in developing the commercial potential of new creative talent.

To explore the role that higher education institutions can adopt in developing environments and alliances that stimulate artistic and creative enterprise, the PACE project supported the Creative Enterprise in Higher Education Conference, which took place on 16 November 2005 at Lancaster University. This was the first national conference in the area of cultural entrepreneurship in higher education. The conference was attended by 140 delegates from right across the performing and visual arts higher education sector.

The conference addressed the policy context for arts enterprise, with a discussion of new national policy and development initiatives promoted by the Department for Culture, Media and Sport, as well as the relationships between higher education institutions and the creative industries at regional level. It also featured a range of approaches to promoting graduate enterprise, including the work of specialist creative enterprise centres within universities, student enterprise clubs and the work of students consulting with small arts companies, professional mentor schemes, teaching resources and new pedagogical research in this field. Initial feedback from the conference suggests that delegates felt that there is now a clearer idea of what arts enterprise is, of what works in this area and potential ways to develop more informed entrepreneurial learning provision in the creative arts.

If performing arts departments are to equip their students with a range of entrepreneurial skills, ways of thinking and behaving, that can enable them to be better prepared for making the transition from student to professional performer, what are the implications for the content of degree courses and the processes of learning? Recent research in the field of teaching and learning entrepreneurship in subjects related to working in the cultural sector suggests that entrepreneurs do not usefully learn from formalized training and support that is generic and de-contextualized, or where trainers lack an understanding or sympathy for specialized creative communities of practice and how they work (Raffo et al., 2000a, p. 362).

Entrepreneurial learning, defined as 'learning that occurs during the venture creation process' (Pittaway, 2004, p. 3), in the context of students learning how businesses actually operate in the creative sector, is most effective when it includes project-based activity where students are:

- able to experiment with ideas, by 'doing' and reflecting on what they are doing;
- collaborating and networking with others (acquiring information and ideas through contacts, adopting and developing ideas from within a community of practice);
- working with more experienced mentors in their sector (Raffo et al., 2000a, p. 356; Penaluna and Penaluna, 2005);
- involved in context-specific training, where practitioners and situated learners learn through the qualitative and reciprocal exchange of ideas in informal settings (Raffo et al., 2000b, p. 228);
- learning from experiences where students take risks and could fail.

The notion of entrepreneurship, particularly as it pertains to innovation, risk and creativity, is often discussed in the arts. These terms are also widely discussed in management schools; indeed, 'creativity' and 'enterprise' are often used loosely and interchangeably in the literature on learning and teaching in both sectors. Similarly, there can be an emphasis on the Romantic models of the isolated 'creative' artist and 'entrepreneur', an emphasis on the inspired individual and the innovative output or product. However, it can also be argued that the innovations of creative individuals in both the arts and industry are better understood in a process model that emphasizes the role of social context (Banks et al., 2002, p. 256). In accordance with this process model of creativity, the following possible teaching strategies were highlighted at the Lancaster University conference that might foster creative and innovative abilities:

- experiential learning;
- projects that involve the production of independent works or artifacts in unpredictable or complex situations;

- safe spaces for creative experiment and innovation;
- networks to connect innovative ideas to contexts.

CONCLUSION

Graduates seeking work in the creative sector face new challenges and opportunities. National and regional development and funding policies are increasingly being directed towards moving artists and performers away from the traditional grant or subsidy culture, and more towards creative and financial independence through entrepreneurial self-reliance. Yet entrepreneurship has not, in the past, been widely encouraged among arts and creative graduates. This chapter has focused on the ways in which higher education institutions in the UK are working to raise the profile of entrepreneurship among arts students and graduates. It has discussed possible ways of enabling students to have the potential to become creative entrepreneurs, rather than just looking for a job, and the ways in which learning and teaching can contribute to this process.

The PACE project and the Creative Enterprise in Higher Education Conference promoted models of entrepreneurial learning in the arts that were based on students learning about their subject in 'real life' projects and contexts, while interacting with those professional contexts with emotional intelligence and through personal reflection. Entrepreneurial learning in the arts was also linked with students' individual feelings through a process model of creativity and innovation.

The six PACE Innovation Projects explored ways of teaching aspiring professional artists the skills of creative enterprise. Students were encouraged to take personal and artistic risks, to evolve, and reflect on their experiences through processes of experiential learning. Performances and projects were designed to mirror 'real-life' business experiences, allowing risk-taking and failure. These projects have had a significant impact on teaching at the institutional level and have been valued by staff, senior management and students. Some students who participated in the projects at Trinity and Sunderland have obtained employment as a direct result of their work on these projects. Furthermore, teaching staff involved in the projects have regarded them as addressing national policy agendas on graduate employment and enterprise, not in terms of 'key skills', but more from a student-centred, reflective perspective, highlighting the ways in which students were engaged on a personal level. The mentor schemes at Trinity and Sunderland, for example, demonstrate the differences between mentoring in the arts and other industries – they are not placements, with students doing other people's jobs for them. They bring students into supportive relationships where they work with professional artists. Mentors provide 'not only subject knowledge, understanding and skills, but also offer guidance on the different approaches and adaptations needed to operate effectively within the different contexts/groups/cultures encountered' (Younger, 2005, p. 1).

This way of working helps foster the skills and abilities needed to generate and market artistic products. As a result, students are better equipped and have more confidence to take the initiative in creating work for themselves and in managing their own artistic product.

NOTE

1. The author would like to thank the National Council for Graduate Entrepreneurship (NCGE) for funding the policy paper from which this chapter has been developed, and Luke Pittaway, Director of the Enterprise and Regional Development Unit, Sheffield University Management School, for his comments on an earlier version of the chapter.

REFERENCES

Ball, L. (2003), *Future Directions for Employability Research in the Creative Industries*, ADC-LTSN, http://www.bton.ac.uk/adc-ltsn/html/issues/Reports/FuturDirectforEm.pdf.

Banks, M., Calvey, D., Owen, J. and Russell, D. (2002), Where the art is: defining and managing creativity in new media SMEs, *Creativity and Innovation Management*, **11** (4), 255–264.

Banks, M., Lovatt, A., O'Connor, J. and Raffo, C. (2000), Risk and Trust in the Cultural Industries, *Geforum*, 31, 453–464.

Brown, P. and Hesketh, A. (2004), *The Mismanagement of Talent: Employability and Jobs in the Knowledge Economy*, Oxford: Oxford University Press.

Burns, S. (2000), Training artists within a higher education context: a case study, *Journal of Arts Management, Law and Society*, **30** (2), 113–123.

Culture Northwest (2004), *A snapshot of the creative industries in England's North West*, available from http://www.englandsnorthwest-culture.com/cultural/news_updates.asp.

Department of Culture, Media and Sport – DCMS (2003), 'Culture and Creativity: The Next Ten Years', *Creative Industries Economic Estimates Statistical Bulletin*.

Gibb, A. (2002), In pursuit of a new 'enterprise' and entrepreneurship' paradigm for learning: creative destruction, new values, new ways of doing things and new combinations of knowledge, *International Journal of Management Reviews*, **4** (3), 233–269.

Gibb, A. and Ritchie, J. (1982), Understanding the process of starting small businesses, *European Small Business Journal*, **1** (1), 26–45.

Graduate Prospects (2005), *Graduates in self-employment*, NCGE, http://www.ncge.org.uk/policy.php?Entry=papers.

Greenlees, R. (2005), *London Centre for Arts and Cultural Enterprise: a collaborative approach to enterprise*. Presentation at the Creative Enterprise in Higher Education Conference, Lancaster University, 16 November, http://www.palatine.ac.uk/events/viewreport/397/.

Hannon, P.D. (2004), Making the journey from student to entrepreneur: a review of the existing research into graduate entrepreneurship, NCGE, http://www.ncge.org.uk/DisplayPage.asp?pageid=7983.

Heeley, J. and Pickard, C. (2002), *Employing Creativity: Skills Development in the Creative Industries in the North West of England*, North West Regional Development Agency.

Higher Education Funding Council for England – HEFCE (2000), *Foundation Degree Prospectus*, Bristol: HEFCE.

Higher Education Funding Council for England – HEFCE (2003), How much does higher education enhance the employability of Graduates? Bristol: HEFCE, available from http://www.hefce.ac.uk/Pubs/rdreports/Downloads/report34.htm.

Higher Education Funding Council for England – HEFCE (2005), *Centres for Excellence in Teaching and Learning*, Bristol: HEFCE.

House of Commons, Culture, Media and Sport Committee (2004), *Arts Development: Dance*, available from http://www.publications.parliament.uk/pa/cm200304/cmselect/cmcumeds/587/587.pdf.

Lambert, R. (2003), *Lambert Review of Business–University Collaboration*, London: HM Treasury, available from http://www.hm-treasury.gov.uk./media/DDE/65/lambert_review_final_450.pdf.

Leadbeater, C. (2004), Britain's creativity challenge. Leeds: Creative & Cultural Skills, http://www.ccskills.org.uk/pdf/britains-creativity-challenge.pdf

Leadbeater, C. and Oakley, K. (1999), The independents: Britain's new cultural entrepreneurs, Demos, http://www.demos.co.uk.

Menger, P.-M. (2001), 'Statistics in the Wake of Challenges Posed by Cultural Diversity in a Globalization Context – Are there too many artists?', *International Symposium on Cultural Statistics*, http://www.colloque2002symposium.gouv.qc.ca/PDF/Menger_paper_Symposium.pdf.

Penaluna, A. and Penaluna, K. (2005), Entrepreneurship for artists and designers in higher education. Unpublished paper presented at the IntEnt Conference, University of Surrey, 10–13 July.

Pittaway, L. (2004), Simulating Entrepreneurial Learning: Assessing the Utility of Experiential Learning Designs. Lancaster University Management School Working Paper, 2004/049.

Raffo, C., O'Connor, J., Lovatt, A. and Banks, M. (2000b), Attitudes to formal business training and learning amongst entrepreneurs in the cultural industries: situated business learning through 'doing with others', *Journal of Education and Work*, **13** (2), 215–230.

Raffo, C., Lovatt, A., Banks, M. and O'Connor, J. (2000a), Teaching and Learning Entrepreneurship for micro and small businesses in the cultural industries sector, *Education and Training*, **42** (6), 356–366.

Summerton, J. (2001), Framing Pictures: creative thinking about creative workers, *Arts Professional*, 11, October, 8–9.

Towse, R. (2001), Cultural economics, copyright and the cultural industries, trends and strategies in the arts and cultural industries, http://www.lib.uni-corvinus.hu/gt/2000-4/towse.pdf.

Wedgwood, M. (2002), Higher education and the creative industry sector of the Northwest. Manchester Metropolitan University, http://www.mmu.ac.uk/externalrelations/papers/creative_industry.pdf.

Wedgwood, M. (2005), *Developing Entrepreneurial Students and Graduates.* Presentation at the Creative Enterprise in Higher Education Conference, Lancaster University, 16 November 2005, http://www.palatine.ac.uk/events/viewreport/397/.

Younger, L. (2005), *Initial tutor reflections: dance apprentice mentor learning and teaching model.* Unpublished draft report for PALATINE.

9. Encouraging creative enterprise in Russia

Linda Moss[1]

INTRODUCTION

Since the collapse of the Soviet system, a demand-led, market economy has been developing in Russia in a very sporadic way. In some sectors the impact has been both profound and immediate (for example, the expansion of the extractive raw materials industry, which accounts for 80 per cent of Russia's export income; the proliferation of multinational retail stores and the growth of private car ownership), but in other areas, change has been slow, difficult and spasmodic. One area in particular which has witnessed slow and spasmodic change is the cultural sector, a sector which is still largely in the hands of large, traditional, long-established arts organizations supported by state funding, and controlled by an administration that has remained intact from the communist period, despite political change. Market forces have had an impact in the field of popular mass culture (for example, publishing, cinema, broadcasting and other media), but the non-profit sector, which constitutes a major part of the cultural economy in many Western countries, remains underdeveloped in Russia. For instance, non-profit museums form 49 per cent of all museums in Austria, and 41 per cent of all museums in Holland; arts employment in Spain is 24 per cent in the non-profit sector. In Eastern Europe, arts employment percentages vary from 3 percent to 5 per cent in non-profit organizations while over 80 per cent of cultural employment is still in the public sector.[2] Despite the support of international finance and expertise to help develop small, mission-driven creative enterprises, and the efforts of Russian creative entrepreneurs impatient with legislation inimical to their formation, cultural provision has become polarized between state and market. In 1996, records indicated that 90 per cent of non-state cultural enterprises were for profit. These constituted 40 per cent of all cultural organizations by number, but these figures mask enormous variations in size (for example the Bolshoi Ballet and a sole trader each count as one organization).[3]

This chapter attempts to explore some of the reasons why this should still be the case after 15 years of transitional economy. The focus is on attitudes, social and historical factors, and on the restrictive legislation and weak infrastructure that frustrate current developments: a discursive, socio-cultural approach that may disappoint economists seeking facts and figures. However, as yet it is difficult to attempt any serious analysis of creative enterprise in Russia because the terrain is yet to be mapped. It has been noted (Toepler, 2000) that the absence of empirical data from Eastern Europe may itself serve to limit the importance placed by analysts on creative enterprise. Organizations start up and then disappear; some are sole traders who do not even realise that they constitute a creative enterprise, so are never recorded as such; poor communications across Russia mean that networks, so crucial to the cultural sector, are fragile and ephemeral, and official statistics are often considered to be unreliable.

The scant literature in this field creates further problems. Many explorations of enterprise development in transitional economies have located the key issues in the fields of economics and management theory, and have discussed them from the standpoints of those disciplines (Feige and Ott, 1999). Questions of definition of 'enterprise' have been related to Schumpeterian or Kirznerian theories, thus focusing on the distinction between the creative disruption of economic equilibrium, and the recognition of opportunity for profit (Schumpeter, 1947; Kirzner, 1973). Dana (2001) argues that barriers to enterprise (so defined) in transitional economies arise from educational systems that do not stress entrepreneurial skills, as well as from low expectations of entrepreneurship among some sectors of the population. All these approaches assume that profitability is the driving force of the shift from the centrally planned economy. The few articles specific to the field of creative industries development in Eastern Europe (Toepler, 2000; Jakobson et al., 2000) note the failure to acknowledge the non-profit cultural sector in more general works on transitional economies.

The significance of the non-profit sector in culture differs sharply between Western and Eastern Europe generally. The concept of creative enterprise is a relatively recent categorization in Western Europe, coming to prominence in the 1980s, particularly in the UK (Myerscough, 1988). It encompasses products that arise as a result of individual creativity, where the prime value is symbolic (for example fashion, advertising, film, media, digital imagery and all the arts). While many of these represent some of the most profitable areas of the UK economy (and have been much promoted as such by its government; DCMS, 2001), others are more likely to be social enterprises: small businesses that are mission-driven, that plough any profit back into the enterprise, but are keen to make sufficient money to pay realistic salaries to employees. They may seek, and receive, some public grant aid; they may be constituted for legal clarity to operate a trading arm alongside overtly non-profit activity. Examples include film-makers who work in areas of urban deprivation; training schemes in new media for unemployed young people; craft workshops in redundant barns in areas decimated by foot and mouth disease. The aims are not primarily economic, except insofar as it can be argued that the economy is culturally, rather than socially, determined (DCMS, 2004). The new emphasis placed on culture as a means of combating social exclusion by several Western European governments (Dubois and Laborier, 2003; Looseley, 2003) lifts this type of activity into the sphere of economic and social development, but not as conventionally understood by economists. However this constitutes a major part of the cultural sector in Western Europe in terms of employment and users.

THE NEED FOR CREATIVE ENTERPRISE DEVELOPMENT IN RUSSIA

In Russia creative enterprise is generally more than just a question of economic diversification. It is also a crucial part of the attempt to embrace a whole new political basis for a country moving from centrist to demand-led social and economic principles. Furthermore, creative enterprise is also a means of safeguarding cultural development in this new, more competitive environment. This sector is also of importance in terms of the diversification of ways of working. To date the diversity discourse in Eastern Europe has been largely concerned with the issue of minorities in relation to the politics of equity. This is not surprising: despite the commitment to equality of opportunity at the heart of communist ideology, progress in this area during the communist period was, in practice, behind that of the West, and now democratically acceptable approaches to representation and access are the priority. But alongside these trends, the development of market mechanisms and private enterprise, and the mix of profitability with social concern – a process that may seem to have little connection with diversity politics – create a different kind of diversity: that of a mixture of types and levels of cultural production and consumption. In societies moving away from paternalistic state-funded provision, with only full-time public posts in culture, social creative enterprises have vast potential to offer a new variety of employment and enterprise opportunities, different ways of making, exhibiting, marketing and consuming culture, more obviously open to minorities, women and unconventional ways of working than was ever the case under Soviet bureaucracy. This is itself is part of the process of enabling diversity.

Another urgent incentive for the development of creative enterprise is the withdrawal of state support for culture. In Russia the state budget for culture fell by 40 per cent from 1991 to 1997 in an erratic fashion, including cuts of 100 per cent to libraries (Jakobson et al., 2000). Attempts to stabilize it by setting a minimum of 2 per cent of federal expenditure failed even at the budget-setting stage. In 1999 it stood at 0.58 per cent (Vladimirov, 2000), although it has grown since 2001. Obviously, the previously heavily subsidized state companies could not sustain this kind of cut or its unpredictability. Ultimately, reliance on a wider basket of funding sources will provide stability at some level, but this basket will have to be created through the development of a wider range of creative activity.

A third reason to encourage creative enterprise is to re-establish one of the prime roles for culture within, rather than outside of, the official economy. It is through culture than we reflect upon, make sense of, and critique our human experience, which is why culture can be such a powerful tool for state propaganda and for revolution. In the Soviet era, culture fulfilled both these purposes in Russia. The critical, dissident culture that helped to overthrow communism was part of the underground economy, but now it needs to be encompassed within a democracy where it can provide legitimate comment on society. It is the non-profit, mission-driven enterprise that can best provide this forum, since it is neither determined by the state nor at the mercy of market forces.

It is into this situation that several Western creative development organizations have ventured, often with EU support, to offer their expertise in the building of a diverse creative economy. But the problems for such development are enormous because the infrastructure of appropriate legislation, education and awareness of what a creative economy might mean are lacking. An assumption that Western methods can simply be transplanted into Eastern Europe can be compounded by a failure to appreciate the scale of historical difference, and by an ignorance of those features of the Soviet-style economies that could actually enable creative enterprise development in ways that would be inappropriate in the West.

THE ROLE OF HISTORIC AND SOCIAL FACTORS IN CREATIVE ENTERPRISE DEVELOPMENT

The basic distinctions between the principles of cultural provision in the communist era in Russia and those of the West are widely understood. In summary, these consisted of almost universal, heavily subsidized state provision, in contrast to a more mixed system of commercial, mission-driven and state-supported culture; and a huge emphasis on the educative, moral, propagandist roles of culture as opposed to its aesthetic, economic and exploratory aspects. For example, artists in Russia tended to divide into those supportive of, and supported by, the state, in contrast with those critical of the state and operating clandestinely and subversively. In contrast, in the West artists are more likely to support themselves by a mixture of means, including teaching, selling, running workshops and non-arts activity, none of which would be overtly political in intent. Their work is usually less directly linked with the politics of culture. It should be no surprise that some of the main protagonists of the Velvet Revolutions of the late 1980s were artists (such as Vaclav Havel in Czechoslovakia); culture was crucially important politically, whether in support of the state or in opposition.

What is less well appreciated is the enormous impact of these differences upon both our understanding of the nature of culture and its management. The move away from paternalistic cultural provision, together with secret cultural subversion, involves a major paradigm shift that questions the very purpose of culture, and the role of the artist, as well as every aspect of its organization. At the most fundamental level, culture ceases to be either the cement that secures the ideology of the state, or the axe that breaks it down; it becomes instead an aspect of lifestyle, and consumer choice. The artist is no longer the upholder of the regime or prophet of doom, but instead is a minor part of the economy. The cultural sector also becomes a much less cosy environment. With generous state subsidy, and no competition (although there were some targets to meet and some 'socialist competitions' between different organizations of the same sector) there was no legal commercial activity in the USSR at all until the late 1980s, with the exception of foreign trade controlled by the central government. In this environment, arts marketing was not an issue and there was no reason to develop expertise in this field. The mixed economy of merchandising, franchised catering and the use of a profit-making arm to subsidize mission-driven activity is also not relevant. More subtly, if consumer durables such as television, video and other home entertainments are unaffordable or unobtainable, there is less to compete with the live arts for leisure-time activity. When this situation began to change from the end of the communist period, the expertise and flexibility to adapt to the new enterprise environment was not already present.

DIFFERENCES IN THE DEVELOPMENT OF CREATIVE INDUSTRIES

In the West creative industries began to grow in the 1970s and 1980s through two main routes. Either they developed organically, at the creative end of the commercial sector, as symbolic goods assumed greater prominence and market share; or they were encouraged by schemes supported by public money. In the first case the type of goods and locations of outlets for them were predicated on market demand (for instance, Greenwich Village in New York, Affleck's Palace in Manchester or, more recently, the Devonshire Quarter in Sheffield). The publicly-funded developments tended instead to be dictated by public policy, and locations for them were predetermined into designated 'cultural quarters', as in Sheffield, or the Albert Dock in Liverpool (Moss, 2002). Where public pump-priming has been successful, the distinctions between these types have broken down as small creative enterprises have become self-sustaining, if not profit-driven, for example, the Northern Quarter in Manchester and the Victoria Quarter in Leeds). This depends on a blurring of boundaries between public and private funding, and between profit, mission-driven and subsidized enterprises. Often all aspects exist within one organization, and various flexible expertises have grown within the organization to benefit from funding, marketing, sales and development opportunities as they arise. All this assumes a basket of differing funding types and a sophisticated, changing and growing demand for symbolic goods. In turn, this presupposes a ready clientele which is accustomed to choosing and buying cultural goods or experiences; has the disposable income to do so; has some confidence in making its selection; and some sense of what different cultural goods indicate or symbolize about their purchasers and their lifestyle.

In Russia, the development of creative enterprise took a rather different route. The traditionally profitable areas (such as advertising, antiques, fashion and popular music production) had almost no role in the Soviet economy. Conversely, state provision for the arts was widespread, affordable and of traditional but very high quality. Culture had a strongly social, even moral, purpose before the breakdown of communism, while the 'creative economy' did not exist. Once the transition to a market economy began, the new areas of culture that could form an obvious part of profit-driven growth (that is, advertising and mass media) developed rapidly, but the non-profit, socially motivated type of creative organization lacked the infrastructure for growth. In 1997, statistics listed only 2076 non-profit cultural organizations across the whole of the Russian Federation. After the fall of communist regimes, such enterprises developed in a sporadic, ad hoc way, often without any coordination or awareness that they constituted creative industries. Alternatives to state funding were not obvious, with no structures for sponsorship, charitable donation or voluntary sector. Ironically, there has been more development in non-metropolitan areas, such as the Republic of Karelia, where policy-makers in a regional capital far removed from Moscow have been able to pursue local initiatives without federal interference. While privatizations of modern media have proceeded apace, the number of creative organizations employing fewer than 50 people has fluctuated wildly (for example from 1550 in 2000, to 1100 in 2001 in St Petersburg alone), and their contribution to the economy in Russia has never reached 2 per cent of that of all small enterprises (Belova, 2002). In other words, there is little evidence of secure, stable growth, although this may be obscured by the number of firms operating in the black economy: estimated to constitute 23 per cent of all service industries, of which the creative industries comprise 25 per cent (Skvoznikov and Azernikova, 2001).

The reasons for such fragility are not difficult to find, and are categorized here for convenience as attitudinal issues and structural disadvantage, although these overlap.

ATTITUDINAL ISSUES

The Market

Cultural consumption assumes some degree of disposable income and the confidence to spend it on cultural goods. In Western Europe there is a long history of both factors, dating back at least to the rise of the merchant classes in the seventeenth century. It is from that time that cultural goods were produced 'off the peg' rather than solely by commission, one of the clearest examples being the growth of a market for small landscape paintings in the Netherlands. All the mechanisms began to develop for the sale, regulation, pricing, exhibition and distribution of non-commissioned cultural goods, such as shops, galleries, trading standards, advertising, shows, and pricing that fluctuated with what the market would sustain. This continued to evolve over hundreds of years, together with marketing and critical comment which informed and encouraged choice and discernment in purchase. But Russia moved directly in 1917 from a virtually pre-industrial social economy consisting still largely of peasants and landowners, with a tiny middle class, to rapid industrialization under communism. Choices during the communist period were limited to the purchase of extremely cheap tickets for traditional performance, and free visits to traditional historic galleries and museums. The mechanisms that inform consumer choice in the West, such as critical debate, reviews and the impact of advertising or editorial coverage in glossy magazines and other media, did not exist. Indeed, little commitment of income was possible, and little choice of material cultural goods was available. Consequently, in Russia, the basic structure for the possibility of cultural consumption was missing or had been lost by 1990: not only were there few outlets for cultural goods, there was little either to regulate, enable or inform their sale. This absence of social convention to encourage expenditure, or informed choice, works alongside falling incomes in post-Soviet Russia to discourage cultural consumption. Household incomes fell by 90 per cent in real terms between 1991 and 1996, and theatre attendances declined by 50 per cent as ticket prices increased after the reduction in state funding (Jakobson et al., 2000). It is interesting that, today, the most conspicuous examples of 'Western' consumption in Russia seem to be cars, casinos and mobile phones: all of which have an obvious utilitarian purpose in addition to any symbolic meaning.

Suspicion of Earned Income

Before the breakdown of traditional divisions between 'elite' arts and 'popular culture' in the later part of the twentieth century, many European countries based cultural policymaking on the presumption that 'arts' were worthy of state support while 'entertainment' could fight its corner in the market. This approach persisted in communist states until (and beyond) their downfall, in that most 'high' culture (opera, ballet, classical music, historic art galleries) is still funded by the state, while mass culture (popular music, media, most publishing) has moved into the market economy. Here, however, the distinction has particular force because of the dominance of the ideological values of culture in support of or in opposition to the state. For dissidents, as for communist propaganda, economic considerations had no role in this, so it was easy to associate commercial viability with a lack of symbolic, ideological or aesthetic value. Such attitudes are reinforced by current legislation and self-description by entrepreneurs (see below).

Conservative Approaches to Culture

Russian legislation describes cultural activity as 'work to preserve, create, disseminate and teach cultural values'. Creative activity is the 'making of cultural values and their interpretation'.[4] There is nothing here about the process of creation that must precede the establishment of value. Both definitions are essentially retrospective: they pertain to activities that follow creation rather than encompass it. Such an approach suffuses state-funded cultural activity, devoted to the preservation and representation of historic and traditional forms, including folk techniques such as enamel work, woodcarving and wood painting. Even the currently planned regeneration of Petrozavodsk, the old industrial satellite town of St Petersburg, is based on traditional woodworking skills. While this has preserved traditional skills, it does not encourage new types of creative enterprise. Individual entrepreneurs on the streets of Moscow hawking Matrioshka nesting dolls from a basket are far more common than small galleries selling contemporary jewellery. This is conservative in two ways: it is a primitive type of enterprise, and what is being sold is itself very traditional.

The impact of all these factors is to maintain a climate deeply prejudicial to creative entrepreneurship, particularly in non-profit, mission-driven organizations, despite official rhetoric to encourage it.

INFRASTRUCTURAL PROBLEMS

Inflexibility of Large Organizations and Training

Most state cultural organizations are large, with staffing structures fixed for decades and little flexibility of employment, since jobs are fixed to the particular area of residence. (For example, you cannot apply for work in Moscow unless you already have a Moscow resident's permit.) Large organizations respond more slowly to change than small ones, and in Russia, this is compounded by the non-competitive allocation of state funding and lack of entrepreneurial skills among long-standing employees. Radical political change in the 1990s had little impact upon the actual staffing of cultural management. Further, in the Soviet period, policy-making was divorced from management, so integrated approaches to policy, marketing and management are not established among senior staff. It is also difficult to acquire this expertise, except by trial and error, since the distinction is maintained in Russian cultural management educational courses. Such courses focus upon a technical approach to the methods of cultural management rather than on the rationales of cultural policy-making and the centrality of marketing to policy in arts enterprises. They also encourage students to make compilations of existing views rather than to develop their own, thus discouraging exploration and opportunism which are crucial to enterprising approaches.

Taxation and Other Financial Disadvantages for Small Creative Enterprises

The perceived distinctions between commercial and non-profit organizations are reinforced in Russia by state law that uses the same distinction, giving tax and tax reporting advantage to the state-funded organization. Commercial activity by a non-profit organization is taxable, while for a state organization, it is tax-free. Similarly, donations to a non-profit organisation are taxable, but not if the gift is to a state-supported body. Restrictions on what counts as non-profit are set by the state and are non-negotiable. This discourages mixes of profit with non-profit activity in the same firm, which makes it difficult to take enterprising approaches to earned income for small mission-driven organizations. The non-profit organizations are allowed to have some commercial activity, but the commercial turnover is limited and the reinvestment of profit is highly regulated. While non-profit enterprises are eligible to apply for grants from state funds, the details of these schemes are circulated only through mechanisms used by state bureaucracies. Conversely, the assumption that such enterprises are non-profit means that they are not eligible for the small business grants available to other new Russian companies. Conflicts between federal and regional legislation, and the custom of interpreting the law by presidential decree as new situations arise, do not engender a stable legislative environment for new types of enterprise (Glinkova, 1999).

Currently, the best way to perform well in the Russian creative enterprise sector is to have two different organizations: one for commercial purposes, and the other for non-profit activity. The administrative and management problems of this are obvious.

The impact of these problems is that the introduction of tried and tested development strategies from the West is unlikely to have any real effect. There is little point in running an arts marketing course if no market exists in the Western understanding of the word. Arguing for flexible approaches to funding by managers will achieve no purpose, while legislation prevents such enterprise, and no mechanisms for certain styles of financial support exist. These may be relevant after the establishment of more fundamental changes in attitude, legislation and funding mechanisms, but it is also possible that Russia will develop in new ways currently not imagined. Perhaps, therefore, it is appropriate to look at the specific conditions of Russia that may help to generate the creative industries in ways that are not available in the West. Ironically, these have developed as a response to some of the difficulties of the communist years.

SPECIAL CHARACTERISTICS OF RUSSIA FAVOURABLE TO CREATIVE ENTERPRISE DEVELOPMENT

One advantage Russia has is the number of small atelier workshops that have existed before and throughout the Soviet period. Originally producing bespoke orders in Tsarist Russia, demand for their output continued as the only means of securing individually made, distinctive items not available through mass production. Mainly high-class tailoring workshops, they produce designer fur apparel, items of leatherwork and some metalwork. These ateliers are accustomed to producing commissioned, unique goods and understand the importance of customer relations and customer service: all values ideal for other types of small creative enterprise. As new social classes emerge and stratify in Russia, and as disposable income grows, people begin to express their style and status through lifestyle choices, as in the West. In Russia, this has not taken place predominantly through home improvements and gardening, as in the UK (very few own their homes, live in houses, and almost none in the cities have gardens), but rather though display of personal goods: clothing, jewellery, cars, personalized mobile phones. This offers huge opportunity for small wearable creative goods to be developed because here there is a ready market for them. Combined with the expertise of ateliers, this provides both the market and the places of production for small-scale designer fashion.

The communist era also gave rise to informal networks of trust and mutual help, since often this was the only way to achieve goals outside state concerns, such as obtaining a rare book or finding temporary accommodation. Much barter took place to mutual benefit. Trust was built on mutual reliance, but also sometimes on the shared knowledge of the illegitimate nature of the help given. This had a tremendous binding force, but it also had the effect of closing ranks to outsiders. The relationship of the cultural sector with the underground economy is ambiguous. On the one hand, its illegal activities were a significant force in the overthrow of communism; but now these same activities are being harnessed for social benefit within the official economy, often by the same protagonists. Strong, informal networks are crucial in the establishment of new types of creative enterprise. The long Russian experience of this way of working may prove a useful training ground for cultural growth.

Voluntary, amateur clubs for cultural purposes also flourished in Russia through the Soviet period. These were one of the few permissible forms of self-organized activity, tolerated because they were assumed to be without political significance. Often affiliated to state-funded institutions, they were able to use their resources and offered opportunities for management experience and policy making to people interested in culture. By 1990, the Russian Ministry of Culture estimated that there were 65 000 such clubs – embryonic non-profit organizations that could become creative enterprises in the post-Soviet period.

WESTERN CRITERIA FOR CULTURE-LED REGENERATION ALREADY WIDESPREAD IN RUSSIA

In addition, several circumstances that favour the growth of creative enterprise have existed for decades in Russia, although in the West they had to be realized, promoted and then specially encouraged and funded over recent years.

Night-Time Economy

In the West urban cultural regeneration often involved promoting the use of the city outside working hours, through lighting, transport policies and encouragement to creative businesses to open in the evening (Mulgan and Worpole, 1987). The notion of a night-time economy was novel; indeed, the term is an invention of Western cultural managers. In Russia, however, it was less of an issue: there has been something of a night-time economy for almost a century. Soviet shops tended to close at about 7 p.m., and this rapidly expanded in the post-communist period into a genuine night-time economy. In a society where everyone is assumed to work, shops are open at night and the city functions commercially and socially as during the day; in fact it is often busier. The circumstances already existed for the creative economy to operate at night time without any special new provision or promotion.

City Centre Living

Another 'discovery' of Western exponents of culturally driven regeneration was the benefit of mixed-use urban developments, including living accommodation in city centres, together with the small shops, services and surgeries that must accompany residential areas. These are believed to keep the city centre safe and animated. In Russia, this is less of a problem: city centre living in flats is the norm, and the services needed to sustain this are to be found in many urban centres, including the heart of Moscow and St Petersburg, although now increasing rentals are driving out this domestic provision. The situation in many Russian cities, however, is that there has never been a 'centre' in the Western sense. Established by planning in the Stalinist era, they consist entirely of complexes of housing, factories and shops, with no obvious central hub for retail, commerce and culture. This poses its own problems for urban renewal, but they are not identical to the problems of Western cities in post-industrial decline.

Café Culture

The small size of Russian urban flats, and the difficulty in buying, carrying and storing ingredients, means that home entertaining is not always an option. Until very recently eating out was also limited by a shortage of stylish cafes and the high cost of distinctive restaurants, but an explosion in café culture is now taking place as supply expands to meet demand, including food styles from all over the world alongside a revival of traditional Russian dishes, presented with a new realization of customer care.

In some ways, then, the urban infrastructure is right for the growth of creative enterprise in Russia. There is less need for the elaborate, slow and very costly plans to restructure the urban environment physically that have formed the basis of many cultural regeneration schemes in the West, (although rising rents in commercially viable areas are a problem both for Russia and the West). Where there are problems, they are not all the same as those that have exercised Western cultural planners, and may not be amenable to Western solutions.

An examination of mission-driven, Russian creative enterprises that have proved successful reveals a mixture of techniques that have been drawn from Western models, while at the same time exploiting Russian advantages. As illustrated below, they also demonstrate an approach to enterprise that goes beyond the notion of simply selling in the hope of profit. However, all these are drawn from Moscow and St Petersburg, where living standards, cultural infrastructure and expectations are far higher than in other parts of the country.

Vladimir Nabokov Museum, St Petersburg

The Vladimir Nabokov Museum in St Petersburg occupies the childhood home of the writer. In 1995, it had a dusty collection of secondary material about Nabokov displayed in one room, which typified the dull presentation of museums in the Soviet era. In 1987, Dmitri Milkov, a new member of its staff, presented an ambitious business plan to its Council of Founders, arguing for a mixed funding package to convert the museum into a lively, interactive cultural centre focused on the author's work. The Council (many of whom had worked only in the Soviet era) rejected it as unrealistic, thus demonstrating the fear and suspicion of enterprise common at that time. Milkov raised the money from private business to buy the building from its state custodians, and jointly with these purchasers set about changing it into a cultural centre for concerts, exhibitions, plays and conferences about Nabokov and related issues. The business sponsors receive corporate benefits such as free tickets, private events, and acknowledgement of their contribution. This was an innovation at the time and had to be explained to sponsors, visitors and the public. Milkov says that the key to their support is high-quality restoration and events delivered on time.

This project has adopted Western concepts of mixed usage, business sponsorship and a recognition of the need for high quality. However, the networks used to achieve this were informal and personal, taking advantage of Russian values. What is unusual (and, indeed, enterprising) is the clear focus on actual and potential users rather than on the existing collection: customer satisfaction was the priority. The collection and its display were secondary to this in a reversal of the traditional Soviet approach to museum culture.

OKA Café and Gallery, Moscow

The OKA Café consists of a small, informal restaurant and a gallery which sells the work of young artists. It is formally set up as a commercial venture (thus escaping the problems of identity outlined above), although, in fact, it is mission-driven: the purpose of the gallery is to provide exhibition space for new work in central Moscow for artists who are unlikely to be offered a show in a traditional commercial gallery. The gallery does not make a profit, although the small commission on sales is intended to cover the gallery costs. At present this does not happen because a discerning, purchasing public has not developed. It is supported by the proceeds of the restaurant. This serves stylish food and drink in a setting of 'industrial chic' with pressed metal stairs and exposed pipe-work. Unlike such decor in the West, this really was done to save money as it is in a redundant warehouse. In 2002, the bar had fruit-crates screwed to the wall to provide shelving. The OKA Café fulfils the need for better cafe culture, but has to put great effort into promotion, not only of its own existence and warehouse location, but also of the very concept of a cafe-gallery. This exemplifies the difficulties of establishing a small creative enterprise; even in central Moscow, there is no social convention of patronizing an unconventional venue, and no infra-structure to inform and encourage the purchase of paintings. The OKA Café has to work to create its own user group. This also shows the type of creative effort that is currently necessary in Russia if 'enterprise' is about changing a social situation rather than merely responding to it.

Club on Brestkaya Street (Klub na Brestkoy)

Set up in 2002 with funding from a consortium of private investors, Klub na Brestkoy occupies an award-winning architectural design in a specially excavated basement beneath an office building in central Moscow. Managed by a team of three, with 40 catering staff, it is just beginning to break even, although the investors were pressing for an early profit. The restaurant is the main source of income, offering affordable business lunches and evening dining. Art exhibitions of work for sale without com-mission are changed every three to four weeks, and the main hall is a venue for the Moscow Film Festival. The clients are an emerging class of young professionals with whom the programme is being developed as usage grows. Much of the custom comes by word of mouth (exploiting the Russian use of informal networks), but the concept of club use is in its infancy and has to be encouraged through editorial coverage, critical reviews and special events. The club is thus tackling some of the fundamental conceptual problems about the expansion of cultural experience in modern Russia, while embracing the notion of the mission-driven organization supported by private enterprise. Like the OKA Café, it is working to bring about social change and expectations, in addition to building a service for the market it is simultaneously creating.

CONCLUSION

It is already clear in Russia that creative enterprise is becoming established in areas that are new and appropriate in the market economy, rather than taking over what used to be provided by the state. At the profitable end, obviously enough, it is popular culture and advertising that have flourished.

Commercial art galleries are well established in Moscow and St Petersburg (where most wealthy 'new Russians' live) but rare elsewhere. The mission-driven creative enterprise, for which there is a real social and democratic need, struggles with a lack of infrastructure and lack of understanding at government level and among users. Traditional state-funded 'high' art provision has hardly shifted (except in cost to the end-user) since the Soviet period, and is clearly distinguished from what creative enterprise is attempting to supply. This sharp differentiation within the creative sector is not helpful to innovation in public provision, networking between public, private and non-profit organizations, or to the sustainability of diverse and mixed ways of working between them. It is evident from the examples and the foregoing arguments that encouraging non-profit creative enterprise in Russia involves much more than providing Western types of training and examples of expertise. The idea that entrepreneurs take advantage of situations, and can be trained to do so, can be effective only when there are suitable situations; for example, some type of market, some user expectations, and a fiscal climate favourable to a mixed economy of profit, social purpose and commercial subsidiary.

The impact of not only the Soviet moratorium on enterprise, but also the lack of any real market economy for most of the population for hundreds of years, cannot be easily dismissed. The current trend towards utilitarian and ephemeral consumer spend suggests that confidence and discernment in cultural choices is in its infancy. It will need development through better information, critical debate in the media, and the gradual establishment of a class of purchasers through the efforts of the enterprising new creative businesses. Advertising is widespread. Stylish presentation in shops and restaurants and a new focus on users rather than on goods indicate that the process has already begun. The limitations of business law can be changed, but this depends on the will and understanding of legislators.

In other words, the current situation is unstable, and likely to remain so for some time. Government will have to make choices about its role in the balance between providing cultural experience or enabling creative growth; consumers of culture will have to become more confident and secure in their choices; creative enterprises will have to work with both government and consumers to bring about these changes, and to work with each other to create a more viable creative economy.

NOTES

1. The author is grateful to Basil Gnedovsky of Moscow State University, and to Lyudmila Taskevich of Surgut University, for comments on an earlier draft of this chapter.
2. Figures quoted in Toepler (2000).
3. Figures from the Aggregate Register of the Russian State Committee for Statistics, as quoted by Jakobson et al. (2000).
4. Law no 3612-1, 9.10.92, quoted in Belova (2002).

REFERENCES

Belova, E. (ed.) (2002), Encouraging enterprise and creativity in St Petersburg. Tacis Programme, EU.

DCMS (2004), Culture at the heart of regeneration. Department of Culture, Media and Sport, HMSO.

Dubois, V. and Laborier, P. (2003), The 'social' in the institutionalisation of local cultural policies in France and Germany, *International Journal of Cultural Policy*, **9** (2), 195–206.

Glinkova, S. (1999), Russia's underground economy during the transition, in Feige, E.L. and Ott, K. (eds) (1999), *Underground Economies in Transition*, Aldershot: Ashgate, pp. 101–106.

Jakobson, L., Koushtanina, E. and Rudnik, B. (2000), The emergence of the nonprofit sector in the sphere of culture in Russia, *Journal of Arts Management, Law and Society*, **30** (1), 19–29.

Kirzner, I.M. (1973), *Competition and Entrepreneurship*, Chicago, IL: University of Chicago.

Looseley, D.L. (2003), Back to the future: rethinking French cultural policy 1997–2002, *International Journal of Cultural Policy*, **9** (2), 227–234.

Moss, L.M. (2002), Sheffield's Cultural Industries Quarter 20 years on: what can be learned from this pioneering example? *International Journal of Cultural Policy*, **8** (2), 221–219.

Mulgan, G. and Worpole, K. (1987), 'Saturday Night or Sunday Morning: From Arts to Industry – new forms of cultural policy', London: Comedia.

Myerscough, J. (1988), The economic importance of the arts in Britain. Policy Studies Institute.

Schumpeter, J. (1947), The creative response in economic history, *Journal of Economic History*, 7, 149–159.

Skvoznikov, N. and Azernikova, K. (2001), Voprosiy Chernoi Ekonomii, *Voprosy Statisktki*, 12.

Toepler, S. (2000), From Communism to civil society? The arts and the nonprofit sector in Central and Eastern Europe, *Journal of Arts Management, Law and Society*, 30 (1), 7–18.

Vladimirov, Y. (2000), Budzhet poderzhal televidenie i izdatelstva. Prospekt Sankt-Peterburga March–April.

10. Human language technologies and entrepreneurship in the creative industries

Brian Kenny and Julia Meaton

INTRODUCTION

The creative implications for information and communications technology (ICT), and human language technologies (HLT) in particular, are exemplified in the efforts to foster related international and pan-European collaboration – both inter and intra – among various government research agencies, higher education and industry. However, HLT research and development is a complex drawn-out process that needs substantial public support. Its application to the creative industries is still in its infancy relative to the potential for exploitation and, furthermore, success cannot be assured by market forces alone.

The elements of risk and uncertainty inherent in HLT software development have been reduced to some extent by networking programmes and the subsequent cross-transfer of knowledge. The impact on entrepreneurial activity has been wide-ranging including the sharing of experience and helping entrepreneurs to find inspiration and advice, access technology and knowledge, or identify partners.

As HLT technology develops, increasing artificial intelligence will be accompanied by larger vocabularies, more complex grammars and greater natural language processing. In this context, research in new media and art practice are important strands that inform the dialogue between practitioners, researchers, creative industries and the public.

Against this backcloth, this chapter describes some popular applications of HLT to the creative industries and examines the R&D performance and technology transfer of selected European states in this field. In addition, case-studies are used to illustrate the development and entrepreneurial activities of two HLT suppliers in the context of entrepreneurship, national vision and social and innovation policies. In the latter respect, the choice of Finland serves to illustrate how success in HLT can be achieved in a 'marginalized' situation; that is, in a state with a relatively small population, limited resources and a restricted (minor) national language. Here, it is seen that HLT innovation policy and entrepreneurial industry potential arise from balancing commercial innovativeness and social welfare.

HLT IN THE CREATIVE INDUSTRIES

Human language technologies (HLT) comprises the group of software components, tools, techniques and applications that process natural human language. This covers the two broad areas of speech processing and natural language processing (NLP) technology, which models the human capacity to comprehend and process the content of human language. The combination of speech and NLP provides powerful technology for improving the interaction between humans and machines, and between humans using machines.

The production of digital content and application to the creative industries is still in its infancy relative to the potential for exploitation. Indeed, the larger organizations in the non-digital text (or print) media, audio-visual entertainment and advertising still appear to dominate at the expense of the more creative, small firms involved in HLT development and application.

Timely and cost-effective delivery of high-quality digital content has opened the relatively narrow software localization industry to a wider range of players who are broadening traditional roles, including publishing houses, film and music producers, and video games developers. Keane (2004) draws attention to the links between knowledge, creativity and diversity and refers to the sub-components of software and digital media and product design as coming within the term 'creative industries' (which he attributes to Mitchell et al., 2003).

The computer has enabled a revolution in contemporary arts where its use may be as a medium or as a tool to produce art, or as an originator of art. A dialogue has been initiated whereby interactivity has become the main purpose of digital artistic tendencies involving the audience in the creative process through the use of active agents. The following examples, although not exhaustive, demonstrate the range of HLT applications and their benefits in the creative industries, starting with what might be considered less commercially attractive developments.

Computer-Generated Poetry

The relationship between language and image within a digital environment has produced such interesting efforts as navigable poems and automatic

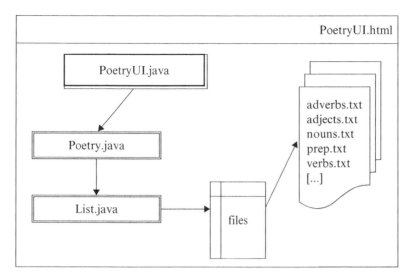

Source: Millan (2001).

Figure 10.1   Relation between classes in ADAM

poem-generators, although low in priority compared with other natural language processing applications. This is, in part, probably due to the more immediate rewards that other applications, such as natural language database interfaces, provide.

Research by Millan (2001) at the University of Birmingham, UK, addressed ADAM (Another Dimension of Artistic Manifestations), a computer program that randomly generates lyrical poems. This illustrates the use of the computer as an originator of art, since the only role of the human artist in this particular case is the one of writing the computer program. ADAM comprises a number of text files containing a limited corpus of words, ordered and classified according to different syntactic categories: adverbs, prepositions, nouns, pronouns, adjectives, verbs and so on. These are called upon when a poem is generated according to the syntactic rules contained in the applet Poetry.java (see Figure 10.1).

Poetry CreatOR II (http://www.prancyhorse.com/servlet/PoetryCreatOR), created by Jeff Lewis and Eric Sincoff at Stanford University's computing labs in the United States, is an Internet-based system through which poems may be randomly or 'theme' generated. The reader can judge from the following poem which is the result of this writer's effort using Poetry CreatOR II and based on the selected title and theme inputs of 'speak to me only with thine eyes' and 'creative industry and natural language processing', respectively:

Speak to me only with thine eyes

A bison emerges from the bored creative industry,
Listless, helpless, but never shouting
Ever briskly, the shiny pate took its toll . . .
The natural language processing danced like a dainty pixy, or a fragile little elf
A chain yelps noisily, but no one ever listens . . .
Nimbuses leave from the ruby spider
How easily did the dream come apart, like a horn of death in one's big toe
Cast me down from heaven for destroying of grangers.
Right here, right now, and for each and every gigolo.

As laymen, we might wish to question the computer program's degree of poetic license and the ability to link in the HLT components in a more meaningful (contextual) way. However, the fundamental creative idea is apparent, and the seriousness of such experimentation is demonstrated by some of the respectable higher education institutions involved in the research arena, as noted above, including the Massachusetts Institute of Technology's work on 'visual language'. In essence, poetry generation as a textual application provides a model for how far the structure of language can be stretched, while remaining reasonably intelligible, functional and, to an extent, enjoyable.

Language Processing and the DJ

ThoughtTreasure (TT) is a commonsense knowledge base and architecture for natural language processing comprising many thousands of English and French words and phrases, concepts and related assertions. The Common Sense DJ (CSDJ), developed at the MIT Media Lab in the United States, uses TT as an aid to selecting music, given certain parameters about the dancers' response level as captured on camera. The CSDJ responds by finding the necessary Common Sense knowledge in TT's database and validating its usefulness. A further application, TextOrgan, aids DJs in the selection of texts – pure and/or visual – based on the mood or themes they wish to develop. The DJ plays his decks, and the TextOrganist uses the MIDI keyboard and a mouse to play the text. Output is then projected onto a screen above the dancers.

Music

The modelling of music notation is an extremely complex problem, which may be used for several different purposes including music analysis, audio coding, sheet-music production, teaching, content query and entertainment. For example, Music Markup Language (MML) attempts to mark music objects and events with a programming language (XML-based) that enables the processing of music documents for various purposes, ranging from music theory and notation to practical performance. With MML it is possible to 'sequence' a piece of music without having to use expensive software and, as it uses human language elements, it is easier to understand than the more popular MIDI (Musical Instrument Digital Interface) software (Technology Reports, 2002).

Advertising

In a maturing advertising industry, new contextual networks are emerging that combine the technology to understand natural language with the real-time artificial intelligence for automated campaign optimization. Advanced contextual technology enables marketers, for example, to more accurately display what they want to market directly at the user target. Chahal (2005) notes that this model benefits all those involved in the online advertising equation. For example: the publisher's interests are served as online ad space is used most effectively and at a premium; advertiser benefits accrue given the increased message response, while the target audience is less likely to see irrelevant advertisements.

Publishing and Broadcasting

Publishing is the process that allows the sharing of knowledge among a wide audience. In this context, electronic delivery is especially important for responding to an international, multilingual market and for the production, localization and cultural adaptation of knowledge. New media publishing on the Internet combines computing, entertainment, broadcasting, music and video production.

Indeed, natural language generation (NLG) techniques have already been successfully applied in a number of publishing areas, the most relevant of which is automatic production of technical documentation and generating texts for knowledge diffusion. This approach has the benefit of knowledge dissemination in the form needed by specific users, expressed with the correct level of detail and in the appropriate language type. A major aim for NLG publishing is to develop tools and techniques that will enable the specialist or technologist, rather than just linguist, to create and customise such information resources.

In broadcasting, automated voice activation has been developed to help the television production process. For example, voice prompts by the presenter may cue in the lights, sound, pre-recorded reports and graphics sequences in a live news programme.

Video Games

Modern video games are complex systems where the user may face intricate rules and simultaneous tactile, visual and audible information. In this sort of environment, as Oberteuffer (2005) notes, speech commands are highly useful and may make novice players more able to progress through the levels of the games, and expert players able to use a wider range of skills and strategies. Indeed, the quality of interactions between non-player characters (NPCs) and the player is an important area of artificial intelligence in games. As a method of improving dialogue between players and NPCs, conversational agents are often used. These are software agents that have the ability to portray emotions and personality through dialogue, and thus, demonstrate believable behaviour. In terms of the benefits, vocabularies and grammars can be created without coding or concerns about speech technology and acoustic models for words or phrases can be generated automatically. For programmers, sample code is provided to make the implementation of speech input fast and reliable.

HLT IN EUROPE

The creative implications for information and communications technology (ICT), particularly HLT, are beginning to be recognized. This is evidenced by the fact that HLT was featured within the EU's key action on Multimedia Content and Tools in the User-Friendly Information Society Thematic Programme – part of the European Commission's 5th Framework Programme (1998–2002) covering Information Society Technologies. In this regard, initiatives set up to encourage and support the application of HLT to the creative industries include:

- RADICAL (Research and Development Informed by Creative Arts Labs) – for establishing a platform for consensus-building between the creative professional, academia and the R&D community. Partners include the UK, France, Ireland and the Netherlands.
- NAMIC (News Agencies Multilingual Information Classification) – news customization services based on XML standards. Partners include Belgium, Italy, Spain and the UK.

As part of the initiative to improve awareness of HLT RTD (Research and Technological Development) projects and accelerate the rate of technology transfer from the research base to the market, the European Commission EUROMAP project reviewed opportunities and challenges for language technology (LT). As a result, EUROMAP Language Technologies was set up in 1996 to promote greater awareness and faster take-up of HLT within Europe. In 2003, the EUROMAP HLT benchmarking study provided the first comprehensive pan-EU perspective on this emerging technology (Euromap, 2003).

The study was based on a benchmarking analysis of the opportunities and achievements of HLT research efforts in Europe. The analysis compared Member States, and created indexes for the two broad measures of 'Opportunity' and 'Benchmark'. The Opportunity Index comprises supply-side and demand-side factors including ease of business formation, access to key channels for HLT, and ability to adopt innovation, ICT infrastructure and capacity to absorb innovation. Benchmark factors include depth and breadth of HLT research, funding commitments by both the public sector and industry, and the breadth of language coverage in research and products.

Mapping the Opportunity Index against the HLT Benchmark produced a summary measure (the HLT Scorecard) showing the relationship between the two indices. In general, countries with the most favourable business environment and the most highly developed infrastructure have the most successful HLT research efforts. The research identified four clusters of countries, as shown in Figure 10.2:

1. Leaders – which were judged to be 'market-ready' for advanced HLT research.

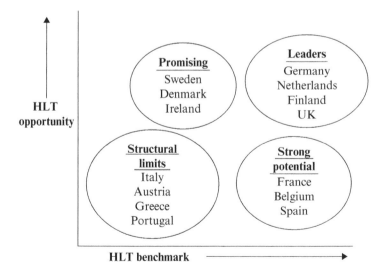

Figure 10.2   HLT national clusters

2. A strong potential group considered to have well-developed research communities, and a significant depth of HLT research, so were in a strong position to exploit HLT.
3. A promising group that had comparable performances in both 'first-generation' HLT R&D and transferring essential results to the marketplace.
4. Countries with structural limits in their existing HLT market situation.

According to Lockwood and Joscelyne (2003), the transfer of first-generation HLT to market moved into the mainstream 'early-majority' stage with applications in telephone-based speech recognition, search engines and machine translation of millions of web pages each day. The Euromap (2003) study concluded that HLT research and development was a complex, drawn-out process that needed substantial public support, and its success could not be assured by market forces alone. Clearly, Europe's progress in the field had been built on public funding in the universities and national research institutes. However, there is no discernable, direct link between robustness of the HLT research effort in any particular language community and actual effectiveness of transfer to market. What factors then would constitute success for a smaller nation dependent on a relatively minor language?

THE CASE OF FINLAND

The development of HLT technology increasingly involves larger vocabularies, more complex grammars and greater natural language processing. In this context, research in new media and art practice are important strands that inform the dialogue between practitioners, researchers, creative industries and the public. Under these conditions, even the relatively less-commercially attractive (but more societally oriented) creative HLT industry sectors are likely to benefit from the encouragement and wider support given to ICT development and associated entrepreneurial activity. What, then, are the conditions for success and the implications for national policy, general competitiveness and impact on industry participants? To explore these issues we consider HLT activity in Finland and the cases of two HLT suppliers. The choice of Finland is appropriate given its strong competitive positioning in HLT and the 'marginalized' conditions under which this has been achieved: for example minor language, relatively small population and limited resources, compared with two of the other HLT leaders: Germany and the United Kingdom. For example, the relatively strong research bases in the

Table 10.1   HTL benchmarking: technology opportunity factors

	Ger.	Neth.	UK	Fin.
RTD & Innovation as % of GDP	2.4	1.9	1.8	3.1
High-Tech Patents per M Population				
Euro Patent Office	29.3	35.8	18.9	80.4
US Patent Office	14.4	19.6	14.4	35.9
Language Technology (LT) R&D				
Research centres	85	27	19	21
Active suppliers	63	15	33	14

Source: Adapted from Euromap (2003).

Netherlands and Finland, where the business environments and infrastructures were judged to be among the strongest in Europe, had, according to the Euromap (2003) study, transferred less HLT technology than might have been expected. However, inspection of selected indicators of the 'leader cluster' countries (Table 10.1) gives rise to some interesting performance comparisons.

A small country like Finland is unlikely to possess the same material and intellectual resources needed for the production or utilization of knowledge as a major European nation such as the UK. Furthermore, it is reasonable to assume that in general, support for application of HLT to the creative industries is unlikely to be a high priority compared with the more pressing ICT programmes where the commercial gains may be both greater and more expedient. Under these circumstances, and, coupling this with Finland's restrictive use of its language, comparative size and economy, its comparative HLT ranking is all the more remarkable and worthy of exploration.

Interestingly, *The Global Competitiveness Report 2000–2004* (WEF, 2004) showed that, from 104 countries surveyed, Finland was ranked the most competitive economy in the world, followed by the United States. The underlying survey attempted to quantify the conditions for sustained growth based on two complementary indexes: the Growth Competitiveness Index analysed the potential of the various economies to sustain economic growth, while the Business Competitiveness Index focused on company sophistication and quality of the business environment. It identifies the factors that relate to high productivity and, thus, economic performance measured by the level of GDP per head of population.

From Table 10.2, it can be seen that Finland's ranking on selected competitive factors is quite remarkable, and more so because of its

Table 10.2   Finland's world competitiveness rankings: selected characteristics

Growth competitiveness index	Rank
Technology	
Technological sophistication	1
Firm-level technology absorption	1
University–industry research collaboration	1
Laws relating to ICT	1
Tertiary enrolment	1
Internet access in schools	1
Company spending on research and development	2
Business competitiveness index	**Rank**
Sophistication of company operations and strategy	
Capacity for innovation	1
Production process sophistication	1
Value chain presence	1
Quality of the national business environment	
Extent of collaboration among clusters	1
State of cluster development	1
University–industry research collaboration	1
Other indicators rank	
Ethical behaviour of firms	1
Prevalence of environmental management systems	1
Government intervention in corporate investment	1
Effects of compliance on business	2
Consistency of regulation enforcement	2

Source: Adapted from WEF (2004, p. 56).

out-ranking of the United States. Five other European economies were ranked among the top ten: Sweden (3), Denmark (5), Switzerland (8), Norway (9) and Iceland (10), while the United Kingdom (11) was up four places from its 2003 position. Both Germany (13), and the Netherlands (25) remained unchanged. Thus, apart from selected Scandinavian countries, there appears to be little correlation with HLT performance rankings.

A major finding of the Euromap report was that the strength and coherence of government policies have an enormous bearing on a country's ranking. The rule of law and existence of efficient public institutions are essential prerequisites for developing conditions under which local entrepreneurship can be fostered and higher levels of national income attained.

By 2003 Finland had developed a strong research base in language technology, and displayed a conducive environment for technology development and transfer, both in its business environment and in the advanced state of its ICT markets and infrastructure. In spite of its limited geographic usage, the complexities of the Finnish language are attributed to the nation's focus on theory in HLT research, giving it valuable potential for developing advanced HLT solutions in many languages. The research community now benefits from programme support and investment from both the national government and the private sector.

POLICY AND TECHNOLOGY TRANSFER

Finland enjoys significant national-level support for its language technology RTD effort. For example, TEKES (Finnish Funding Agency for Technology and Innovation) is the main financing organization for applied and industrial R&D in Finland, providing funding and expert services for R&D projects for companies and universities and co-ordinating Finnish participation in international technology initiatives.

The Finnish Network for Language Technology Studies – funded by the Ministry of Education – links university departments specializing in language technology, with the aim of increasing the number of professionals and scientists working in the HLT field. The network includes 29 departments in ten universities, covering computer science, cognitive neuroscience, information sciences, computational and applied linguistics. This initiative has been very effective in awareness and community building for the HLT research base, and it has seen a tenfold increase in the number of HLT students studying language technology either as a major or minor subject. In addition, Finland has a well-established funding structure for HLT technology transfer assistance. For example, new HLT companies benefit from well-established science parks, as well as from organizations that incubate and support licensing and commercialization of scientific research results. Funding is provided in the form of capital investment and pre-seed funding and through the commercialization stage of product development.

Furthermore, the nation has been especially successful in creating small, niche companies to exploit its high-quality academic research results. The Nokia company, with its substantial R&D facilities including speech-processing research, represents a strong attraction and encouragement for language technology transfer.

CASE-STUDIES

Connexor

Connexor is a small Finnish company (16 employees) providing multilingual language technology to application developers in fields such as knowledge management, interaction, learning, translation and speech. For the first three years of its operation Connexor was funded with the help of one long-term private financier, but it has been self-supporting since 2000. The company was founded in 1997 by three former natural language processing researchers from the University of Helsinki who began to commercialize successful academic research that they carried out during the 1990s. Initially, Connexor concentrated on customized projects and on the development of end-user products such as terminology tools and language checkers, but eventually the focus was shifted to OEM (original equipment manufacturers) licensing Connexor technology to developers of a wide variety of language processing applications.

From the initial development of English language-based Linux operating systems, Connexor systems now support French, German, Spanish, Italian, Dutch, Danish, Norwegian, Swedish and Finnish. These cover a variety of operating systems and platforms, ranging from hand-held to mainframe computers.

In September 2002, Connexor announced a license agreement for embedding Connexor's syntactic analyser of Swedish in Namni's mobile service platform for entertaining mobile products and services. From 2003, Connexor had virtually a monopoly position in the high-end area of HLT, covered by the Machinese parser product family and including semantic analysis capabilities. By the end of 2004 Connexor was providing language analysers (French, German and Spanish) for text-to-speech synthesis to Toshiba and licensing Machinese text analysers for human genome database creation to the University of Tokyo.

According to Arppe (2004), the company is a prime example of firms adopting what was the new paradigm of IT business in Finland. Contrary to the older HLT engineering companies, it both exploited external private capital and directly targeted the international IT corporate market from the outset. In contrast, the tradition was to start little by little from Finland, followed by Sweden and Germany, then the rest of Europe, culminating with the American market. Arppe (2004) also notes that, as in the case of Connexor, a considerable number of key owners and actors in language engineering companies have remained consultants or active teachers and researchers in Finnish academia.

Imagetalk

Finland-based company Imagetalk specializes in mobile applications with customizable symbols-based content. The core product is communication software for individuals with various speech and language disorders and its core competence has been extended to related types of mobile company software products and solutions. The company was established in 2000 and was spun-off in summer 2002.

In February 2005, Lingsoft (another Finnish company) and Imagetalk entered into an ownership and financing arrangement, where Lingsoft became a major shareholder of Imagetalk. Both faster growth and synergy potential were seen in the arrangement where Imagetalk products could be enriched with Lingsoft language technologies, and conversely, Imagetalk could utilize its mobile user interface concepts in products and services based on Lingsoft language solutions.

Lingsoft was established in 1986 and based its business on word and sentence analysis methods, with applications in language and speech technology, translation and language service, and e-library systems and e-books. A major customer of Lingsoft is Microsoft, to which the company has licenced its language tools.

Venture capitalists Innofinance Ltd and Finland's Industrial Investment Ltd both invested in Imagetalk in order to help marketing and related localization needs of the software, as well as making the product known in the software business. Additional funding was granted from the government technology body TEKES in the form of a loan for product development.

In April 2005, Imagetalk released Imagetalk Symbol Writer, a full-featured touch-screen, symbols-based communication software application for the Nokia 7710 Smartphone, which comprises entertainment and organizer multimedia capabilities. When loaded with Symbol Writer software, these features are easily recognizable and instantly usable by customers with speech and language limitations.

By 2005, Imagetalk had expanded its European activities through a number of collaborations. For example, a technology agreement with Helpicare, one of Italy's leading producers and distributors of assistive technologies which has collaborative agreements with the University of Pisa, for the research and development of new products and a European network of enterprises for the development of synergies necessary to improve products and the market. Helpicare also exports its technologies to the UK, Germany, France, Sweden, Holland and Austria.

Imagetalk also entered into agreement with the German company Reha Media GmbH for distribution of its software. Reha Media is a pioneer in the field of assistive communication devices, and its distribution network covers the whole country.

FOSTERING ENTREPRENEURSHIP IN HLT

While Connexor's early internationalization may be viewed merely as a necessary economic move, the entrepreneurial implications are worthy of further exploration. For example, internationalization may not only mean access to a larger market but activity across different markets can help achieve and sustain competitive advantage over firms operating in one country only (COM, 2004).

Clearly, Connexor's intellectual property rights and associated licenses reflect considerable competitive advantage if, indeed, their 'virtual monopoly' mentioned above might be debatable. In contrast to this relative degree and speed of success, Romijn and Albu (2002) noted from their study of British high-technology small and medium-sized organizations (SMEs), that patentable innovations could not be created overnight, and that the innovations upon which such ventures are based carried high risks and had very long gestation periods. The risk and time-to-market aspects, including the risk for outside funders, are not insignificant factors faced by both Connexor and Imagetalk.

However, from the SME owner's perspective the risk factor may, in this case, be as much a matter of attitude. For example, from the extent to which entrepreneurs have more confidence, or more optimism, in their expectations than those of non-entrepreneurs, then they will be seen to take on more projects than the latter; 'this appearance may then be mistaken as greater risk tolerance than average' (Norton and Moore, 2000).

The elements of risk and uncertainty inherent in information software development, and HLT in particular, have been reduced to some extent by networking programmes and the subsequent cross-transfer of knowledge. The impact on entrepreneurial activity has been wide-ranging, including the sharing of experience and helping entrepreneurs to find inspiration and advice, access technology and knowledge, or identify partners.

While Oviatt and McDougall (1994) point to the network structure as one of the new ventures' most powerful resource-conserving alternatives to internalization of SMEs, Bell (1995) suggests that networking is a better explanation of the internationalization process of these firms. The latter proposition seems well supported in the case of Imagetalk.

It is evident that in the wider, national and international policy arenas, the knowledge and technology transfer impact is of prime importance.

Dana et al. (2004) refer to the importance of public policy and international expansion of high-technology SMEs. Knowledge transfer between knowledge institutions and private parties is clearly becoming increasingly important as a channel for matching knowledge supply and demand. In Connexor's case the founders' academic research origins clearly played an important part in the transfer process. In support of this view, Hughes (2003) highlights the need for a policy focus on technology transfer to be embedded in a wider framework. He emphasizes that this must necessarily address the ability of firms engaged in knowledge transfer to employ appropriately qualified staff and to absorb, implement and exploit that knowledge. In Finland the main responsibility for the utilization of knowledge rests with the public sector. While considerable measures have been taken to strengthen its capacity for carrying out these increasingly demanding expert and development tasks, it is acknowledged that the government previously had no clear development strategy for social innovation, nor was entrepreneurial activity considered to be at the desired level – although the legislative framework was said to favour entrepreneurship and innovation (Science and Technology Policy Council of Finland, 2003).

A MODEL OF SOCIAL ENTREPRENEURSHIP?

Castells and Himanen (2002) have described Finland as a paradigmatic model of societal transformation. In their view, the Finnish case demonstrates that a competitive information society creates the economic basis of the welfare state, while effectively fostering the educational, health and social services for those employed in the economic sector. In this context, the authors point out the importance of the production and use of ICT in changing the economic structure, increasing productivity and promoting economic well-being.

While acknowledging that Finland may be lower down the list in terms of the use of ICT (Pelkonen, 2004), Sipilä (2004) notes that Finnish researchers are at the leading edge of developments in a number of ICT fields. For example, the neural network concept developed by Professor Teuvo Kohonen is probably the single most widely disseminated Finnish scientific achievement to date, together with Internet encryption systems and other information and communications technology products.

Of particular note is the Linux computer operating system developed by Finn Linus Torvalds, which is an example of social innovation driven by entrepreneurs in the world of digital technology: the so-called Open Source movement (Himanen, 2001). The principle is that anybody is free to improve or modify the software source-code, provided that they make the new source-code available when they publish the software. Torvalds originally created his operating system software in 1992, as a then 21-year-old student at Helsinki University.

Interestingly, Himanen explains this 'hacker ethic' as the passion for technology that drives Torvalds, and others like him, to spend considerable time developing software, often at their own expense. He includes creativity within this ethic and relates the behaviour to values that would apply to social entrepreneurs more generally. Supporting this societal notion, Drayton (2002) notes that it is only the entrepreneur who literally cannot stop until he or she has changed the whole society. In this respect, integrity and ethics can be seen as an integral part of entrepreneurial culture in which the values of innovation and creativity are nurtured towards making a positive impact on society, often at the expense of personal gain.

Golden et al. (2003) contend that the existence of national systems of innovation (NSI) should promote entrepreneurship within an economy, given that they seek to foster innovation, and entrepreneurship has innovation as a central component. Even though their paper draws no firm conclusions about the relationships between NSI and entrepreneurship, it is reasonable to assume that a positive relationship exists and, thus, can be subsumed in any discussion.

Many of the entrepreneurial characteristics and aspirations discussed above are reflected in Finland's strategy, as demonstrated in its 'shared vision' for an information and knowledge society. In this respect, society develops and utilizes the opportunities in order to improve the quality of life, knowledge, international competitiveness and interaction in an exemplary, versatile and sustainable way (Science and Technology Policy Council of Finland, 2003). This vision is set to drive strategy towards technology and infrastructure innovation through a network economy and public sector processes, as shown in Figure 10.3.

In the Finnish strategy, all national actors (individuals, organizations and the public sector) are encouraged to participate in the further development of the information society. The single most important emphasis is on users' needs with the mutual aim to build an information society for all people, so that it can be continuously accessed by all concerned from anywhere. In this sense we can refer to Leydesdorff's (2006) triple helix model which, in the context of the knowledge-based economy, represents the role of university (for example via Connexor's founders' HLT research PhDs), industry and government, as key pieces of the process of innovation development within a complex structure of interaction between the three.

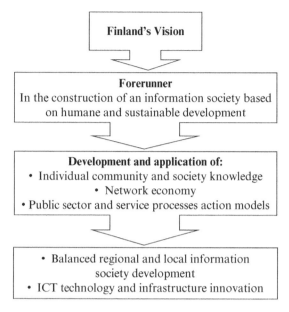

Source: Adapted from Lavikainen (1999, p. 3).

Figure 10.3   Finland's ICT strategy model

CONCLUSION

As HLT technology develops, increasing artificial intelligence will be accompanied by larger vocabularies, more complex grammars and greater natural language processing. These will be available for engaging in sophisticated interactive dialogues and communication, such as virtual reality entertainment applications comprising speech interaction and emotional content in their virtual worlds. In this context, research in new media and art practice are important strands that inform the dialogue between practitioners, researchers, creative industries and the public.

As information processing and storage gets cheaper by the decade, computer technology is likely to continue to reshape society, and this will create substantial economic and social opportunity for natural language and speech technology, while stretching the creativity of researchers, developers and entrepreneurs alike. It will also further the questioning about the social acceptance of developments such as the role of digital input and output methods, say for example, the 'languages' of human gesture and gaze.

The International Federation of Arts Councils and Cultural Agencies (IFACCA) notes that practices in new media culture are no longer restricted to audiovisual and interactive media content, but acknowledge the wider social, urban and global context of the information society, through evolving networked projects (IFACCA, 2004). Within such networks, media arts and cultural organizations act as the necessary intermediate R&D force, coordinating activity between the academic and creative industry sectors.

Overall, the evidence shows that even in a 'marginalized' situation, a country's strength in ICT and HLT innovation policy and entrepreneurial industry potential arises from balancing commercial innovativeness and social welfare. In turn, this is reflected in high investment in infrastructure, a highly skilled population and a functioning social welfare sector. The result is a sound basis for socio-economic development, where all potential resources – including the entrepreneurial base – and creative HLT innovations can be utilized as promoters of competitiveness and welfare. Under these conditions, even the relatively less commercially attractive, but more societally oriented creative industry sectors will be afforded the opportunity to benefit from the encouragement and wider support given to HLT development and associated entrepreneurial activity.

REFERENCES

Arppe, A. (2004), Finnish lessons: no single path to market. Accessed 20 February 2005 from www.hltcentral.org/page-969.0.shtml.

Bell, J. (1995), The internationalisation of small computer software firms: A further challenge to 'stage' theories, *European Journal of Marketing*, **29** (8), 60–75.

Castells, M. and Himanen, P. (2002), *The Information Society and the Welfare State. The Finnish Model*, Oxford: Oxford University Press.

COM (2004), 70 final. Action Plan: The European Agenda for Entrepreneurship, Commission for the European Communities, Brussels, 11.02.2004. Accessed 3 January 2005 from http://europa.eu.int/eur-lex/en/com/cnc/2004/com2004_0070en01.pdf.

Chahal, G. (2005), Contextual advertising: a win/win/win. Accessed 20 January 2005 from http://www.imediaconnection.com/content/4875.asp.

Drayton, W. (2002), The citizen sector: becoming as competitive and entrepreneurial as business, *California Management Review*, **44** (3), 120–132.

Euromap (2003), Benchmarking HLT progress in Europe. Accessed 10 December 2004 from www.hltcentral.org/page-243.shtml.

Golden, W., Higgins, E. and Lee, S.H. (2003), National innovation systems and entrepreneurship, CISC Working Paper No. 8. Accessed 10 December 2004 from www.nuigalway.ie/cisc.

Himanen, P. (2001), *The Hacker Ethic*, London: Vintage.

Hughes, A. (2003), Knowledge transfer, entrepreneurship and economic growth: some reflections and implications for policy in the Netherlands. Retrieved 14 April 2004 from http://www.cbr.cam.ac.uk/pdf/wp273.pdf and http://www.prancyhorse.com/servlet/PoetryCreatOR, accessed 3 April 2004.

IFACCA (2004), Strategy document on international development of new media culture policy, Helsinki, August 24. Accessed 10 January 2005 from http://www.ifacca.org/files/040916Helsinki_agenda_final.pdf.

Lavikainen, J. (1999), Probing the Information Society: converging objectives in Finnish and pan-European development, Finnish National Fund for Research and Development. Retrieved 3 January 2004 from http://194.100.30.11/tietoyhteiskunta/suomi/eu_ist_ohjelma.htm.

Leydesdorff, L. (2006), The knowledge-based economy and the triple helix model, in Dolfsma, W. and Soete, L. (eds), *Reading the Dynamics of a Knowledge Economy*, Cheltenham, UK and Northampton, MA, USA: Edward Elgar, pp. 42–76.

Lockwood, R. and Joscelyne, A. (2003), Benchmarking HLT progress in Europe, Euproject, HOPE (IST 1999-12595). Accessed 16 June 2004 from http://www.enabler-network.org/reports.htm.

Millan, N. (2001), Computer generated poetry and visual arts. Unpublished MSc dissertation, University of Birmingham, September.

Mitchell, W., Inouye, A. and Blumenthal, M. (2003), *Beyond Productivity: Information Technology, Innovation and Creativity*, Washington: National Academies Press.

Norton, Jr, W.I. and Moore, W.T. (2000), Entrepreneurial risk: have we been asking the wrong question?, *Small Business Economics*, **18** (4), 281–287.

Oviatt, B.M. and McDougall, P.P. (1994), Toward a theory of international new ventures, *Journal of International Business Studies*, 25 (1), 45–64.

Pelkonen, A. (2004), Questioning the Finnish model: forms of public engagement in building the Finnish information society. STAGE (Science, Technology and Governance in Europe) Discussion Paper, 5 June. Accessed 11 November 2004 from http://www.stage-research.net/STAGE/documents/5_ICTFinlandcase_final.pdf.

Romijn, H. and Albu, M. (2002), Innovation, networking, and proximity: lessons from small high-technology firms in the United Kingdom, *Regional Studies*, **36** (1), 81–86.

Science and Technology Policy Council of Finland (2003), Knowledge, innovation and internationalization. Retrieved 5 June 2004 from http://www.minedu.fi/tiede_ja_teknologianeuvosto.

Sipilä, K. (2004), A country that innovates. Department for Communication and Culture/Unit for Promotion and Publications, Finland. Accessed 12 July 2005 from http://virtual.finland.fi/netcomm/news/showarticle.asp?intNWSAID=25818.

Technology Reports (2002), XML and Music. Accessed 14 June 2004 from http://xmlcoverpages.org/xml/music.html.

World Economic Forum – WEF (2004), *The Global Competitiveness Report 2003–2004*, New York: Oxford University Press.

11. Developing relationships between higher education, enterprise and innovation in the creative industries

Calvin Taylor[1]

INTRODUCTION

Once the exclusive touchstone of cool city lifestylists and urban regenerators, it seems that everyone is now a creative – even academics. In public policy, creativity has been linked to intellectual property (IP) (Department of Culture, Media and Sport – DCMS, 1998, 2001), and forward-thinking university business managers have clearly detected an opportunity. It is now not unusual to see universities set up graduate creative entrepreneurship programmes, invest in incubator and spin-out programmes and, perhaps most commonly, enter into innovation partnerships with creative enterprises from the private, public and third sectors.[2] The Queensland University of Technology has gone so far as to create a Faculty of Creative Industries with a strategic remit to work with the creative industries sector of the state. The interest that universities now have in the creative industries, as the UK in particular illustrates, has been the regional turn in economic development policy.[3] Since the region has taken off as the apparently most effective geographic unit for operating in the global economy (Scott and Storper, 1992; Saxenian, 1994; Braczyk et al., 1998), the priority to stimulate regional productivity through enterprise and innovation has created opportunities for universities to develop relationships with a range of IP-based sectors, including the creative industries.[4]

On the surface, therefore, there appears to be something of a virtuous circle drawing in the growth of the creative industries, regionalization in economic policy and higher education strategies for engagement with business through enterprise and innovation. With this in mind, this chapter reflects on the developing role of universities in relation to the creative industries in the context of research in the areas of the creative industries, regional development and knowledge transfer.[5] More detailed consideration of knowledge transfer is given below, but for our purposes here it refers to the application of research-generated knowledge outside of the traditional academic context.[6] The chapter concludes by suggesting that if higher education strategies for engagement with the creative industries are to make a significant and real impact on regional strategies for enterprise and innovation, then a number of challenges need to be met by both institutions and policy. The first set of challenges concerns the implications for higher education practice of the organizational characteristics of the creative industries, together with their associated business models. The second concerns the evolving role of institutions within regions as loci of enterprise, innovation and adaptive learning. The third concerns the models of business engagement (and their associated performance measures) that are currently being advocated by central governments, and their appropriateness for encouraging universities to work with the creative industries. The central argument of the chapter is that if universities are to work with this sector in a meaningful way, then both institutional practice and wider higher education policy need to develop rapidly.[7] Universities around the world are being encouraged to think more closely about how their work has wider social and economic impact – with possible commercial benefits to institutions. There is a critical issue here, of how institutions understand and respond to this demand in terms of, for example, attitudes towards IP exploitation and protection and institutional support practices. These could go a number of different ways. It would be deeply ironic if the very globalization process that encourages the development of flexible, distributed and innovative models of enterprise in industry and in society more generally were to be met by a largely mass production-style response from higher education.

The next section discusses the organizational characteristics of the creative industries and the types of business models within which they work. This is followed by a consideration of the role of institutions in regional development, particularly in relation to the development of enterprise and innovation. The knowledge transfer role of universities and their possible relationship to the creative industries is then discussed. The final section concludes by setting out some of the main issues that need to be considered by both institutions and policymakers if there is to be an effective relationship between universities and the creative industries.

DEFINING THE CREATIVE INDUSTRIES

There are a number of different definitions of the 'creative industries' in use around the world. However, the one developed in the UK by the Department for Culture, Media and Sport (DCMS) is useful from the point of view of discussion and, despite some criticisms, is also quite widely adopted. In this chapter, creative industries are defined as:

> those industries which have their origin in individual creativity, skill and talent and which have a potential for wealth and job creation through the generation and exploitation of intellectual property. This includes advertising, architecture, the art and antiques market, crafts, design, designer fashion, film and video, interactive leisure software, music, the performing arts, publishing, software and computer games, television and radio. (www.culture.gov.uk)

This definition gives some clues as to the underlying motives for encouraging the creative industries: international competitiveness, economic modernization, urban regeneration, economic diversification, national prestige and economic development (Myerscough, 1988; Lewis, 1990; Frith, 1991; Bassett, 1993; Bianchini and Parkinson, 1993; Griffiths, 1995; McGuigan, 1996). What these motives all share in common is a view that the creative industries, as well as their underlying business models and organizational characteristics, are claimed to be typical of the industries and business models that can flourish in the post-Fordist economic landscape. Some of the early commentators (for example, Schapiro et al., 1992; Lash and Urry, 1994) have gone as far as to suggest that such business models and organizational characteristics are paradigmatic of this new economic landscape.

This interest in the specificity of the organizational characteristics and business models of the creative industries is also linked to a new social understanding of the workings of contemporary economies, much of which focuses upon the phenomenon of local and regional industrial clusters. Although the typical business models and organizational characteristics tend to suggest a single path or model of creative industry economic development, the experience around the world is diverse. Many commentators link the particular character of the development of the creative industries in specific localities to specificities of place, that is, local identities, business cultures, ethnic diversity, institutional cultures and practices, and local customs. Furthermore, reference is often made to the neo-classical economist Alfred Marshall, and the 'industrial atmosphere' of a given location (O'Connor and Wynne, 1997, 1998; Pratt, 2002; Nevarez, 2003). It is the growing importance of these intangible qualities, often referred to in regional economics as 'untraded interdependencies' (Storper, 1995, p. 192), that offers the creative industries a competitive advantage over other sectors. Concomitantly, it is the difficult to replicate place-specific qualities of the creative industries that give localities a competitive edge. The business models and organizational characteristics of the creative industries on the one hand, and their particular amenability to place-specific economic development on the other, present universities with challenges if they are to partner effectively with this sector.

The typical business models underpinning the creative industries have been commented upon by a variety of authors (Bilton, 1999; Pratt and Jeffcut, 2002). They point to the existence of a number of common characteristics that may distinguish the creative industries from other kinds of enterprise. For the purposes of this chapter these characteristics will be summarized under four headings: supply and value chains (including IP), markets, the role of risk and working patterns.

The earliest writers (Christopherson and Storper, 1986; Shapiro et al., 1992; Cornford and Robbins, 1992; Lash and Urry, 1994) on the business models underpinning the creative industries linked what they saw happening to the structure of advertising, the film industry and audio-visual industries to the shifts happening in the wider economy. Out-sourcing, downsizing, the growth of a few very large transnational corporations sitting on top of large pools of independent companies and the growth of micro-enterprise and freelancing all suggested that the creative industries were part of a much larger set of economic processes. The typical size of creative industry businesses is an important consideration for initiatives designed to encourage universities to work with them. In the UK in 2004 the British government (Department of Culture, Media and Sport, 2005) estimated that there were approximately 115 000 businesses[8] in the creative industries sector, accounting for approximately 7 per cent of all UK businesses. Of this total, approximately 99.6 per cent[9] are classed as small or medium-sized enterprises (that is, they employ less than 250 people), and approximately 90 per cent of the total employ less than ten people.[10] Of the 500 or so large enterprises, the majority are based in London. In short, in the main, universities that work in a regional context with the creative industries will be working with small and medium-sized enterprises.

Another important consideration is the type of activities undertaken across the creative industries supply chain. A number of models have been developed to explain the principal stages in the cycle of creative production and consumption. Most of these revolve around a multi-stage model usefully described by Pratt as a 'production-cycle' model (Pratt, 1997). In the UK, the government department responsible for the creative industries is considering adopting a six-stage model of the cycle that includes the stages of creation, making, distribution, consumption, education and understanding, and archiving and preservation. When populated with the kind of statistical data referred to above, this model provides an analysis of the typical size of business working in each of the major stages. In one of the English regions where this model has been tried – the South West

(Burns Owen Partnership and University of Leeds 2003) – what became apparent was the extent to which the processes of original creation were dependent upon small-scale enterprises, with any larger enterprises distributed across the other stages of the cycle. Whilst innovation can take place across the cycle, the moment of creation has a particular status that separates it out from the other stages, if for no other reason than that it is here where new IP is created. Again considering the role of universities, organizations that have become very aware of their own status as creators of new IP, institutions need to consider how their work can interact with small-scale IP production if they are to work effectively with the creative industries.

The second feature of the creative industries that apparently identifies them with the new economic landscape is the nature of their markets. Until the age of mass reproduction, the market for art operated as a series of niches, each with its own patrons, artistic styles and schools, systems of taste, connoisseurship and agents, galleries and critics (Becker, 1982). In the age of mass reproduction, cultural consumption assumed the shape of its industrial origins – routinized, homogeneous and subject to large-scale economies of scale with the consumption of art relegated entirely to private patronage or ordered by the routines of state intervention. What the last 20 years has seen is the return of the niche – partly as a result of changing fashions and cultural demands, but also critically as a result of the possibilities offered by new technologies.

Inspired by Piore and Sabel's *The Second Industrial Divide* (1984), there is a widespread view that the markets for creative industry products and services are typical of the kind of post-Fordist systems of production and consumption they describe. The apparent return of small-scale, independent, flexible and specialized production as a mode of industrial organization creates the conditions within which creative industries can develop. Flexibility refers to three interrelated processes: the ability to swap production activities between niche markets; the ability to innovate existing products and services; and the ability to adjust to varying levels of demand. What particularly facilitates this is the advent of low-cost information and communications technologies (ICT). ICTs mitigate the drive to achieve economies of scale in production systems, thus enabling even small producers to compete in complex, shifting markets. Specialization refers to the ability of a particular locality to capture such flexible economies for itself. Again, the interaction of a flexible business model with economic and social environments favours the creative industries.

The nature of the markets for creative products and services then leads to a particular consideration of the nature and role of business risk in this sector (Bilton, 1999; O'Connor et al., 2000). For example, Bilton (1999) argues that creative products and services engender a type of business risk that is qualitatively different to that experienced by other industrial sectors. What distinguishes creative products from other types of use-value is that their economic value exists in an unstable relationship with their symbolic value. As digital technologies have permeated the production cycle, the materiality of products and services has become a residual consideration. Once value is linked with symbolic values and experiences, the variables in the underlying business model become resistant to prediction. Creative enterprises, therefore, have to adopt strategies for managing this risk. These strategies again distinguish creative industries from other sectors. Bilton's (1999) analysis of how businesses deal with this type of risk and uncertainty depends both on their place within the production cycle or value-chain and also on their size. Larger businesses working in the film or publishing industries have developed strategies that try to make markets for creative products behave like markets for traditional material products. Branding, the star system, and the cultivation of the celebrity actor or author are all ways of creating a semblance of economic predictability. However, since such proxies are not infallible, the film and publishing industries look to manage a wide portfolio in which the potential super-profits from the next blockbuster can be used to soak up the losses made within the rest of the portfolio – with obviously hope of a net gain. This tends to drive larger organizations towards the distributive stage of the production cycle and makes them more dependent for product on the large number of smaller independent and quasi-independent producers. This encourages relationships between the larger corporate players and the smaller independent organizations. The independents know that they have to establish a relationship with the larger players. They do this by developing more 'emergent' strategies that allow for flexible responses to the opportunities that circulate through networks (Bilton, 1999). The nature of risk in the creative industries also needs to be understood by universities as part of their engagement with the sector.

The working patterns of the creative industries and their labour markets have also been widely commented upon. In this regard, the processes of vertical and horizontal supply chain disintegration have contributed to the current profile of the sector as one with a very small number of large organizations and a very large pool of small enterprises, the vast majority of them employing less than ten people. These smaller enterprises range from the small owner-managed business, with the objective of achieving relative stability, to more complex enterprises that mix core staff with bought-in services from freelancers that can expand and contract in light of market conditions and opportunities (Caves, 2000; Benner, 2002).

INNOVATION, INSTITUTIONS AND THE CREATIVE INDUSTRIES

The adoption of the creative industries into regional development strategies has been justified on a number of bases, for example, employment creation, contribution to gross domestic product and business start-up strategies. But to what extent can the creative industries contribute to the idea of regions as drivers of enterprise and innovation? Again, the role of place becomes important here, particularly in relation to territorial proximity and the formation of industrial clusters of specialized economic activity. A number of different approaches towards understanding territorially based enterprise and innovation have been offered, including collective learning or regional innovative capacity (Nelson and Winter, 1982; Lawson and Lorenz, 1999), the *milieu innovateur* (Camagni, 1991b, 1995), the learning region (Asheim, 1996; Simmie, 1997) and the regional innovation system (Cooke et al., 1997; Braczyk et al., 1998). What the approaches share is the idea that enterprise and innovation, as well as their development and adoption into industrial activities, occur most effectively when they are grounded in sets of territorially based relationships. To that extent they all acknowledge that economic development is a socially mediated process dependent upon the nature, type and quality of social relationships within an economy (Grabher, 1993a). Where they differ is in their respective understanding of the type of relationship that best leads to innovation. The collective learning and *milieu innovateur* approaches emphasize the collective learning capacities of a given location based, in the main, on business-to-business relationships. The learning region and regional innovation systems approaches place the emphasis on the type and quality of relationship between businesses and the wider set of institutions – educational, technological, political – that impact upon business in a given locality.

It is the role of institutions in regional innovation that poses the question of how universities can work with the creative industries. The idea that institutions become important in flexibly specialized regions was acknowledged by Piore and Sabel in their original formulation. However, the idea has been refined in ways which allow a more focused understanding of the potential relationship between universities and the creative industries.

To understand the role of institutions, we first need to understand the primary reasons why businesses tend to cluster. In this regard, Amin and Thrift (1994) identify five reasons why small business economies need this clustering or agglomeration. Firstly, firms themselves are relatively loose in their practical organization and therefore cannot be easily distinguished from the wider business context. Secondly, business decision-making in small businesses, as Bilton (1999) also points out above, may be more ad hoc than at first appears. Thirdly, businesses are not as stable as organizational theory suggests. Fourthly, small businesses are porous and are open to two-way influences. And fifthly, agglomerations are the link between the individual firm and the wider market.

Clustering works through two processes that are important for understanding the potential role of universities in the creative economy. First, agglomeration can deliver significant external economies of scale for a given group of businesses that have connections with each other (Asheim, 1992; Bellandi, 1989; Brusco, 1986). However, it is the second set of agglomeration processes that are important for enterprise and innovation. For example, the diffusion of innovation, the regulation of labour markets and the formation of a culture of trust between firms create the kinds of difficult-to-replicate 'untraded interdependencies' that allow regional economies to specialize. Clustering becomes most effective when it enables levels of cooperation and coordination that collectively mitigate the negative consequences of open competition. Without a certain level of cooperation and coordination, competition will continually threaten the small firm with extinction, thus forcing a short-term survivalist attitude to innovation and risk-taking that may undermine successful risk-taking in the future.

What, then, is the role of institutions? Clustering processes are achieved by a combination of formal and informal means. At the formal level this includes defined relationships between a wide range of organizations: 'firms; financial institutions; local chambers of commerce; training agencies; trade associations; local authorities; development agencies; innovation centres; clerical bodies; unions; government agencies providing premises, land and infrastructure; business service organizations; marketing boards' (Amin and Thrift, 1994). Informal clustering is more personalized and includes detailed personal contacts, membership of associations, and what are often described as the 'cafeteria effects' of close-proximity working.

The ability of institutions to function effectively within the regional context of flexibly specialised industrial sectors is dependent upon three factors. The first is that the institutions must be 'actively engaged with and conscious of each other. These contacts and interchanges are often embodied in shared rules, conventions and knowledge which serve to constitute the "social atmosphere" of a particular region' (Amin and Thrift, 1994, p. 14). The second is that a clear coalition is formed that ultimately produces the collective representation of what are 'normally sectional and individual interests' (Amin and Thrift, 1994). The third factor is the practical awareness that institutions bring to their collective purpose. The successful adaptation of institutions to their regional role will result in six benefits:

1. the persistence of local institutions;
2. the local accumulation of codified and tacit knowledge;
3. institutional flexibility;
4. a commonly enjoyed innovative culture;
5. the extension of trust and reciprocity with the concomitant ability to adapt as circumstances allow or demand.

There are no prescriptive reasons why any one form of successful institutionalization should be preferred over another. However, a number of different models have emerged that centre upon the levels of relative formality with which relationships are formed and embedded. In his review of the industrial districts literature, Raco (1999) identifies two typical models. The examples of industrial districts in California (Silicon Valley and the San Francisco Bay Area) are examples of what might be described as 'grassroots' industrial districts:

> in that the impetus for collaboration, co-operation and innovation transfer has come from within the districts themselves rather than through federal or state-led programmes. Thus, the Californian model is primarily market-driven and based on informal co-ordination. By contrast the example of Baden Wurttemburg (BW) illustrates the types of actions that might be taken by a closely engaged state sector. (Raco, 1999, p. 959)

> The local industrial milieu is supported by governance structures that devolve power to regional, Lander governments. In contrast to the American model, development in BW is supported by active local state institutions that supplement the existing socio-economic links between firms. The Lander government provides direct subsidies to SMEs for specific technical development projects. It also co-ordinates the infrastructure of institutional resources available to firms such as education, state-sponsored consultancy, export promotion and trade fairs. (Raco, 1999, p. 961)

The UK context has elements of both these models. The regional institutions are intended to work with the private sector and to give the private sector a leading role. They also have a coordinating role across a range of policy agendas. However, they do not have the directive role found in Baden Wurttemburg. For example, a range of agencies manages the education sector. Universities, however, are independent organizations accountable to their governing bodies. They have accountability to the national funding body for the work that is funded from that source. In all other respects they are independent.

KNOWLEDGE TRANSFER AND THE CREATIVE INDUSTRIES

Under the combined pressures of growth in the higher education system, changes to the funding of universities and new policy emphases, the relationship between university-based activities and the wider economy and society have risen up the public policy agenda. One of the strengthening facets of these changes is the role that universities play in economic development. The direct economic impact of universities on their local economies is relatively well documented (Williams, 1997). However, as we saw in the previous section, the development of adaptive local and regional economies based on enterprise and innovation places a new responsibility on institutions with possible implications for how they work and communicate with the local and regional economies.

The pattern of engagement with the wider economy and society by British universities appears to be conditioned by a number of factors: the nature and type of institution (Chatterton, 2000), pre-existing relationships between the institution and the local and regional economies (Williams, 1997), and policies at the local, regional, national and in many cases European levels. In addition to the direct and indirect economic impact of universities on their local and regional economies, Williams also identifies a group of activities that he regards as having more intangible impacts upon the local and regional economies. This group of activities: 'technology and non-technology transfer, the growth of new firms emerging from university activities and the additional income generated by the existence of universities in a locality' (Williams, 1997, p. 99) is what was, for a time, termed 'third arm' or 'third leg' activities but what is now more commonly termed knowledge transfer. Universities have been involved in technology transfer and spin-out company activities for decades, but there has been a tendency to only acknowledge these activities where they originate from science, engineering and technology. The development of the creative industries as a significant economic sector challenges this tendency.

In a survey of UK universities' interaction with business in 2001–2002 (HEFCE, 2003), one of the most commonly reported institutional intentions was to work with the cultural and creative industries. More specifically, a study sponsored by the UK Treasury (HM Treasury, 2003), commissioned specifically to examine the opportunities and achievements of university–business collaboration and to make recommendations for policy, noted:

> There are many excellent examples of collaborations involving the creative industries and universities or colleges of art and design. Policy-makers must

ensure that policies aimed at promoting knowledge transfer are broad enough to allow initiatives such as these to grow and flourish, and that the focus is not entirely on science and engineering. (HM Treasury, 2003, p. 45)

However, whilst a broad range of types of institution acknowledge their work with the cultural and creative industries, it was most marked within the 'new' universities sector, a sector that also more explicitly identifies its purpose with the local and regional economies (Goddard et al., 1994; HEFCE, 2003).

Over the last few years, universities and businesses within the creative industries around the world have examined how they might work together. Moreover, the region and, in many contexts, regional development institutions appear to be a common element in the development of strategy. Initiatives range across the full spectrum of university activities: learning and teaching, research and knowledge transfer.[11] Initiatives abound that encompass one or more of these activities. Below, a few from the UK context are mentioned by way of example.

The Northern Way initiative, combining the efforts of the three northern regions of England, has proposed to develop a pan-regional Centre for Professional Excellence focusing on the creative industries. The University of Warwick already offers a taught postgraduate programme in Creative and Media Enterprises. Some initiatives focus on business support, for example New Media Knowledge based at the University of Westminster. Along a similar theme, the Cultural Industries Development Service (CIDS) in Manchester grew out of a combined local authorities and universities initiative in the late 1990s. Some initiatives focus explicitly on enterprise in the creative industries – for example at Dartington College of Arts students and working professionals are supported by the Centre for Creative Enterprise and Participation. By contrast, the CultureLab at the University of Newcastle and the Digital Research Unit (a collaborative venture originally between the University of Huddersfield and the Kirklees Media Centre) focus more explicitly on the role of research in knowledge transfer. The range of disciplines reflected in these activities is also very wide and not just confined to arts and humanities subjects but also includes media and communications, design, computing and a range of technological disciplines. The interface between universities and the creative industries may also be a rich field for interdisciplinary work.

As the knowledge transfer activities that universities undertake with the creative industries grows, so will the demand for a greater understanding of how these kinds of knowledge transfer activities take place together with an understanding of how their impact is to be evaluated. This will become more urgent as the demand for public investment to facilitate this work also grows. As the Lambert Review of university–business interactions points out, knowledge transfer is now a concern beyond its established fields in the sciences, technology and engineering and this calls for a distribution of funding for this type of activity that reflects this pattern (HM Treasury, 2003).

The academic literature on knowledge transfer (and its related fields of knowledge management and innovation) is vast and too extensive to summarize effectively here.[12] Conversely, there is, as yet, very little literature on knowledge transfer and its related fields with specific reference to the creative industries. Therefore, it is only possible to consider some speculative ideas about the typical characteristics of knowledge transfer and its possible implications for assessing its impact. This speculation may also shed light on the questions of whether or not (and if so, to what extent) the typical characteristics of knowledge transfer with the creative industries are the same as those that characterize knowledge transfer in the sciences, engineering and technology.[13]

A useful starting point for this speculation is to consider why, despite the obvious enthusiasm that universities have for working with the creative industries (as evidenced by the institutional submissions to the Lambert Review)[14] that such work does not appear as highly on the agenda as, say, technology transfer work or the successful launch of a spin-out company. There may be a number of causes for this relative under-acknowledgement. In the first instance, there may simply be under-reporting of knowledge transfer activities in the disciplines that are cognate with the creative industries. This may be allied to an issue of under-recognition in institutional terms that discourages academics from declaring their activities. This under-recognition may also be linked to variation in the terms that are used to describe knowledge transfer-type activities. Knowledge transfer activities in disciplines in which practice plays an important intellectual role may be being recognized through other framing devices such as collaborative work, practice-based research and practice as research. As such, they may not be reported as knowledge transfer activities.

The organizational characteristics of the creative industries and their traditional relationship to higher education (especially the art school and conservatoire models) may also have an impact on the visibility of knowledge transfer activities with the creative industries. For example, the tradition of dual job holding in practice-based creative disciplines (and the associated practice of bringing practitioners into the academy) undercuts the conventional transactional model of a transfer of ownership of knowledge between a vendor and a buyer. The widespread perception that hitherto knowledge transfer has been primarily commercially driven within a particular scientific-technological paradigm may also inhibit recognition of alternative styles and drivers of knowledge transfer more appropriate to the creative industries. In relation to this, the emergent indicators and metrics being developed for evaluating knowledge transfer (largely based on financial measures – consulting revenues, spin-out company valuations, and so on) may themselves be inappropriate for evaluating the impact of knowledge transfer on the creative industries.

This kind of speculation tends to suggest that there may be important qualitative differences between knowledge transfer activity within the creative industries compared with that undertaken within, for example, engineering and technology industries. While some knowledge transfer activities with the creative industries appear to follow well-established organizational models (for example, consultancy and applied research), there are grounds for considering knowledge transfer in the cultural sphere to possess some divergent characteristics.

The first concerns the financial ecology of the creative industries itself. Significant parts of the creative industries are linked into programmes of public investment and are not overtly constituted to fulfil a commercial function, although many institutions and enterprises working within the sector seek to develop commercial income streams. For example, public art galleries are an essential feature of urban cultural strategies that seek to employ creativity in their role within a local economy. However, they are, in the main, funded directly through systems of local and national cultural funding. A second cause for thinking that knowledge transfer with the creative industries is different is based on concepts of intellectual property. Traditional models of knowledge transfer largely rest upon a clear specification of the underlying intellectual property which is to be transferred. As indicated earlier in this chapter, much of the intellectual property of the creative industries consists of 'know-how' that circulates through professional networks, and is often uncodified and typically tacit within any given activity (Kong, 2005). In most cases it is also unprotectable. This leads us to consider that knowledge transfer with the creative industries may itself be a cultural construct of the particular communities of practice that straddle higher education and the creative sector.

The assessment of value in the creative sphere is a deeply contentious and contested issue. Financial measures are not in themselves especially regarded as effective. Although there is an acknowledgement of the underlying economics of creative activity, this is generally not seen as part of the frame of value that surrounds creative activity. Since a large part of the creative sector that universities deal with lies within the publicly funded sphere, the sources of potential finance for knowledge transfer work are heavily circumscribed. The models of commercial investment (for example venture capital-funded models) used to appraise technology roll-out programmes are only exceptionally relevant. Indeed it is the spillover effects from these activities that may have a greater impact upon regions and their economic development than the more formalized activities of licensing and spin-out company activity (Goldstein and Renault, 2004). Finally, there is evidence that much knowledge transfer in the creative industries takes place within dense webs of micro-interactions between individual academics, their personal and professional contacts and networks in the industry or community that lead to collaborative projects, new creative work, student placements, consultancy contracts, and so on. As we saw earlier in the chapter, extensive micro and small enterprise working is typical of this sector and not especially amenable to being captured within the formalized legal structures of university–industry interaction.

Whilst these factors and characteristics point in the direction of needing to treat knowledge transfer, innovation and entrepreneurship with the creative industries as exceptional, there is a growing trend in the innovation literature that encourages caution before drawing this conclusion. In their review of the historical evolution of models of innovation across a broad range of technological disciplines, Dodgson et al. (2005, p. 36) chart a departure from a simple supply-side model of innovation through a number of stages to an integrated model of demand and supply mediated by complex networks. It is in this model that 'we see greater appreciation of the role of knowledge, creativity, and learning as sources and outcomes of innovation'. With particular reference to IP:

> Value is increasingly determined not so much by the ownership of particular assets but by the connectedness of those assets in networks and is realised in new forms of project organisation and project-based firms. (Dodgson et al., 2005, p. 37)

If connecting rather than simply exploiting assets is the route to value, then not only do knowledge transfer and entrepreneurship in the creative industries seem less exceptional than they first appeared, but they may indeed be in the vanguard of the complex industrial and organizational changes that are happening around us.

CONCLUSION

Around the world, a wide range of public and private agencies take an interest in the development of the creative industries and their potential for economic and social impact. The development of regional strategies has given further impetus to universities to engage with this sector. However, there are a number of considerations that universities and public policymakers need to make if they are to engage with this sector in a productive way. First, universities have to consider how their own processes of knowledge production and dissemination are appropriate for the creative industries. In a sector in which tacit knowledge plays such a crucial role, and considering the role of tacit knowledge and other forms of untraded interdependency in regional development, universities need to understand their own role in the creation and circulation of such knowledge. In practical terms, this means universities have to consider: how they interact with businesses, especially with the SME community; how they make their work accessible, and how they allow businesses and organizations into their own processes. At a time when universities are pursuing quite proprietorial strategies towards their IP, the kind of connected strategies being advocated by Dodgson et al. (2005) may be difficult to realize fully. Second, there is some claim for variation in the engagement with the creative industries according to type of institution, with the 'new' universities appearing to be more conscious of the creative industries and of the styles of working required for regional engagement. However, this should not preclude the engagement of research-intensive institutions. The future of the creative industries will become ever more closely tied to new technologies and the styles of enterprise and innovation that they will facilitate. If knowledge and creativity are fusing in the ways described, then institutions will need to consider how their own knowledge production processes can engage with and incorporate creative imperatives. Similarly, successful creative organizations and individuals will economically depend ever more closely on connecting with knowledge assets, and they in turn will need to learn how to engage with universities. Third, wider public policy needs to consider more specifically the characteristics of innovation and, in particular, its social dynamics. The creative industries in particular trade heavily on the role of social interaction and, as Nevarez (2003) claims, universities may make more appropriate 'chambers of commerce' for the creative industries than those of the traditional variety. Dodgson et al. (2005) affirm the implications of this for public policy:

> Policies need to focus on support for the collaborative nature of innovation and the integrated technology that supports it. There are serious and persistent market failures in collaboration, and government can help here by supporting research that cuts across boundaries and disciplines and that fits uneasily into traditional industry or sectoral policies or, indeed, disciplinary peer review and research assessment exercises. (Dodgson et al., 2005, p. 200)

Finally, there is a strong sense that we, as yet, do not know enough about how the models of flexible, distributed and collaborative innovation and entrepreneurship work, or indeed, how we should fully describe and evaluate them. A key area for further research is a comparative analysis of innovation processes both in the creative industries and in other new and advancing industrial activities to identify common and divergent practices, methodologies and models of evaluation.

NOTES

1. The author gratefully acknowledges the finanical support of the Arts and Humanities Research Council, provided under its Impact Evaluation Fellowship Programme.
2. Apparently first formulated within Australian cultural policy, the creative industries are identified as a priority industrial sector in economies as diverse as the UK, China, the most recent European Union accession states and Canada. There is developing interest within the Americas (the USA, Mexico, Colombia and Brazil) and the European Union is increasingly using this nomenclature within its discussion of intellectual property policy. The creative industries are also being identified for their development potential in Africa (South Africa, Mali and Tanzania in particular).
3. See Taylor (2006).
4. In the UK the creative industries have been adopted into all nine English regional strategies and the economic development strategies for Scotland, Wales and Northern Ireland.
5. The chapter mainly draws upon UK experience.
6. Although this definition could be regarded as something of a 'straw man', as a model it continues to dominate much public policy thinking, for example the Higher Education–Business Interaction Survey conducted by the Higher Education Funding Council for England.
7. How the entrepreneurs and businesses of the creative industries view higher education is a related but separate issue. Until higher education knows how to present itself to the creative industries, then the current exemplars of good practice will not be generalized.
8. The statistics only include those businesses that earn revenues above the threshold for registration to pay value-added taxes or who voluntarily register for value-added tax on a regular basis or who collect income taxes from employee earnings on behalf of the revenue authorities.
9. These estimates are based on UK government data collected by the Annual Business Survey (Office for National Statistics).
10. These proportions have remained relatively unchanged since 1999.
11. Once conceived as a discrete activity, 'third arm' or 'third leg' activities such as knowledge transfer are now becoming seen as integral to the main activities of learning, teaching and research. This issue is not addressed in this chapter.
12. For a systematic analysis of the range and types of knowledge management transfer activities see the summaries included in Holsapple and Jones (2004, 2005) to get an indication of just how broad the field is. See also Easterby-Smith and Lyles (2005).
13. Similar considerations are also being undertaken in the social sciences (see Bechhofer et al., 2001).
14. 'Successful events to date have included a workshop on creative media business opportunities between researchers in the School of Art and Design, local creative industries and Venture Capitalists' (University of Ulster, 2003). This is not untypical of the kinds of comments that were made in submissions to the Lambert Review that were published on the web during the review process.

REFERENCES

Amin, A. and Thrift, N. (1994), *Globalisation, Institutions and Regional Development in Europe*, Oxford: Oxford University Press.
Asheim, B.T. (1992), 'Flexible Specialisation, Industrial Districts and Small Firms: A Critical Appraisal', in Ernste, H. and Meier, V. (eds), *Regional Development and Contemporary Industrial Responses: Extending Flexible Specialisations*, London: Belhaven Press, pp. 45–63.
Asheim, P. (1996), Industrial districts as 'Learning Regions', *European Planning Studies*, 4, 379–400.
Bassett, K. (1993), Urban Cultural Strategies and Urban Regeneration: A Case Study and Critique, *Environment and Planning A*, 25, 1773–1788.
Bechhofer, F., Raymann, B. and Williams, R. (2001), The dynamics of social science research, *Scottish Affairs*, 36, 124–155.
Becker, H. (1982), *Artworlds*, Berkeley, CA: University of California Press.
Bellandi, M. (1989), 'The industrial district in Marshall', in Goodman, E., Bamford, J. and Saynor, P. (eds), *Small Firms and Industrial Districts in Italy*, London: Routledge.
Benner, C. (2002), *Work in the New Economy: Flexible Labour Markets in Silicon Valley*, Oxford: Blackwell.
Bianchini, F. and Parkinson, M. (1993), *Cultural Policy and Urban Regeneration: The West European Experience*, Manchester: Manchester University Press.
Bilton, C. (1999), The new adhocracy: strategy, risk and the small creative firm. A Working Paper of the Centre for the Study of Cultural Policy, Warwick: Centre for the Study of Cultural Policy, University of Warwick.
Braczyk, H.J., Cooke, P. and Heidenreich, M. (eds) (1998), *Regional Innovations Systems: The Role of Governance in a Globalised World*, London: UCL Press.
Brusco, S. (1986), 'Small Firms and Industrial Districts. The Experience of Italy', in Keeble, D. and Wever, E. (eds), *New Firms and Regional Development in Europe*, London: Groom Helm.
Burns Owen Partnership and University of Leeds (2003), *Creative Industrial Mapping and Economic Impact Study: stage one data and Technical Report*, Bristol: South West Regional Development Agency and Culture South West.
Camagni, R. (ed.) (1991a), 'Local Milieu', Uncertainty and Innovation Networks: Towards a New Dynamic Theory of Economic Space', in Camagni, R. (ed.), *Innovation Network: Spatial Perspectives*, London: Belhaven Press.
Camagni, R. (ed.) (1991b), *Innovation Network: Spatial Perspectives*, London: Belhaven Press.
Caves, R.E. (2000), *Creative Industries*, London: Harvard University Press.
Chatterton, P. (2000), 'The Cultural Role of Universities in the Community: Revisiting the University–Community Debate', *Environment and Planning*, **32**, 165–181.
Christopherson, S. and Storper, M. (1986), The city as studio; the world as back lot: the location of the motion picture industry, *Environment and Planning D: Society and Space*, 4, pp. 305–320.
Cooke, P.M., Uranga, G. and Extabarria, G. (1997), Regional innovation systems: institutional and organisational dimensions, *Research Policy*, 26, 475–491.
Cornford, J. and Robbins, K. (1992), Development strategies in the audio-visual industries: the case of North East England, *Regional Studies*, 26, 421–435.

Department of Culture, Media and Sport (1998), Creative Industries Mapping Document, London, DCMS.

Department of Culture, Media and Sport (2001), Creative Industries Mapping Document, London, DCMS.

Department of Culture, Media and Sport (2005), Creative Industries Economic Estimates Statistical Bulletin, London: DCMS.

Dodgson, M., Gann, D. and Salter, A. (2005), *Think, Play, Do: Technology Innovation and Organisation*, Oxford; Oxford University Press.

Easterby-Smith, M. and Lyles, M.A. (2005), *Handbook of Organisational Learning and Knowledge Management*, Oxford: Blackwell.

Frith, S. (1991), Knowing One's Place: the Culture of Cultural Industries, *Cultural Studies*, 1, 134–155.

Goddard, J., Charles, D., Pike, A., Potts, G. and Bradley, D. (1994), *Universities and Communities*, London: Committee of Vice-Chancellors and Principals.

Goldstein, H. and Renault, C. (2004), Contributions of universities to regional development: a quasi-experimental approach, *Regional Studies*, 38, 733–746.

Grabher, G. (1993), *On the Socio-economics of Industrial Networks*, London: Routledge.

Griffiths, R. (1995), The politics of cultural policy in urban regeneration strategies, *Policy and Politics*, **21** (1) 39–46.

Higher Education Funding Council for England – HEFCE (2003), *Higher Education Business Interaction Survey 2000–2001*, Bristol: Higher Education Funding Council for England.

HM Treasury (2003), *Lambert Review of Business–University Collaboration: Final Report*, London: Her Majesty's Stationary Office.

Holsapple, C.W. and Jones, K. (2004), Exploring primary activities of the knowledge chain, *Knowledge and Process Management*, **11** (3), 155–174.

Holsapple, C.W. and Jones, K. (2005), Exploring secondary activities of the knowledge chain, *Knowledge and Process Management*, **12** (1), 3–31.

Kong, L. (2005), The sociality of cultural industries, *International Journal of Cultural Policy*, **11** (1), 61–76.

Lash, S. and Urry, J. (1994), *Economics of Signs and Space*, London: Sage.

Lawson, C. and Lorenz, E. (1999), Collective learning, tacit knowledge and regional innovation capacity, in *Regional Studies*, **33** (4), 305–317.

Lewis, J. (1990), *Art, Culture and Enterprise: The Politics of Art and the Cultural Industries*, London: Routledge.

McGuigan, J. (1996), *Culture and the Public Sphere*, London: Routledge.

Myerscough, J. (1988), *The Economic Importance of the Arts in Britain*, London: Policy Studies Institute.

Nelson, R. and Winter, S. (1982), *An Evolutionary Theory of Economic Change*, Cambridge, MA: Harvard University Press.

Nevarez, L. (2003), *New Money, Nice Town: How Capital Works in the New Urban Economy*, London: Routledge.

O'Connor, J., Banks, M., Lovatt, A. and Raffo, C. (2000), Risk and trust in the cultural industries, *Geoforum*, **31** (4), 453–464.

O'Connor, J. and Wynne, D. (1997), From the margins to the centre: post-industrial city cultures, in Sulkunen, P. et al (eds).

O'Connor, J. and Wynne, D. (1998), Consumption and the Postmodern City, *Urban Studies*, **35** (5–6), 841–864.

Piore, M.J. and Sabel, C.F. (1984), *The Second Industrial Divide: Possibilities for Prosperity*, New York: Basic Books.

Pratt, A.C. (1997), The cultural industries production system: a case study of employment change in Britain 1984–1991, *Environment and Planning A*, **29** (11), 1953–1974.

Pratt, A.C. (2002), Hot jobs in cool places: the material cultures of new product spaces: the case of south of the market, San Francisco, *Information, Communication and Society*, **5** (1), 27–50.

Pratt, A.C. and Jeffcutt, P. (2002), Managing creativity in the cultural industries, *Creativity and Innovation Management*, **11** (4), 225–233.

Raco, M. (1999), Competition, collaboration and the new industrial districts: examining the institutional turn in local economic development, *Urban Studies*, **36** (5–6), 951–968.

Saxenian, A. (1994), *Regional Networks: Industrial Adaptation in Silicone Valley and Route 128*, Cambridge, MA: Harvard University Press.

Schapiro, D., Abercrombie, N., Lash, S. and Lury, C. (1992), Flexible specialisation in the cultural industries, in Ernste, H. and Meier, V. (eds), *Regional Development and Contemporary Industrial Responses: Extending Flexible Specialisations*, London: Belhaven Press, pp. 45–63.

Scott, A.J. and Storper, M. (1992), Regional development reconsidered, in Ernste, H. and Meier, V. (eds) *Regional Development and Contemporary Industrial Responses: Extending Flexible Specialisations*, London: Belhaven Press, pp. 45–63.

Simmie, J. (ed.) (1997), *Innovation, Networks and Learning Regions?*, London: Jessica Kingsley.

Storper, M. (1995), The resurgence of regional economies ten years later: the region as a nexus of untraded interdependencies, *European Urban and Regional Studies*, **12** (3), 191–221.

Taylor, C. (2006), Beyond advocacy: developing an evidence base for regional creative industry strategies, *Cultural Trends*, **15** (1), 3–18.

University of Ulster (2003), Response to the Lambert Review of Business–University Collaboration. University of Ulster.

Williams, C.C. (1997), *Consumer Services and Economic Development*, London: Routledge.

12. Conclusions

Colette Henry

The creative industries represent a vital, exciting and rapidly changing field of activity; one which is now recognized as a key growth sector in the knowledge-based economy. Creative enterprises are essentially a subset of knowledge-intensive industries and are defined as 'those activities that have their origin in individual creativity, skill and talent, and which have a potential for wealth and job creation through the generation and exploitation of intellectual property' (DCMS – Department of Culture, Media and Sport, 2001, p. 5).

By researching the nature of entrepreneurship in the creative industries, we can gain valuable insights into the creative entrepreneurial process, and strengthen our knowledge and understanding of the range and type of businesses that make up this complex and dynamic sector.

This edited collection of chapters, which has discussed creative entrepreneurship across 14 different countries, has endeavoured to offer some new dimensions to the current creative entrepreneurship research agenda. In so doing, the valuable economic and social contribution of the creative sector has been highlighted and the challenges for policymakers, educators and trainers have been platformed.

While the chapters in Part I of this book considered 'The Nature of Creative Entrepreneurship', providing insights into the various industries within the creative sector across a range of countries, those contained in Part II focused on 'Supporting the Creative Industries Sector', discussing how such industries are and potentially could be funded, supported, encouraged and developed. A number of key themes have emerged.

DEFINING THE CREATIVE INDUSTRIES

A fundamental difficulty with the creative industries is how they are actually defined. While the term 'creative industries' has been widely adopted in the UK and the Commonwealth countries, some European countries, such as Finland, Spain and Germany, prefer the term 'cultural industries'. As Hui pointed out in Chapter 2, Japan and South Korea have opted for 'cultural' rather than 'creative' industries, but the component industries in these countries differ substantially from one another, and attract different levels of government support. For example, in Japan, cultural industries are divided into two main sectors: media contents and arts and culture. While advertising, architecture and design are also part of Japan's cultural industries, they do not appear to be supported by government policy to the same extent. In South Korea, cultural industries primarily comprise literature, fine arts, music, dance, theatre, film, entertainment, traditional music, photography, language and publishing. However, the sector also includes visuals, games, broadcasting, advertising, design, crafts, characters, video, animations and digital content. In both Japan and South Korea different agencies are charged with looking after different industries within the cultural and creative sector, thus resulting in different priority areas and different levels of support.

In Chapter 4, Rae suggested that the creative industries are now defined much more broadly compared to the original restricted definition embodied in 'the arts'. According to the Department of Culture Media and Sport (DCMS), the term 'creative industries' represents a classification of 13 sub-sectors ranging from fine art and design, through to dance, entertainment, advertising and media. In contrast, the term 'creative economy' embraces the entire production chain from creation through to marketing, retailing and consumption. In this regard, Rae introduced the theme of networks and relationships, because any cultural endeavour will require the involvement of a group of independent enterprises acting interdependently in complex and specialized ways.

Taylor, in Chapter 11, suggested that the aforementioned DCMS definition is particularly useful because it contains some clues as to the underlying motives for encouraging the creative industries: international competitiveness, economic modernization, urban regeneration, economic diversification, national prestige and economic development (Myerscough, 1988; Lewis, 1990; Frith, 1991; Bassett, 1993; Bianchini and Parkinson, 1993; Griffiths, 1995; McGuigan, 1996). However, regardless of how they are defined, it appears that the creative industries are quickly becoming understood as a catalysing sector which attracts other sectors along with a highly qualified workforce (Florida, 2002; Pratt, 2002, as cited by Fleming in Chapter 7).

RECOGNIZING THE IMPORTANCE OF THE SECTOR

The development of the creative economy is of general cultural, societal and economic concern, as Rae has pointed out in Chapter 4. Due to their perceived high growth potential and their ability to build attractive communities, the creative industries have even become highly fashionable as an agent of policy. Growth in the creative industries can help renew the mainstream economy through increasing the core value-adding factors of innovation and design. In this regard, Rae cited Newcastle and Gateshead in the UK as examples of successful creative development strategies that have resulted in changing cultural identity and attracting visitors.

The economic value of the creative industries cannot be ignored. UK statistics, as cited in Chapters 4 and 7 by Rae and Fleming respectively, indicated that the creative industries collectively generated revenues of £112.5 billion in 2000, employed almost 1.9 million people in 2003, and grew at a rate of 6 per cent per annum between 1997 and 2003 (DCMS, 2001, 2004; DTI, 2005). In Chapter 2, Hui reported that the creative industries generated revenues of ¥36 300 billion in Japan in 1999, over NT$570 billion in Taiwan in 2000, and HK$46 101 million in Hong Kong in 2001. Elsewhere in the book, commentators offered revenue and employment figures for various sub-sectors of the creative industries, ranging from the music industry in Denmark: US$233 million sales in 2000 with 3057 full-time employees in 2002; in Finland: US$300 million in sales, and employing around 5000 joint-venturing entrepreneurs in 1999; in Norway: NOK905 million in sales 2003, and employing about 9000 people in 1999 (as cited by Aggestam in Chapter 3); and in Ireland: €478 million in sales in 2001, with 10 000 full-time employees in 2003 (as cited by Ó Cinnéide and Henry in Chapter 5). The computer game, design, software and related digital applications sector was cited by Rae in Chapter 4 as being of critical importance to the UK and constituting 37 per cent of the global creative economy (DTI, 2005). In Chapter 6, de Bruin reported on the growth of the New Zealand film industry, where the government has set targets of NZ$400 million per year within a five-year period, to have ten companies each with a turnover of NZ$50 million, and another 20 companies with turnovers of NZ$10 million per year. In Russia, as reported by Moss in Chapter 9, it is the popular culture and advertising sectors that have flourished, with commercial art galleries now well established in Moscow and St Petersburg. While, according to Kenny and Meaton in Chapter 10, it is the human language technologies (HLT) sector, comprising the group of software components, tools, techniques and applications that process natural human language, that has the most creative potential for the future.

As can be seen from the above, it is extremely difficult, if not impossible, to compare the performance of the creative industries or their various sub-sectors from country to country, due to differences in the definitions and data sources used. However, there is no doubt that the creative industries offer an opportunity for countries and, indeed, specific regions therein, to develop strengths in particular creative and cultural areas, allowing them to become global leaders in niche but growing areas within the creative cultural milieu.

THE CREATIVE ENTREPRENEUR

As Aggestam pointed out in Chapter 3, while defining an entrepreneur in any business sector continues to be problematic in the entrepreneurship research literature, defining an entrepreneur in the creative sector is even more difficult, a point reinforced by de Bruin in Chapter 6. Referring mainly to art-entrepreneurs, Aggestam suggested that such entrepreneurs can generally be conceived as holders of 'tacit knowledge that is realized as part of human capital and includes individual skill, competence, commitment and creativity based mindsets'. She also posited that art-creating entrepreneurs are creative in unique and sometimes unexpected ways rather than simply in conformist ones, and that they possess a harmonious set of skills that enable creative and expressible performance.

The concept of creative entrepreneurs, through their creations and productions, having the power to influence the lives of others is also introduced in the book. The music industry was presented as a good example of this in both Chapters 3 and 5, where the positive influence of creative entrepreneurs in the music industry is considered in the context of Scandinavia and Ireland. Ó Cinnéide and Henry reported on the phenomenal economic and cultural success of *Riverdance*, demonstrating the ability of the music industry to provide an attractive platform for entrepreneurship and to renew traditional cultures.

The notion that creative entrepreneurs are different to traditional entrepreneurs was threaded throughout many of the chapters in this book. As the authors of Chapter 5 explained, creative entrepreneurs have long been seen as part of a new and emerging social group (Fussel, 1983), representing valuable new knowledge workers (Drucker, 1993) and forming a new type of creative class (Florida, 2002). In addition to the obvious core characteristics of inspiration, creativity and innovation, other key attributes of creative entrepreneurs include risk-taking, locus of control, perseverance, self-reliance, flexibility, adaptability, autonomy and achievement motivation. As Rae in Chapter 4 explained, entrepreneurs in the creative industries come from different backgrounds, are often self-employed, may operate micro or very small enterprises that are capital-intensive (both from a human and a financial perspective), and depend on tightly wrought networks of workers.

To explain the nature of creative entrepreneurship and the complex skills-set required by creative entrepreneurs, the concept of the 'creative industries value/production chain' or 'entrepreneurship continuum' was introduced by a number of the chapter authors. For example, Rae (in Chapter 4) suggested that the creative economy embraces the entire process from creating the artefact to its marketing, retailing and consumption. In this process, the creative entrepreneur will need to join forces with production and distribution companies to sell their talent. Aggestam's chapter on the music industry presented creative entrepreneurship as an entrepreneurial venturing process which leads to the commodification of products and services. She described the variety of entrepreneurs within the sector, each of whom contribute to the end product, adding value along the way. As de Bruin explained in Chapter 6, while the inputs of creative entrepreneurs are dissimilar to those of other more traditional entrepreneurs in that the 'humdrum inputs respond to ordinary economic incentives' (Caves, 2003, p. 73), the value-adding process of the creative industries requires the combination of both types of inputs. New Zealand film-maker Peter Jackson was presented by de Bruin as an example of a creative entrepreneur who has successfully merged creative (that is, actors, scriptwriters, costume designers, music composers) with humdrum inputs (that is, finance, organization, coordination, project management) to produce a portfolio of blockbusters. Interestingly, de Bruin also included the external environment for creative entrepreneurship in her value chain, with the entrepreneur (the individual level), the state (the national level) and the community (the regional level) combining to make up an entrepreneurship continuum.

In Chapter 7, Fleming suggested that considering the creative industries in terms of Pratt's (2004) value chain can help us assess the value of a creative industries sector. Creation and content origination, manufacture, distribution and mass production, and finally, exchange are the four key links in the chain. Considering the creative industries in this way also helps to inform investment and support decisions better.

BARRIERS FACING CREATIVE ENTREPRENEURS

The creative industries literature identifies a range of barriers facing creative entrepreneurs, and this book is no exception. According to Rae (Chapter 4), one of the key difficulties encountered by those operating in the creative sector is the fundamental challenge of building and sustaining a business from creative activities, given that the sector has a low incidence of creative companies which grow to dominate their market sector (Cox, 2005). Creative entrepreneurs often have to balance conflicting interests, making tough business decisions while trying to maintain their creative dynamic. In fact, according to the authors of Chapter 5, this is one of the most problematic aspects of engaging in creative entrepreneurship. Self-promotion and marketing are also key difficulties for creative entrepreneurs, as most have difficulty promoting their expertise to their audiences. Funding would appear to be a particular difficulty as, despite the potential of the sector, there is still a lack of understanding of creative entrepreneurship among investors. Furthermore, artists have difficulty in pitching their idea to potential funders, and tend to focus on the aesthetic rather than the business case.

Of course, creative enterprises will also face the same challenges as traditional enterprises, and these include finding and building the market, growing the demand for their products and services, attracting suitable staff, securing financial and technical resources – particularly at the start-up and early stages of the business – and making strategic choices on how to compete in their particular environment. However, one set of difficulties that faces the creative entrepreneur more than any other type of entrepreneur is that associated with intellectual property (IP), copyright and contractual agreements. While every new business is faced with legal considerations, those facing the creative entrepreneur can be considerably more complex. The music, design and software industries are obvious examples of sectors where IP is of paramount importance.

In Chapter 7, Fleming identified a number of barriers facing the creative industries, particularly those enterprises that are ideas-based and content-generating. He suggests that risk factors are greater for such businesses in terms of securing finance. Creative businesses often lack the track record necessary for investors, and, as a result, cannot be assessed according to 'gone concern' protocols. Among other issues facing the creative sector, Fleming highlighted the fact that creative industries entrepreneurs prefer to: retain control and ownership of their business; resist expansion; pursue commercial objectives that are complimentary to lifestyle objectives (which, in turn, places growth constraints on the business); produce content on a project-by-project basis, thus limiting distribution; and work within a restricted client base (Crewe and Forster, 1993).

Notwithstanding the above, the chapter by Moss, which dealt with the creative industries in Russia, presented a unique set of barriers and challenges for creative entrepreneurs. Not only is the support environment for Russian creative industries somewhat lacking, but there is also a lack of understanding on the part of both the government and the consumer of what creative entrepreneurship represents. The situation is exacerbated considerably by the fact that the concept of creative industries as a separate categorization is relatively new to Russia; there is a lack of a cultural consumption tradition, significant tax disadvantages exist for small creative enterprises, and the state has adopted a rather conservative definition of what actually constitutes culture.

EDUCATION AND TRAINING

The theme of education and training is just as strong within the creative industries as it is within the general entrepreneurship literature. Using the example of arts courses, Brown (Chapter 8) highlighted the particular need for entrepreneurship to be embedded in educational curricula from the outset. While the number of students on arts and performing arts courses is growing, there are only a small number of employment opportunities available in these areas. It is for this reason, perhaps, that a considerable percentage of those working in the creative sector are self-employed. In fact, the tendency for graduates of arts, performance and creative courses in the UK to become self-employed (at some point in their career), work on a freelance basis, operate on temporary contracts and work part-time is, it seems, considerably higher than for graduates of other more traditional courses. Thus, it is possibly more important for students of creative courses to learn entrepreneurial skills since they are more likely to need them than graduates of other courses, including business courses. However, this stark realization has uncovered the lack of suitable enterprise teaching material that can adequately meet the needs of students studying the creatives. In this regard, the PACE Innovation Projects were presented as a possible step towards equipping students for work in this sector. These projects are of particular interest because, although designed for performing arts courses, the projects comprise a range of elements that would clearly benefit entrepreneurship teaching across a range of courses, that is: the apprentice–mentor system; learning by doing; the creation of real-life challenges across a range of contexts; creativity workshops; experiences from successful alumni; and promotion of the flexible portfolio employment model. However, it could be argued that such elements are somewhat easier to deliver in practically as opposed to theoretically based courses, where the teaching environment is often less restricted and more akin to the development of creative flair.

In Chapter 11, Taylor called for better relationships between the educational sector and creative industries. He argued that if universities are to work with the creative sector in a meaningful and productive way, then both institutional practice and higher education policy need to develop rapidly. Universities need to consider how they essentially interact with the creative industries; question whether their own processes of knowledge production are appropriate for the creative sector; and realize that they can potentially make more appropriate 'chambers of commerce' for creative entrepreneurs than those of the traditional variety. The clustering nature of enterprises provides universities with a greater role in economic development and, indeed, a greater opportunity to interact with and influence creative industries at the regional level. It was also noted that more recently universities, particularly the newer ones, have expressed greater enthusiasm for working with the creative industries than they have done in the past (Lambert, 2003).

THE ROLE OF GOVERNMENT AND FUNDING AGENCIES

Without exception, each of the countries discussed in the book has established policies and strategies to encourage and support the creative industries or sub-sectors thereof, although it must be acknowledged that, in the case of Russia, the support structures have not kept apace with economic, social and political developments overall.

In Chapter 2, Hui discussed the different types of government support for the creative industries in various parts of Asia. Here it was evident that some policies were more developed than others. Those countries with more coherent creative industries policies, which have identified priorities within the sector and have targeted a 'niche' in the creative milieu, would appear to have the greatest opportunity for growth. In this regard, the international success of South Korea's film, TV and music sector is a good example. In contrast, Singapore, Taiwan and Hong Kong seem to be lagging behind – still searching for their particular niche in the global arena.

In Chapter 7, Fleming criticized the public sector's piecemeal approach to creative industries support and investment in the UK. He highlighted the difficulties with current support initiatives for the creative industries, and questioned the rationale behind investment in the sector to date. Fleming also called for the coordination of a range of supports that can respond to the distinctive business profiles of different types of creative businesses. He suggested that while continued support and investment in the sector is important, it should be positioned to compliment existing initiatives so that a coherent landscape of investment opportunities is provided.

In Chapter 4, Rae also highlighted the lack of strategic thinking by the UK's public sector with regard to creative industries support, but suggested that the creative and mainstream economies will have to converge if current discontinuities are to be overcome. If, as Rae has suggested, the creative sector can contribute to the regeneration of the mainstream economy by stimulating creativity, innovation and growth, then the role of government becomes even more pivotal.

The call for a more structured, comprehensive approach to creative industries support was also echoed by de Bruin in Chapter 6 in relation to the New Zealand film industry. Again, the notion of a country carving out a niche for itself in order to compete successfully in a highly competitive global marketplace would appear to be embedded in the creative industries strategies of the more successful nations.

THE WAY FORWARD

Given the increasing popularity of the creative industries, it is likely that the fundamental difficulty of how actually to define the creative sector will remain a problem for both researchers and policymakers for some time. According to the NESTA Report (2006), the definition of the creative industries adopted by the DCMS (2001) – often the most frequently cited in both theoretically and empirically based research studies – is flawed in several respects. Firstly, it is too broad, allowing activities that would not normally be viewed as creative to be included in the definition, thus skewing statistics for the sector. Secondly, it fails to differentiate between sectors on the basis of size or capacity, resulting in very small sectors with no or low growth potential being included. Finally, the DCMS definition is too descriptive and does not facilitate accurate quantitative analysis (NESTA, 2006, p. 53). Indeed, it has been suggested by NESTA (2006) that the creative industries ought to be recategorized into four key groups: creative service providers (those who devote their time and intellectual property to other businesses, that is, advertising agencies, architecture practices, design consultancy and new media agencies), creative content producers (those who produce copyright-protected intellectual property which they distribute to customers, that is, film, television, fashion designers, publishers), creative experience providers (those who sell the right for consumers to experience or witness specific activities or performances, that is, theatre, opera, dance and live music organizers) and creative originals producers (those involved in the creation, manufacture or sale of one-off physical artefacts, that is, craft makers, visual artists and design makers) (NESTA, 2006, p. 54–5).

Notwithstanding the above, in some respects, the creative industries are beginning to be mainstreamed and may, in the future, no longer even be seen as a specialist sector (Creative Clusters, 2006; Cliche and Mitchell, 2002). This is due to the fact that they make up such a broad range of businesses; cut across several industry sectors which have, in the past, been categorized separately; are based on creativity – a key component of any enterprise; and possess the inherent potential to break down social, cultural and economic barriers. This latter aspect positions the creative industries high up on political agendas, allowing them to respond to both social and economic challenges at the international level (Metier Report, 2002). As already suggested in Chapter 1, with equality and diversity at the forefront of new millennium political correctness, music, sport, art and dance suddenly become vehicles for promoting social inclusion, encouraging cultural diversity and supporting the needs of minority groups, adding a new and interesting dimension to the creative sector.

While it is widely accepted that the education and training sectors have an important role to play in developing the potential of creative entrepreneurs, it is now recognized that promoting individual creativity and flair needs to be balanced with developing core business skills. Thus, in the future, creativity should be encouraged alongside the acquisition of transferable skills that include financial management, marketing, negotiation and presentation skills (Wilson and Stokes, 2005, p. 375). This is particularly important in the context of arts courses, since, as pointed out by Brown in Chapter 8, most graduates of arts disciplines become self-employed at some point in their careers. However, in terms of entrepreneurship education per se, it must be remembered that there is still an ongoing debate in the literature as to whether we can actually teach students to be entrepreneurs (Fiet, 2000, p. 1). In this regard, the creative industries are fascinating because they embody the very essence of enterprising behaviour, representing the art in the 'art and the science of entrepreneurship' (Jack and Anderson, 1998). Indeed, it is the art part, which relates to the creative and innovative attributes of entrepreneurship, that does not appear to be teachable in the same way as the business and management functional skills, that is, the science part of entrepreneurship (Henry et al., 2005, p. 164). In addition, it is also accepted in the mainstream entrepreneurship education and training literature that there is a considerable difference between creativity, innovation and business management (Henry et al., 2003, p. 31; Wilson and Stokes, 2005, p. 366). In this regard, there will continue to be a clear role for education providers in helping to embed entrepreneurship within arts curricula. However, as Moss cautioned in Chapter 9, translating Western training models to Eastern creative enterprises is possibly not the optimum solution to encouraging creative entrepreneurship in places like Russia. Education and training must be tailored to the particular sub-sector within the creative industries, and must also reflect the particular economic, political and cultural climates for which it is intended.

We should remember that the creative industries have traditionally been typified by micro and small businesses, employing few staff, often relying on voluntary input and lacking relevant support networks (Metier Report,

2002). Thus, future strategies and support mechanisms need to be tailored to these particular aspects. Perhaps it is time for a renewed policy approach for the creative industries that would include a coherent infrastructure to identify, develop and support future world-class creative businesses. Such an infrastructure would have many dimensions, from education and training, to business support, investment incubation, expert consultancy, to support for exporting and international trade regulations (NESTA, 2006, p. 44). Greater emphasis is also required on promoting innovation in the creative industries and on realizing the potential benefits that can result. According to the DCMS, in the future, creative businesses should seek complementary partnerships with other creative businesses, and consider what value their business can add to other sectors of the economy, particularly those based upon the exploitation of knowledge. More networks and collaborative activities also need to be supported (DCMS, 2006, p. 48). Furthermore, the impact of technology on the creative sector and, in particular, the importance of ICT (information and communications technology) should not be underestimated. As highlighted by Kenny and Meaton in Chapter 10, there is a particular role for HLT (human language technologies) in the creative sector to facilitate sophisticated interactive dialogues such as virtual reality applications. Such technologies will no doubt help to drive forward the multimedia and entertainment sectors of the creative industries. In this regard, the role of education and training in helping creative entrepreneurs to keep up to date with new technologies will be critical.

While successfully supporting the creative industries into the future represents a major challenge for governments worldwide, there is no doubt that, for a range of reasons, this sector will continue to present itself as an interesting topic for research on an international scale, particularly with respect to entrepreneurship.

REFERENCES

Bassett, K. (1993), Urban cultural strategies and urban regeneration: a case study and critique, *Environment and Planning A*, 25, 1773–1788.
Bianchini, F. and Parkinson, M. (1993), *Cultural Policy and Urban Regeneration: The West European Experience*, Manchester: Manchester University Press.
Caves, R. (2003), *Creative Industries: Contracts between Art and Commerce*, Cambridge, MA: Harvard University Press.
Cliche, D. and Mitchell, R. (2002), The Landscape of Women Artists and Media Professionals in Europe, Bonn, Germany, European Research Institute for Comparative Cultural Policy and the Arts.
Cox, G. (2005), Cox review of creative business: building on the UK's strengths, www.hm-treasury.gov.uk/cox.
Creative Clusters (2006), www.creativeclusters.com, accessed 27 October 2006.

Crewe, L. and Forster, Z. (1993), Markets, design and local agglomeration: the role of small independent retailers in the workings of the fashion system, *Environment and Planning D: Society and Space*, 11, 213–229.

DCMS – Department of Culture, Media and Sport (2001), Creative Industries Mapping Document, London, DCMS.

DCMS – Department of Culture, Media and Sport (2004), Creative Industries Toolkit, www.dcms.gov.uk.

Drucker, P.F. (1993), *Post-Capitalist Society*, New York: Harper Business.

DTI – Department of Trade and Industry (2005), Economic Paper No. 15, Creativity, design and business performance, DTI, London, November.

Fiet, J.O. (2000), Theoretical side of teaching entrepreneurship theory, *Journal of Business Venturing*, **16** (1), 1–24.

Florida, R. (2002), *The Rise of the Creative Class*, New York: Basic Books.

Frith, S. (1991), Knowing one's place: the culture of cultural industries, *Cultural Studies*, 1, 134–155.

Fussell, P. (1983), Class: a guide through the American status system, New York: Simon & Schuster.

Griffiths, R. (1995), The politics of cultural policy in urban regeneration strategies, *Policy and Politics*, **21** (1), 39–46.

Henry, C., Hill, F. and Leicth, C. (2003), *Entrepreneurship Education and Training*, Aldershot: Ashgate.

Henry, C., Hill, F. and Leicth, C. (2005), Entrepreneurship education and training: can entrepreneurship be taught?, *Education and Training*, **47** (2–3), 98–111 and 158–169.

Lambert, R. (2003), *Lambert Review of Business–University Collaboration, Final Report*, Norwich: HMSO. Available from http://www.hm-treasury.gov.uk/media/DDE/65/lambert-review-final-450.pdf.

Lewis, J. (1990), *Art, Culture and Enterprise: The Politics of Art and the Cultural Industries*, London: Routledge.

McGuigan, J. (1996), *Culture and the Public Sphere*, London: Routledge.

Metier Report (2002), Arts and Diversity in the Labour Market – a baseline study of research into the training and development needs of Black, disabled and female arts practitioners, managers and technicians in England, April, http://www.metier.org.uk/research/diversity_in_the_labour_market/display.php?section=8, accessed 15 December 2006.

Myerscough, J. (1988), *The Economic Importance of the Arts in Britain*, London: Policy Studies Institute.

NESTA – National Endowment for Science, Technology and the Arts (2006), Creating growth: how the UK can develop world-class creative businesses, April, available from www.nesta.org.

Pratt, A. (2002), Hot jobs in cool places. The material cultures of new media product spaces: the case of south of the market, San Francisco, *Information, Communication Society*, **5** (1), 27–50.

Pratt, A. (2004), 'Creative Clusters: Towards the Governance of the Creative Industries Production System?' Media International, Australia.

Wilson, N.C. and Stokes, D. (2005), Managing creativity and innovation: the challenge for cultural entrepreneurs, *Journal of Small Business and Enterprise Development*, **12** (3), 366–378.

Index

ABBA, impact on Swedish music industry 47–8
Adalsteinsson, G. 44
advertising 163
agglomeration strategies for investment 121–2
Albu, M. 172
Amin, A. 184–5
Arppe, A. 170
art-entrepreneurs
    barriers faced by 77–8
    characteristics of 78–9
    and corporate venturing 35–6
    defining and identifying 31–2
    definition 95
    in Denmark's music industry 39–40
    in Finland 42, 43
    in Iceland 44
    in the music industry 32–4, 39
    in Norway 45–7
    research into 49–50
    in Sweden 47–9
    see also creative entrepreneurs
artists and entrepreneurs 95–6
arts students
    commercial awareness of 128
    employment status of 127–8
    enterprise teaching of 129
Asia
    China 27
    compared to UK 10
    Hong Kong 21–6
    Japan 10–11
    Singapore 14–18, 20
    South Korea 12–14, 27
    Taiwan 18, 20–21, 22
Auckland 99
audiences and cultural diffusion 69
Audretsch, D. 96

barriers faced
    by creative entrepreneurs 77–8, 201–3

by creative industries 77–8
by new businesses 109
Bell, J. 172
Bilton, C. 182
Björk 44
Bjorkegren, D. 34
Blue Fish Design 66
broadcasting 163
Brown, P. 126
Bugge, M. 45
business networks 62
business risk in creative industries 182–3
business sector, mainstream, issues for in UK creative economy 60

cafe culture in Russia 153–4
Castells, M. 173
Caves, R. 33, 94
Chahal, G. 163
China 27
city centre living 153
Club on Brestkaya Street, Moscow 155–6
cluster/agglomeration strategies for investment 121–2
clusters 180–81
    and innovation 184
    need for 184–5
Common Sense DJ 162
competitiveness of European countries 166–8
Connexor 170
consumption, cultural 182
    in Russia 156–7
    Russia and the West compared 148–9
consumption and production, distinction between 63
copyright industries in Singapore 17–18, 19

corporate venturing
  and art entrepreneurs 35–6
  in the music industry 37–9
  Swedish music industry 48
cost leadership of UK economy 61–2
Cox Review 55, 57, 58, 60, 70
creative entrepreneurs
  and artists 95–6
  barriers faced by 77–8, 201–3
  characteristics of 78–9, 200–201
  as special case for investment 111–12
  see also art-entrepreneurs
creative entrepreneurship
  and economic development 75–7
  fostering in human language
      technologies (HLT) 172–3
  teaching of 129–33
creative industries
  academic research into 73
  barriers faced by 77–8
  business models 180–81
  business risk in 182–3
  business size 181–2
  definition of 179–80, 197–8, 205
  development in Russia and the West
      146–8
  economic value of 11
  flexibility of 182
  growth of 73
  importance of 198–200
  increasingly mainstreamed 205–6
  international collaboration in 74
  investor's lack of confidence in 75
  market intelligence 113
  markets of 182
  measuring economic value of 9
  organisational characteristics
      180–81
  as part of global economy 1–2
  perception of 60, 62–3
  as priority sector for government
      74–5
  recategorisation of 205
  size of sector in New Zealand 93
  support for in the future 207
  type of activities undertaken 181–2
  value chain 118–20
  work patterns in 183
  see also investment in creative
      industries

creative networks 62
creative service companies 118–19
creativity
  developing understanding of 131
  relevance and value of in society
      70–1
cultural consumption 182
  in Russia 156–7
  Russia and the West compared
      148–9
cultural diffusion 63–9
cultural entrepreneurship in higher
      education 135–8
cultural goods and services, UNESCO
      definition 21, 28
cultural industries, term used in Asia
      9–10
  see also creative industries
cultural provision in Russia and the
      West 145–6
culture, creative and mainstream
      organisations 61
customers and cultural diffusion 69

de Bruin, A. 93, 94, 96
Denmark, music industry in 39–41
design, investment in (UK) 60
Dewey, J. 63
diffusion, cultural 63–9
DiMaggio, P. 35
Dodgson, M. 191, 192
Drayton, W. 174

Eastern Europe, scarcity of data and
      literature 143
economic contribution
  Hong Kong 23–4
  Irish music industry 81–2
  Japan 10
  Singapore 14–15, 20
  South Korea 14
  Taiwan 21, 22
economic development and creative
      entrepreneurship 75–7
education and training
  developing understanding of
      creativity 131
  development of resources 133
  employers concerns over 126
  enterprise teaching 129, 203, 206

influence of entrepreneurship in 85
issues faced in UK creative economy
59
mentoring 130–1
New Zealand reforms 97
real-life project performances 130
reflective practice 130
responsibility for enterprise
education 133–5
Singapore 17
teaching cultural entrepreneurship
129–33
United Kingdom 61
see also higher education
employment
of arts graduates 128–9
in creative industries 183
Denmark's music industry 41
freelance and self employment
25–6, 127–8, 203
Hong Kong 24–6
Ireland 97
Irish music industry 82
New Zealand 97
New Zealand film industry 93
Norway's music industry 47
portfolio working patterns 132
US entertainment industry 76
enterprise education
in higher education 135–8
PACE projects 129–33, 138
responsibility for 133–5
entrepreneurs
and artists 95–6
barriers faced by 77–8
characteristics of 78–9
issues faced in UK creative economy
58–9
Peter Jackson as example 100
entrepreneurship
cultural, teaching of 129–33, 135–8
defining and identifying art-
entrepreneurs 31–2
definition 94
and economic development 75–7
fostering in human language
technologies (HLT) 172–3
innovation as part of 96
mindsets of 35
municipal-community 97

music industry in Scandinavia 31
potential for in Hong Kong 25
public 97–8
research into 49–50
equity market and investment 112
European Union (EU)
competitiveness within 166–8
human language technologies (HLT)
164–6
Eurovision Song Contest 33, 82

film industry
competition between production
centres 90
decentralisation of 89–90
NZ Film Commission 97–8
NZ regional clusters 98–9
and public entrepreneurship 97–8
start of in New Zealand 90–91
success stories of New Zealand 88
Film New Zealand 92–3
financial support 77
Finland
competitiveness of 166–8
Connexor 170
human language technologies (HLT)
in 166–75
ICT strategy model 175
Imagetalk 171–2
as model of social entrepreneurship
173–4
music industry in 41–3
neural network concept 173
flexible entrepreneurs 131–3, 182
Fredriksen, L. 41
freelance employment 127
funding sources 77
language technology in Finland 169

Games Workshop plc 66
*Global Competitiveness Report 2000-
2004* 167
Golden, W. 174
government support 204–5
of film industry in New Zealand
91–2
Hong Kong 26
Japan 10–11
language technology in Finland 169
NZ film industry 97–8

Singapore 15–17
South Korea 12–14
Taiwan 18, 20–21
see also public sector
growth rates
of creative industries 73, 74
Hong Kong 23–4
New Zealand film industry 93
Singapore 17–18
South Korea 14
Taiwan 21

Hallencreutz, D. 37
Hanrahan, S. 93
Henry, C. 95
Hesketh, A. 126
higher education
creative enterprise in 135–8
and the creative industries 178–9
cultural entrepreneurship in 135–8
enterprise teaching in 127
institutions, role of 184–6
issues faced in UK creative economy 59
and knowledge transfer 187–91
performing arts courses 126–7
relation to the labour market 126
responsibility for enterprise education 133–5
see also education and training
Himanen, P. 173, 174
Home Stagers® 66
Hong Kong
CCPR Report 21, 23–4
creative industries in 76
economic contribution of creative industries 23–4
employment in creative industries 24–5
government policy 28
potential for entrepreneurship in 25
self-employment in 25–6
Howkins, J. 95
Hughes, A. 173
human language technologies (HLT)
and advertising 163
application of 159–60
computer-generated poetry 160–62
Connexor 170
European Union (EU) 164–6

in Finland 166–75
fostering entrepreneurship in 172–3
Imagetalk 171–2
language processing and DJs 162
modelling of music notation 162–3
natural language generation (NLG) 163
potential of 160
in publishing and broadcasting 163
video games 164

Iceland, music industry in 44–5
Imagetalk 171–2
India, creative industries in 76
innovation
and clusters 184
as part of entrepreneurship 96
Peter Jackson as example 100
in the UK 60
institutions, role of 184–6
intellectual property rights
IPR-led companies 119–20
music industry 37
investment in creative industries 75, 77–8
accounting for differences and specialisms 120–121
approaches to public sector intervention 108–9
arts funding mentality 116–17
and barriers for new businesses 109
and businesses in other sectors 111–12
cluster/agglomeration strategies 121–2
creative service companies 118–19
difficulty raising 112–13
IPR-led companies 119–20, 121
as last resort 122
and local or global orientation 115–16
need for coordination 120
need for special support services 117–18, 121
public sector policy towards 122, 207
readiness initiatives 110
regional strategic funding 110
size and growth potential 113–15
value chain 118–20

IPR-led companies 119–20
Ireland
  creative industries as economic
    contributors 76
  critical issues 75
  economic significance of music
    industry 81–2
  entrepreneurial development after
    Riverdance 83–4
  Eurovision Song Contest 82
  music and dance in 80–81
  Riverdance 82–3

Jackson, Peter 100
Japan 10–11
Joscelyne, A. 166

Kickul, J.R. 77
knowledge transfer 187–91
Kohonen, Teuvo 173

labour market of creative industries
  183
Lambeth Report 60
language processing and DJs 162
Leadbetter, C. 61, 63
Linux operating system 173–4
Livesay, H. 31, 75
Lockwood, R. 166
Lorenzen, M. 41

MacMillan, I. 35
mainstream business, issues for in UK
  creative economy 60
market intelligence 113
markets of creative industries 182
McDougall, P.P. 172
McGrath, R. 35
mentoring 130–131
Milkov, Dimitri 154
Mitchell, C.J. 76
municipal-community
  entrepreneurship 97
music industry
  art entrepreneurs in 32–4, 39, 94
  characteristics of entrepreneurs
    78–9
  corporate venturing in 37–9
  Denmark 39–41
  domination by multinational

corporations 41, 42–3, 44
  Finland 41–3
  growth and dynamism of 79–80
  growth of 34
  Iceland 44–5
  impact of technological change 34
  intellectual property rights 37
  international scope 30
  in Ireland 80–84
  Norway 45–7
  processes within 80
  in southern Sweden 36–7
  studies of 36–7
  supporting industries 37
  Sweden 47–9
  unpredictability of market 34–5
Music Markup Language (MML)
  162–3
music notation, modelling of 162–3

natural language generation (NLG)
  163
networks, creative and business 62
neural network concept 173
Nevarez, L. 192
New Zealand
  Auckland 99
  education and training reforms 97
  Film New Zealand 92–3
  government support of film industry
    91–2
  regional clusters in film industry
    98–9
  size of creative industries sector 93
  start of film industry 90–91
  success stories of film industry 88
  Wellington 99
night-time economy of Russia 153
non-profit sector
  in Russia 147–8, 150–1
  significance of in Western Europe
    143–4
Norway, music industry in 45–7

Oakley, K. 61, 63
OKA Café and Gallery, Moscow 155
Oviatt, B.M. 172

PACE *see* Performing Arts Creative
  Enterprise (PACE) projects

performing arts courses 126–7
Performing Arts Creative Enterprise
  (PACE) projects 129–33, 138, 203
Phoenix Fabrications 68
Piore, M.J. 182
poetry, computer-generated 160–62
policymakers
  issues faced in UK creative economy
    59
  renewed approach 207
portfolio working patterns 132
Power, D. 37
Pratt, A.C. 181
production and consumption,
  distinction between 63
public entrepreneurship in the NZ film
  industry 97–8
public sector
  approaches to intervention 108–9
  policy towards investment 122, 204
  readiness initiatives 110
  regional strategic funding 110
  support for language technology in
    Finland 169
  see also government support
publishing 163

Ragnarsdottir, H. 44
readiness for investment initiatives 110
record companies
  Denmark 41
  Finland 42–3
  Iceland 44
  Norway 46–7
  Sweden 47
reflective practice 130
regional development 178
  and innovation 184
research into creative industries 73
risk
  in creative industries 182–3
  and investment 112
Riverdance 82–3, 84
Rogers, E.M. 63
Romijn, H. 172
Russia
  amateur clubs 152
  atelier workshops 151–2
  attitudinal issues 148–50
  cafe culture 153–4

characteristics favourable to creative
    enterprise 151–6
city centre living 153
Club on Brestkaya Street 155–6
conservative approach to culture
    149–50
cultural provision in compared to
    the West 145–6
development of creative industries
    147–8
inflexibility of large organisations
    150
infrastructural problems 150–151
introduction of Western strategies
    151
need for creative enterprise
    development 144–5
networks of trust and help 152
night-time economy 153
non-profit sector 147–8, 150–151
OKA Café and Gallery, Moscow
    155
polarisation between state and
    market 142, 156
scarcity of data and literature 143
slow change in cultural sector 142
suspicion of earned income 149
tax and finance disadvantages for
    small enterprises 150–511
Vladimir Nabokov Museum, St
    Petersburg 154–5

Sabel, C.F. 182
Say, J.B. 100
Scandinavia
  Denmark 39–41
  Finland 41–3
  Iceland 44–5
  international scope of music
    industry 30
  Norway 45–7
  Sweden 47–9
Schumpeter, J.A. 79, 95–6
self employment 203
  of arts graduates 127–8
  in Hong Kong 25–6
service companies 118–19
Shires FM 66, 68
Singapore 14–18, 20
  film industry 90

Sipilä, K. 173
social entrepreneurship 173–4
South Korea 12–14, 27
  film industry 90
stakeholders, issues for in creative
  economy 58–60
states
  entrepreneurship of 97–8
  role of regarding entrepreneurship
    96–7
Stinchcombe, A. 37
Sweden
  impact of ABBA on music industry
    47–8
  music industry in 47–9
  southern, music industry in 37

Taiwan 18, 20–21, 22
tango music 42
Thrift, N. 184–5
Thurik, R. 96
Torvalds, Linus 173–4
Trinity College of Music 131

United Kingdom
  compared to Asia 10
  cost leadership of economy 61–2
  Cox Review 55, 57, 58, 60, 70
  creative and business networks 62
  design and innovation in 60
  differences between creative and
    mainstream organisations 61
  discontinuities in creative economy
    60–63
  education and training 61
  growth of creative industries 55–6,
    74

issues for stakeholders 58–60
Lambeth Report 60
political attention to creative
  industries 57–8
production and consumption,
  distinction between 63
traditional industries 57
United States, employment in
  entertainment 76
universities
  and the creative industries 178,
    191–2, 203–4
  institutions, role of 184–6
  and knowledge transfer 187–91
University of Sunderland 130–131
University of Winchester 133

value chain 118–20
video games 164
Virtanen, H. 41
Vladimir Nabokov Museum, St
  Petersburg 154–5

Wall, G. 76
Wellington 99
Welsch, H.P. 77
Western Europe
  cultural provision in compared to
    Russia 145–6
  development of creative industries
    146–7
  significance of non-profit sector
    143–4
Wolf, M.J. 74
work patterns in creative industries 183

York St John College 131–3

Printed and bound by CPI Group (UK) Ltd, Croydon, CR0 4YY

23/04/2025

14660962-0002